Travels in Tandem

Also by Susanna Hoe

Lady in the Chamber (Collins 1971)

God Save the Tsar (Michael Joseph/St Martin's Press 1978)

The Man Who Gave His Company Away: A Biography of Ernest Bader, Founder of the Scott Bader Commonwealth (Heinemann 1978)

The Private Life of Old Hong Kong: Western Women in the British Colony 1841–1941 (Oxford University Press 1991)

Chinese Footprints: Exploring Women's History in China, Hong Kong and Macau (Roundhouse Publications Asia 1996)

Stories for Eva: A Reader for Chinese Women Learning English (Hong Kong Language Fund 1997)

The Taking of Hong Kong: Charles and Clara Elliot in China Waters (with Derek Roebuck) (Curzon Press 1999; Hong Kong University Press 2009)

Women at the Siege, Peking 1900 (HOLO Books 2000)

At Home in Paradise: A House and Garden in Papua New Guinea (HOLO Books 2003)

Madeira: Women, History, Books and Places (HOLO Books 2004)

Crete: Women, History, Books and Places (HOLO Books 2005)

Watching the Flag Come Down: An Englishwoman in Hong Kong 1987–97 (HOLO Books 2007)

Tasmania: Women, History, Books and Places (HOLO Books 2010)

Travels in Tandem

The Writing of Women and Men Who Travelled Together

Susanna Hoe

HOLO BOOKS
THE WOMEN'S HISTORY PRESS

Published in 2012 by The Women's History Press
A division of HOLO Books
Clarendon House
52 Cornmarket, Oxford OX1 3HJ
www.holobooks.co.uk

www.centralbooks.co.uk

British Library Cataloguing in Publication Data
A catalogue record for this book is available from the British Library

ISBN 978-0-9544056-9-4 paperback
ISBN 978-0-9544056-8-7 Kindle
ISBN 978-0-9544056-4-9 epub

Designed and produced for HOLO Books by
Chase Publishing Services Ltd, 33 Livonia Road, Sidmouth EX10 9JB
Printed in the European Union

In memory of and with thanks to

Diana Shipton Drummond
Doreen Ingrams
Ella Maillart
Barbara Greene Strachwitz

Contents

List of Illustrations

Preface

Between 1664 and 1973 at least 20 couples travelled together and recorded separate impressions of their journey. The discovery of that phenomenon – of complementary accounts, one by a woman, the other by a man – was the inspiration for this book. I was helped in an understanding of that relationship by my own experience as a 'travelling wife' in Papua New Guinea where my husband went to teach law in 1982, and in Hong Kong where we lived between 1987 and 1997 for the same reason. From both places we were able to travel easily and widely in the Pacific and Asia, sometimes in the footsteps of women who had travelled there. I was brought up in Africa.

I hoped at first to write separate chapters about all 20 couples who appear on the list overleaf. That was over-ambitious and would have been too cramped to provide any real insights or enjoyment. Instead, somewhat arbitrarily, I have selected ten couples, excluding, for example, those who travelled in Europe, such as Effie and John Ruskin, Sophie and Nathaniel Hawthorne, Sir Richard and Lady Fanshawe, and Lord and Lady Londonderry. Europe, even in 1664, did not stretch the traveller the way Africa or Central Asia did in the nineteenth and early twentieth centuries. Those who do not have a chapter of their own are given a voice in the more thematic Conclusion.

Then there are the couples who travelled together to the same place but produced only one book – either by one of them or jointly. Some of them help to provide questions in the Introduction.

When I started planning the book many of the accounts, particularly of the women, were out of print. Interest in travel and in women's writing has in the meantime increased; now, happily, many more of them are accessible as the list shows. And much work has been done on the genre 'Women and Travel', some of it, for example, juxtaposing women, travel and empire.

Some of those who travelled and who have chapters of their own were still alive when I was first researching the book. Four women responded warmly to my approach. Doreen Ingrams and Diana Shipton Drummond lived in England and generously and unreservedly gave me their time, hospitality and friendship. Barbara Greene Strachwitz and Ella Maillart lived abroad but replied by return and with great kindness and patience to my letters. Unfortunately, they are now all dead but their involvement gives a cooperative feel to the book that I could not have dared hope for when I started it. I dedicate the book to their memory.

Since I first contacted those four women travellers and, indeed, wrote an earlier draft of the book, some years have passed, and I have, for this final draft, been in touch with the adult children of three of them. They, too, have added to my understanding, as have descendants of other travellers.

Did my husband, Derek Roebuck, and I write complementary travel accounts? His books and articles about Papua New Guinea and Hong Kong are academic law; I have published records of both places which incorporate the lives of us both, and we did write the symbiography of an earlier husband and wife in China waters.

Acknowledgements

I wrote the first draft of the book some years ago in Hong Kong before the advent of email and the internet. Although I was able to do the initial research in London, being subsequently so far away from my usual haunt of the British Library was made easier by the responsiveness of authors, librarians and booksellers. Much of the information I gleaned then would have been easily found on the internet today; in those days, informants often went to some trouble to help. I would like to thank those who did so, in addition to the 'characters', family members and descendants mentioned in the preface, by linking them to the relevant travellers.

Lucy Atkinson remained something of an enigma for a long time outside the pages of her book, but not for want of the help of Professor Anthony Cross who wrote the introduction to its reprint; nor the keeper of manuscripts at the Guildhall Library, London, to whom I wrote about the register containing the record of the Atkinsons' marriage, hoping that their son's baptism might also be there with details of Lucy's background that could have been followed up; nor the cultural attaché at the British Embassy in Moscow. That was then. Since then, via the internet and email, much more has come to light, particularly through the meticulous research and generosity of Sally Hayles whose initial interest was in Thomas Atkinson. I have also been helped by descendants of Lucy or her siblings, Belinda Brown, the late Robert Perkins, and Marianne Simpson. And I was grateful to discover Annette Peach's updated entry for the *Oxford Dictionary of National Biography*.

The late Dr Sione Latukefu, Pacific historian, added to the wisdom he tried to impart to me as a mature student at the University of Papua New Guinea by his answers to my questions concerning the Patons. My friend Professor Mary Hiscock Allan, then of the Law Faculty of the University of Melbourne, let slip that she knew a descendent of the Patons and from that source came Maggie's birth date which had previously eluded me. From a librarian at the same university came Eleanor Lattimore's date of death, and from Nina McCoy in the Department of Alumni Relations at Northwestern University, Illinois, came Eleanor's birth date and other details. Since then, however, I have been able to add information both from introductions to reprints by the Lattimores' son, Professor David Lattimore, and by correspondence with him.

The editor of Florence Baker's diaries and letters, Anne Baker, responded most courteously and in detail to my persistent queries, as did the late Richard Hall, author of *Lovers on the Nile*. A biography of Florence has since been published by Pat Shipman which answers some questions. More recently, thanks to my friend William Twining enabling me to contact the family again, Anne Baker has given her permission to quote from Florence's diary, and her son Peter Baker has read the updated chapter to her.

John Randall brought Anna and Henry Forbes to my attention, and found their books for me. And I thank Henry Barlow for permission to use the map from his chapter about Anna, in spite of my disagreeing with some of his interpretation. It was David Chilton of Taikoo books who told me about Diana and Eric Shipton and Jan Slater of Oxus who put me in touch with Diana. More recently, the Shiptons' son Nick has read the chapter.

Leila Ingrams has added to the help her mother gave me, keeping me on the straight and narrow most kindly regarding her parents, and been to the trouble of providing me with a collage of historic photographs of their time in Arabia. Kate Grimond, daughter of Peter Fleming, has renewed the permission to quote given by the family when I originally published the chapter about him and Ella Maillart; more formally, that copyright permission is granted by the 'Estate of Peter Fleming'. Jeremy Lewis, author of *Shades of Greene*, put me in touch with Barbara Greene Strachwitz's son Rupert Strachwitz who, after reading the chapter about his mother, provided invaluable support and information. He put me in touch with Tim Butcher, author of *Chasing the Devil* (following in the Greenes' footsteps) who also read the chapter and provided digital illustrations.

I thank those 'children' both for their faith in their parents and their travels, and for permission to use extensive quotations from their works. I thank Robin Hanbury-Tenison for reading the Conclusion and giving me permission to quote from his and Marika's accounts. More formal permission has been given to quote from Lucy Atkinson's letters in the John Murray Archives, and from the travel accounts still in copyright published by John Murray as follows: Doreen Ingrams, *A Time in Arabia* (1970); Freya Stark, *The Valleys of the Assassins* (1934); Freya Stark, *A Winter in Arabia* (1940); Percy Sykes, *Ten Thousand Miles in Persia* (1902). I apologise for any permissions I have failed to obtain.

Ruth Dipple, librarian at Lady Margaret Hall, Oxford found me much-needed details about Ella Sykes. Sue Purver of Somerville College Library was also helpful for the Atkinson chapter. The late H. Montgomery Hyde, author of *The Londonderrys*, would have lent me any of his books. There are few greater generosities than that.

More generally, I thank the librarians and staff at the British Library, the School of Slavonic and East European Studies, the School of Oriental and African Studies, the London University Library at Senate House, the Royal Geographical Society, Rhodes House and the Bodleian Library, Oxford, the libraries of the University of Papua New Guinea and of the University of Hong Kong, and the archivist at the John Murray Archives.

I thank Brenda Stones for encouraging me to take the manuscript out of my bottom drawer and refresh it with a new title, Annie Warburton of the Australian Broadcasting Corporation who, interviewing me about my writing at the time of the launch of *Tasmania: Women, History, Books and Places* (2010), drew me out about this work so that there was no going back, and Gail Rebuck who, many years ago, asked the questions that open the Introduction.

Anka Ryall was initially mentioned to me as someone knowledgeable about Lucy Atkinson; when I contacted her she was prepared to read the whole manuscript. Her insights have been invaluable. Caroline Moorehead was also approached out of the blue, even more importunately. I thank them both for the generosity of their response.

I thank Ray Addicott for the patience and flair with which he has taken my manuscript and produced this book, and Tracey Dando for her careful and caring text-editing. I thank, too, Dawn Higgs for her sensitive colouring of the front cover lithograph.

Finally, I thank my husband, Derek Roebuck – historian, feminist and my travelling companion of 33 years. I thank him for being my editor, for his sharp mind and eye, and for his never failing concern. I will not, for ideological reasons, say, like Eleanor Lattimore, that I could not have travelled or written without him, but he adds immeasurably to the fun.

Oxford, February 2012

Author's Note

The internet and digital printing have made a difference to bibliographies. When I first drafted this book, I scavenged, at some expense, the originals of most of the books by the travelling couples. Some readers will remember the thrill of the chase, and the pleasure of ownership. Some titles have since been reprinted, often with a useful introduction; many can now be obtained print on demand (PoD).

Unfortunately, PoD versions have made it almost impossible to obtain the originals. Not only do PoD versions not resemble the attractiveness of the original, but they are often poorly scanned. I have only noted originals and traditional reprints. All is not lost for the internet user, though: often the originals can be obtained online which saves expense or treks to the library. The date of the version I have used is in bold at the top of each chapter.

On the first page of the Introduction, I have called Barbara Greene's 1938 book *Too Late to Turn Back*; the title when it was first published was, in fact, *Land Benighted*, but this was because Barbara misunderstood the words of the Liberian national anthem and the later title is the one by which it is better known. It would have spoiled the music of my opening to explain that there!

The chapter here on Ella Maillart and Peter Fleming 'A Born Traveller', appeared in my *Chinese Footprints: Exploring Women's History in China, Hong Kong and Macao*, under the title 'Different Wavelengths'.

Although I have not used the portraits of Sir Richard and Lady Fanshawe housed with other Fanshawe family portraits in the Valence House Museum (a house once lived in by the family), I should like you to know that they are there.

Updates of my books and relevant articles can be found on www.holobooks. co.uk.

Travelling Companions and their Writing

1664   Lady Fanshawe, *Memoirs* (1829; 1979)
       Sir Richard Fanshawe, *Original Letters ... During his Embassies in Spain and Portugal* (1702)

1817   Rose de Freycinet, *Realms and Islands: The World Voyage of ... in the Corvette Uranie 1817–1820* (ed. Marie Bassett, 1961)
       Louis de Freycinet, *Hawaii in 1819: A Narrative Account* (ed. Marion Kelly, 1978)
       J. Arago, *Narrative of a Voyage Round the World* (1823; 1971)

1836   Lady Londonderry, *Russian Journal 1836–37* (eds W.A.L. Seaman and J.R. Sewell, 1973)
       Marquis of Londonderry, *Recollections of a Tour in the North of Europe in 1836–1838* (1838)

1839   Lady Londonderry, *A Journal of a Three Months' Tour in Portugal, Spain, Africa etc.* (1843)
       Marquis of Londonderry, *Journal of a Tour in the Southern Part of Spain ... Performed in the Autumn of 1839* (1840)

1848   Lucy Atkinson, *Recollections of Tartar Steppes and their Inhabitants* (1863; 1972)
       Thomas Witlam Atkinson, *Oriental and Western Siberia* (1858; 1970)
       Thomas Witlam Atkinson, *Travels in the Regions of the Upper and Lower Amoor* (1860; 1971)

1849   Effie Ruskin, *Young Mrs Ruskin in Venice* (ed. Mary Lutyens, 1965)
       John Ruskin, *Ruskin's Letters from Venice 1851–1852* (ed. J.L. Bradley, 1955)

1865   Maggie Whitecross Paton, *Letters and Sketches from the New Hebrides* (1896; 1994)
       John G. Paton, *Missionary to the New Hebrides* (1889; 1994)

1869   Sophia Hawthorne, *Notes in England and Italy* (1869)
       Nathaniel Hawthorne, *Passages from the English Notebooks* (1870)

1870   Florence Baker, *Morning Star: FB's Diary of an Expedition to Put Down the Slave Trade on the Nile 1870–1873* (ed. Anne Baker, 1972)
       Samuel Baker, *The Albert N'yanza* (1866)
       Samuel Baker, *The Nile Tributaries of Abyssinia* (1868)
       Samuel Baker, *Ismailia* (1874)

1876 Lady Brassey, *A Voyage in the Sunbeam* (1878; 1984)
Lord Brassey, *Voyages and Travels* (ed. S. Eardley-Wilmot, 1895)

1882 Anna Forbes, *Insulinde: Experience of a Naturalist's Wife in the Eastern Archipelago* (1887; 1987)
Henry O. Forbes, *A Naturalist's Wanderings in the Eastern Archipelago* (1885)

1888 Mrs M.L. Stevenson, *From the Saranac to the Marquesas and Beyond* (1903)
Robert Louis Stevenson, *In the South Seas: Being an Account of the Experiences and Observations in the Marquesas etc* (1888)

1890 Fanny Stevenson, *Our Samoan Adventure* (1956)
Mrs M.L. Stevenson, *Letters from Samoa 1891–1895* (1906)
Robert Louis Stevenson, *Vailima Letters* (1895; 1972)

1894 Ella Sykes, *Through Persia on a Side Saddle* (1901)
Percy Sykes, *Ten Thousand Miles in Persia* (1902)

1917 Louise Bryant, *Six Red Months in Russia* (1918; 1982; 2002)
John Reed, *Ten Days that Shook the World* (1919; 1977; 2006)

1927 Eleanor Holgate Lattimore, *Turkestan Reunion* (1934; 1975; 1994)
Owen Lattimore, *High Tartary* (1930; 1975; 1994)

1934 Doreen Ingrams, *A Time in Arabia* (1970; Arabic trans. 2011)
Harold Ingrams, *Arabia and the Isles* (1942; 1966; 1998)

1935 Barbara Greene, *Too Late to Turn Back* (1981; published as *Land Benighted*, 1938)
Graham Greene, *Journey Without Maps* (1936; 1971; 2010)

1935 Ella Maillart, *Forbidden Journey* (1937; 1949; 1983; 2003)
Peter Fleming, *News From Tartary* (1936; 1951; 1994; 2001)

1946 Diana Shipton, *The Antique Land* (1950; 1987)
Eric Shipton, *Mountains of Tartary* (1951)

1973 Marika Hanbury-Tenison, *A Slice of Spice: Travels to the Indonesian Islands* (1975)
Robin Hanbury-Tenison, *A Pattern of Peoples: A Journey Among the Tribes of Indonesia's Outer Islands* (1975)

Introduction

'Do women write with more immediacy?' a woman asked when she heard of my proposal to look at the writing of women and men travelling companions. 'And', she added '... with more colour, more empathy and more attention to detail?' Of course, there is more to travelling together than style of recording impressions but it is a useful place to start, and Graham Greene tells a story in his autobiographical *Ways of Escape* (1980) that opens up a subject with many diverging paths.

He was writing 45 years after his famous trek through Liberia and discussing the style of the book, *Journey Without Maps* (1936), he wrote as a result. He remembers looking at his sketchy notebooks on his return; 'I was haunted by the awful tedium of A to Z' was his retrospective verdict.

He did not feel able to produce a conventional travel book nor, because of the nature of the journey, could it be an adventure story like those of Peter Fleming that were popular at the time, for his own was only a 'subjective adventure'; the reality was exhaustion, fever and, worst of all, tedium.

Greene decided, therefore, to write a journey inside himself to parallel the external one. That decision allowed him to suggest, at the end of a night of illness spent in Zigi's town, when his travelling companion Barbara Greene thought he would die, that he woke up in the morning much better and 'completely convinced of the beauty and desirability of the mere act of living'. Quoting that mystical claim all those years later, he asks, 'Did I learn the lesson of Zigi's town?' And then admits, 'I doubt it' (p43).

With that admission as part of a map, it is possible to begin a historical exploration of the differences between men and women's travel writing, for Barbara Greene unselfconsciously wrote *Too Late to Turn Back* (1938) A to Z. What differences there are, apart from gender, between the women and men who travelled in tandem – such as age, background, education, experience – will emerge in the chapters that follow and be further explored in the Conclusion.

Relying for the moment only on Graham Greene's frank and rather endearing admission, can one conclude that men tend to tell 'a story' for reasons of style or image; and that women (looking at his cousin's more straightforward account) tell it as it was? Is one more truthful than the other, more valid than the other, more interesting, and to whom? Because of their history, do women relate to their surroundings more directly because they are less sure of their right to twist, for effect, what actually happened?

And is that the phenomenon caught by Mary Ward in her novel *Robert Elsmere* (1888) when a woman promises not to interrupt the telling of an anecdote unless 'You put in too many inventions'? And the man replies, 'You invite me to break the first law of story telling ... Every man is bound to leave a story better than he found it' (pp33–4).

All these questions are more than superficial, for style has many aspects: not only how something is written but also what the writer chooses to write about. Then there is perception – how a person sees – and when does that become perspective: from what angle? And what lens is used to focus, wide angle or close-up?

Thomas Brassey (1836–1918) completed the last book of his wife Annie Brassey (1839–1887) who had died of malaria as they travelled. Introducing her life and work in *The Last Voyage* (1889), he wrote:

> The book grew out of a habit, early adopted when on her travels, of sitting up in bed as soon as she awoke in the morning, in her dressing-jacket, and writing with pencil and paper an unpretending narrative of the previous day's proceedings to be sent home to her father ... the instruction and knowledge conveyed, if not profound, are useful and interesting to readers of all classes. (pxix)

'An Unpretending Narrative' will serve as a heading for this whole aspect of style and content.

0.1   Lady Brassey (from Brassey, *A Voyage in the Sunbeam*)

Readers of this book will want to make their own comparisons between the travel writings that follow in ten chapters about ten couples. But, as I have chosen extracts to conform to my own responses to reading the travel books as a whole (as well as other writings), some explanations might be helpful.

As far as practical, each chapter follows a pattern which will be picked up in the sub-headings of the Conclusion. The titles of these – such as the one from Thomas Brassey just quoted – highlight issues which seem to me the most obvious and appropriate for discussion. And this is more a study of people than of places; it is an aspect of women's history rather than an elaboration of places visited. It also investigates the relationships between the sexes. To fully enjoy the fascinating places you should read the travellers' accounts.

The Dictionary of National Biography entry for Isabel Burton (1831–1896) provides the title for the next area to watch out for. The writer says of Isabel's marriage to Richard Burton (1821–1890), 'henceforth, she shared her husband's life in travel and in literature *so far as a woman could* [my italics].' Isabel Burton herself was a collaborator in this attempt to belittle, through her, all women. Her biographer, Jean Burton, quotes her as rhapsodising, 'I wish I were a man. If I were, I would be Richard Burton; being only a woman, I would be Richard Burton's wife' (p9).

How big a difference is there between two different types of women travellers, and is it important? The best known women travellers of the nineteenth and early twentieth centuries travelled alone; often they were unmarried. *Travels in Tandem* deals, until the Conclusion, with women who travelled with men, often their husbands. Being a woman, womanliness, femaleness, femininity and feminism then have a different context. Joanna Trollope gives a sense of the difference when she writes in *Britannia's Daughters: Women of the British Empire* (1983):

> The quality of endurance in the diaries and letters of a Victorian missionary's wife makes hard reading ... spinster missionaries were another matter altogether. Freed from emotional loyalty to another human being and the encumbrance of setting up house, they were, like the lady travellers, very much their own mistresses. (pp191–2)

Is it possible to imagine Isabella Bird (1821–1904), or Gertrude Bell (1868–1920) writing like Isabel Burton? Did companions take second place because they were that kind of woman or did the fact that they were companions put them in second place? And how does that second placeness manifest itself in their published writing? Here are some examples from other women who travelled with men but who do not qualify technically to have a chapter of their own. They suggest a pattern of self-denigration dressed up as modesty in introductions to their travel accounts. Does it differ from male self-deprecation?

Caroline David (1856–1951) met her geologist husband Edgeworth David on a voyage to Sydney to take up her post as principal of Hurlstone Training College for female teachers. *Funafuti* (1899), an account of the three-month expedition led by him to an island in the Pacific Ellice Group, is nicely humorous, and that is no doubt how Caroline meant the opening of her preface; but it can be read differently:

This does not claim to be a literary production but merely an accurate, though unscientific account of the 1987 Funafuti coral-boring expedition … The leader of the expedition says that as my MS. has thrice made him fall asleep, the book will probably prove an infallible cure for insomnia and is worth publishing as such.

Mabel Bent (Mrs Theodore Bent; 1872?–1929), who was left on her husband's death in 1897 with an account of their Arabian journey to produce, combined his notebooks with her 'chronicles' and hastened to explain in her introduction to *Southern Arabia* (1900) that 'the least part of the writing is mine'.

Katherine Routledge (1866–1935) attended Somerville College, Oxford, and later wrote the massive and original study *The Mystery of Easter Island* (1920). Yet she observes in *With Prehistoric People: The Akikuyu of East Africa* (1910) (written at a time when today's formal discipline of anthropology through fieldwork was still in its infancy), 'An apology is due for the fact that my own share of the work was undertaken purely through interest of circumstances, and, apart from some slight knowledge of our own early constitution, without any technical knowledge' (pxvii).

0.2   Katherine Routledge (from Huie, *Tiger Lilies*)

Mabel Cook Cole (d. ca 1978), wife of the anthropologist Fay-Cooper Cole (1881–1961), writes in *Savage Gentlemen* (1920) of how she came to accompany him to the Philippines: 'Woman-wise I asked questions and when I was assured that asking questions was the chief part of the anthropologist's business, I accepted at once' (p3).

A neat, though telling, twist to this genre are the sentiments expressed by astronomer David Gill on behalf of his wife Isobel Gill (1849–1919) in his introduction to *Six Months in Ascension: An Unscientific Account of a Scientific Expedition* (1878), her record of accompanying him to observe the near approach of Mars and calculate its distance; it starts well enough:

> A scientific expedition may be said to have two histories. The one treats of the special object of the expedition, the other of the personal adventures of those concerned in it. It is only the former which finds permanent record in the transactions: the other too often remains unwritten.
>
> For many reasons I think this is a matter of regret … on my expedition to Ascension last year, however, I had the good fortune to be accompanied by my wife, who found much pleasure and interest in making a daily record of our life and work there. This little book [285 pages], compiled from her journal, she now lays before the public with much diffidence … She hopes that the faults incidental to a first work will meet with lenient judgement.

Following these modest remarks on her behalf, David Gill then takes up a further 46 pages of her little book explaining his work. We shall see whether or not the spirit of the modest introduction pervades the rest of a woman's account.

Is it possible to suggest that, through travel, the accompanied woman, seeing the position of women in other parts of the world, became more critical of her own position in her own society? Or perhaps they were so ethnocentric that they did not relate the two?

The sub-heading in the Conclusion 'So Far As a Woman Could' will look not only at how the travelling companions saw themselves, and how they saw the position of other women, but also at how their male companions saw and treated them and the women they observed.

The words 'so far as a woman could' suggest that she was in some way too physically weak or prone to sickness to keep up; is that implication borne out by the facts? We know, for example, that Isabella Bird was an invalid at home and fit and energetic when she travelled, often in places full of physical demands and dangers. The mountaineer Lin Rutland maintains that 'Women find it easier to acclimatize because of their ability to build up red blood cells, but other things may work against them. Pre-menstrual tension can make a woman very tired and prone to germs' (Russell 1986 p109).

Women of the nineteenth and early twentieth centuries were not much given to discussing their bodily functions in print; as far as they do, however, they may have some bearing on women's stamina and ability to keep up.

It is not easy to be concerned about appearance when travelling but, since another feminine weakness is supposed to be vanity, it may be interesting to see if it is so and how it shows itself.

Assuming a woman could keep up, what else did she contribute to the enterprise? Did she feel, as Helen Saker (1821–1885), a missionary who arrived with her husband, Alfred, in the Cameroons in 1844, expressed it in her autobiography, that 'The man's work is the woman's memorial' (Trollope pp188–9)? Or in the end can she be said to have existed in the partnership 'In Her Own Right'?

To answer that sub-heading, we need to ask, why did travellers travel? Women who travelled alone were always having to justify why they did so. A woman who travelled with a man usually went to be with him, though it cannot always be so narrowly defined. Men usually travelled for professional reasons but there was undoubtedly more to it than that. Paul Fussell in *Abroad: British Literary Travelling Between the Wars* (1980) suggests that British men then, including Graham Greene and Peter Fleming, wrote richer travel books than any other nationality because of 'a powerful strain of lawless eccentricity and flagrant individuality' (p78). He does not distinguish between individuality and individualism. Colin Thubron, in a 2011 *Guardian* article, uses a phrase I like even more: 'heroic self-posturing'.

How far British women conform to the Englishman's tradition will be looked for, for example, in Barbara Greene's writing (in relation to that of her cousin). And, as for foreign women, we shall see how far the Swiss, Ella Maillart, usually a lone traveller, appreciated the individualism of her companion Peter Fleming. Perhaps what most women travelling alone were seeking, through the rebelliousness not only of their manner of travelling but also the decision to travel itself, was not so much individualism – outside society – as their own individuality – or identity – within society. Their persona had previously been imposed on them. Did it continue to be imposed on women travelling with a man?

How did travelling companions make their mark? Often, practical women or young women full of energy and determined to be part of the enterprise took the organisational burden off the man; she was the housewife or administrator of the expedition. But there were more intangible contributions. In the introduction to Mabel Cook Cole's book, George A. Dorsey writes, 'Mrs Cole not only went where Dr Cole went but her presence helped smooth rough trails and also broke new ones never before available to whites' (ppxiv–xv).

That leads into another area of interest. W. Scoresby Routledge (1859–1939) writes in his part of the preface to their book on the Kikuyu, 'It was in addition possible for my wife to visit among the huts and thus come in touch with the women and domestic life' (pxiii). And she writes, 'I frequently induced my native friends to give me information by telling them that when we were back in England the white women would wish me to tell them about the women of Kikuyu, for we all now belonged to the same great white chief' (pxviii).

For all the real or imagined weaknesses or disadvantages of travelling companions, when it came to looking at women in traditional societies, often Islamic, the position was reversed. It was written of the author of the classic *The Fellahin of Upper Egypt* (1927), Winifred Blackman (1872–1950), 'And she had, lastly one great advantage in her favour: she was a woman ... Miss Blackman was enabled as a woman to go where no man would ever be allowed' (Tiltman 1935 p272). Isabel Burton put it in her inimitable way (thereby providing another sub-heading) 'I have followed my husband everywhere, *gleaning only women's lore*' (my italics).

Mrs Hugh Fraser (Mary Crawford Fraser, 1851–1922) confirms the pattern and leads into the next theme when she writes in her introduction to *Seven Years On the Pacific Slope* (1914):

> In this book it has been necessary to give, as it were, two individual stories, which sometimes merge into one, sometimes take their separate ways. In no other fashion could the account of the place and our experiences there be made in any way complete. There are always in primitive places, two little worlds, the one of the men, the other of the women. They have points of contact, but the fact remains that women will open their hearts to a woman and men to a man in a fashion quite distinct from that which one sex will accord to the other. So, to give any true impression of the only bit remaining of the far West, it was necessary that my son and I should describe things as they were shown to us individually. (p7)

From a purely practical point of view, there is also the sharing of the burden of work in producing an account in cases where only one book is written. As Xavier Hommaire de Hell (1812–1848) puts it in *Travels in the Steppes of the Caspian Sea* (1847), 'My wife [Adèle, 1819–1883], who braved all the hardships to accompany me in most of my journeys, has also been the partner of my literary labours in France. To her belongs all the descriptive part of this book of travels.'

As well as the literary compensations, Hommaire de Hell implies another form of complementing or companionship, one aptly described by Eleanor Lattimore in *Turkestan Reunion* (1934). Soon after finding her husband, after a gruelling 17 days' journey across the Siberian wastelands on a sledge laden with matches, she observed, providing an appropriate sub-title, 'We were jogging along on the road from Chuguchak to Urumchi, and travelling with a husband is *a lot more fun* [my italics] than travelling alone.' It is unlikely that the joys of companionship were all one way but how well did most couples relate, apparently and in reality, to each other, and how does it affect their accounts?

Finally, what did the individual female companion, in the end, get out of her travels, apart from 'a lot more fun'? What is each woman like as a person at the beginning and at the end? Experience, particularly endurance, has traditionally been said to make a man of a youth. How far, therefore, did the vicissitudes of often girlish travellers succeed in 'the making of a woman'? To put it another way, travel is said to broaden the mind; so, were the attitudes of individual women modified or changed by their experiences? Were particular women less ethnocentric, patronising, colonial, racist, or more sisterly or feminist on the last page than on the first, given that women tended to write chronologically and contemporaneously?

Leading from that, is it possible, over time, to observe female attitudes in general changing? Mary Russell, in *The Blessings of a Good Thick Skirt: Women Travellers and their World* (1986), supplies a good contrast to illustrate this point when she quotes Annie Taylor (1855–1922), a missionary to China and Tibet in the 1890s: 'I was shocked to see men and women near Ta'ri'si prostrating themselves the whole length of the road ... Poor things, they know no better; no one has ever told them about Jesus.' And then Alexandra David Neel (1869–1968) who, observing the same scene 50 years later, carefully explained that:

> Many of the pilgrims went round the mountain, prostrating themselves at each step, that is to say, stretching their arms as they lay on the ground, and marking with their fingers the length they had covered with their bodies. They would get up and stand at the exact place which their fingers had touched, after which they would prostrate themselves and measure their length once more, and so on, all the way round. (Russell 1986 pp44–5)

By the same token, does Ella Maillart's account of her visit to Chinese Turkestan show her to be less ethnocentric in 1935 than Maggie Paton was in the Pacific in the 1860s? If the answer is yes, can this begin to be construed as a cumulative change, one connected with general intellectual and ideological progress for women?

Although some of the travelling women's books discussed in the following chapters are more available than they were when I first planned this book, Barbara Greene's *Too Late to Turn Back* (originally published as *Land Benighted*) was last reprinted in 1991, and is expensive to get hold of. Graham Greene's *Journey Without Maps* is, meanwhile, still in print (2010). To question this discrepancy, Barbara's book was included in the 2003 *Lost Classics* (eds Michael Ondaatje and others) with a two-page piece by Russell Banks. It ends appropriately, 'The great pleasure is to read them in tandem, his first, then hers' (p8). When you have read Chapter 8, you decide the order!

Part I
Nineteenth Century

1 – A Little Streak of Wilfulness

Lucy Atkinson, *Recollections of Tartar Steppes and their Inhabitants* (1863; **1972**)
Thomas Witlam Atkinson, *Oriental and Western Siberia* (1858; **1970**); *Travels in the Regions of the Upper and Lower Amoor* (1860; **1971**)

1.1   Lucy, Thomas and baby Alatau Atkinson with Chinese officials (from Atkinson, *Recollections of Tartar Steppes*)

Lucy and Thomas Atkinson explored Siberia together on horseback between 1848 and 1853 – the first English travellers to visit the area and write about it. But in the two books that made him famous in London from the late 1850s Thomas not only fails to mention Lucy's name but he does not even hint at her presence. Describing his departure from Moscow he does not have Lucy beside him on the sledge but a dog.

Does that suggest how he thought of her? Not if one reads her account. She never criticises his treatment of her in her letters though, in her published introduction to them, she does write of his books:

There is no allusion in them to the adventures we encountered during those journeys, and, especially, there is no mention of the strange incidents that befell myself, often left alone with an infant in arms, among a semi-savage people, to whom I was a perfect stranger. (pvi)

Otherwise, to the unsuspecting reader some of the thoughtlessness he displays is no more pronounced than that of many a travelling man.

TABLE OF DATES.

1848		1851	
Feb. 13	Left Petersburg.	May 23	Left Irkoutsk for the mountains in the north.
„ 22	„ Moscow.		
March 21	„ Ekaterinburg.		
April 4	Arrived in Tomsk.	Sept. 6	Returned to Irkoutsk.
June 3	Left Tomsk.		
„ 7	Arrived in Barnaoul.		
July 9	Left Barnaoul for Altin-kool.	1852	
Sept. 2	Left the Altai viâ Zmeinogorsk for Kirghis steppe.	May	Left Irkoutsk.
		July	Arrived in Barnaoul.
1849		1853	
Sept. 3	Returned to Zmeinogorsk from Kirghis steppe.	February	Left Barnaoul for Ekaterinburg.
October	Left Zmeinogorsk for Barnaoul.	June 11	Left Ekaterinburg for the Oural Mountains.
		August	Returned to Ekaterinburg.
1850			
June 16	Left Barnaoul for the Yenissey River.		
Aug. 30	Arrived in Irkoutsk.	Dec. 24	Arrived in Petersburg.

1.2   Lucy Atkinson's chronology of Siberian travel
(from Atkinson, *Recollections of Tartar Steppes*)

It was not the first time she had faced strangeness, however. Lucy Sherrard Finley Atkinson (1817–1893) writes in her preface, 'Being one of a large family it became my duty, at an early period of life, to seek support by my own exertions' (pv). Born in Sunderland, County Durham, to Matthew and Mary Ann Finley, Lucy was the fourth child and eldest daughter of ten children. Her father was a school teacher and the family, which had moved back to Mary Ann's home place, Stepney, London, between 1824 and 1826, was impecunious. Thus, in her early twenties, at the end of the 1830s, she went to Russia as governess to the only daughter of General Muravyev. Young Englishwomen had been going to Russia as governesses for at least a century – since Elizabeth Justice arrived there in 1734 – but you would hardly have gone if you came from a comfortable background with good marriage prospects. Lucy stayed with the Muravyevs for eight years.

Lucy's career as a governess and her fine writing style suggest that she was well-educated – hardly surprising as the daughter of a school teacher. She must have arrived in Russia in about 1838, and was content enough there until

1846 when she was 29 years old. It is known that she met Thomas Atkinson in that year. He was 47 and had established himself as an architect, though not without a struggle.

Thomas (Witlam) Atkinson (1799–1861) was of humble origin but was taken under the wing of the Spencer Stanhope family of Cannon Hall, Cawthorne, Yorkshire, where his father had been head mason and his mother a housemaid. He worked under his father from the age of eight, first as a mason's labourer. Soon he was a skilled stone-cutter and then self-taught draughtsman; in his early twenties he was walking five miles each way to work as a stone-carver at St George's Church in Barnsley.

He first came to the Stanhope family's notice when he designed a headstone for his mother in Cawthorne churchyard (she died in 1817). Anna Maria Pickering (née Spencer Stanhope) takes the story further in her *Memoirs* (1903): 'At the time of my grandfather's death, he made a design for a tomb for him which showed so much talent that my Uncle Charles sent for him and told him that he had his fortune at his fingers' ends, but not as a mason.' In a letter of 7 May 1825, Anna Maria's mother, Lady Elizabeth Stanhope (née Coke), noted that her husband had introduced the 26-year-old Atkinson to the famous sculptor Richard Westmacott (the elder, an associate of her father). The Stanhopes were to maintain an interest in their protégé until Thomas's death.

With this encouragement, Thomas went to London and 'engaged himself to a good architect'; by 1827 he had a practice as a church architect and he rose rapidly in his new profession, obtaining work and commissions throughout the country, particularly in the Manchester area. Aged 30, in 1829, Thomas published his first work, on Gothic ornaments, cathedrals and churches, but then his fortunes must have declined: an 1841 record shows that he was in a debtors' prison in London. By 1842 he had been released for in May that year Hamburg was devastated by a great fire and there was work for him there. During his time in Germany, he met Humboldt in Berlin and learned of unexplored Siberia. By a happy chance, and according to Anna Maria Pickering, though not more formal sources, his work was noted and admired by Nicholas I of Russia passing through Hamburg, and in due course – following travels in Greece and Egypt – he was invited to St Petersburg. It was there, with a special pass from the Tsar, that his career as traveller and artist took off. He left for Siberia in March 1847.

Atkinson's contemporary, Francis Galton, wrote of that privilege, at a time when journeys to and within Russia were subject to much constraint, 'Possibly the Tsar wished for unbiased and independent evidence as to certain matters in South Siberia and Atkinson may have acted as a secret agent' (p76). Certainly much of what Thomas described would have been of interest to the Central Government; and the Tsar was to show his appreciation with gifts of jewellery, the first a ruby ring. Some information, such as visits to armament factories and details of the border between Siberia and Chinese Turkestan, would also have interested the British Government, as part of the so-called Great Game. There is evidence in Foreign Office papers that Thomas offered his services to the British Consulate in Moscow. The year after his return from Russia the two countries were at war.

At the end of 1847 Thomas returned from Siberia and married Lucy in the new year (18 February) in the chapel of the Russia Company in Moscow. Three days later he set off back to Siberia with her. He does not mention breaking off his Oriental journey; he does not even hint that he was married, nor that for the next five years he was accompanied by a wife and, seven months after that second journey began, a child. He writes only, 'Passing by the long winter I will speak of Barnoul in the spring-time. I ought to call it early summer' (*Siberia*, p277). That is when he arrived back in Barnoul with Lucy, on 7 June, as is shown in the chronological table in her book and in her letters; he was not there that winter at all.

Why did he suddenly go back to Moscow and marry Lucy, and then take her on his travels? Was it because he could not live without her? There may have been an element of that. Was it that she spoke Russian and he found he could not manage without an interpreter in a land that was mainly non-Russian-speaking but where officialdom was Russian? Was it that as a self-educated man he felt an educated woman would help in his ambition of eventual publication? Was it that he wanted a travelling housekeeper and cook? Perhaps it was lonely work travelling in the depths of a barbaric country for months on end. But would she not have held him up and even more so if a baby was to be born? And why did he fail to mention her in his narrative? Must it have been to emphasise that he had undertaken, alone, a long, hazardous and totally original journey – one that required great reserves of manly strength, stamina and courage? Or was there another reason? Did he fail to mention Lucy in his books because he was already married to someone else?

When he died in 1861, seven years after their return – a time when they lived in London off the Old Brompton Road, while he wrote his books and basked in the acclaim which accompanied their publication – Lucy applied to the treasury for some money owed to her husband. It was then she discovered that the wife he had married in 1819, and whom he must have told her was dead (he is described as a widower in the register of marriages now in the Guildhall, London) was, in fact, alive. Rebecca (Rebekah) Atkinson had not heard of him for some years, until she was told by a friend of his death; thus she resurfaced.

And it was then that Thomas and Lucy Atkinson's smart London friends such as Francis Galton confirmed that 'Atkinson had avoided bringing his wife (as we thought of her) to the forefront, and it had been remarked at the time of the publication of his book of travels that he made the scantiest references to her, and never used the word "wife"' (pp176–7). Those 'scantiest references' are beyond detection.

This makes one look at Lucy and Thomas Atkinson's writing with new eyes. Lucy's account of their travels was published two years after his death and it proved a time-bomb to his reputation, for in her simple and open account is an unspoken refutation of much that he claimed about his adventures in new areas; and the ethnographic information he collected in the far east of

Siberia now seemed to be plagiarism from an earlier source. The question is, did she know what she was doing? It seems unlikely, from what little we have to go on, that she was a party to the bigamy, so she had already lived through the hurt and humiliation that must have followed his death. Did she publish her letters, with their definite chronology and unvarnished details, knowing that her account would expose him to any but the most casual reader?

There is no hint of that in the small cache of unpublished letters in the archives of her publisher, John Murray, starting in January 1862. She writes openly of financial difficulties; indeed Murray offers her guidance. But of any other troubles there is just a hint in a letter of 26 June 1862 when the publisher is waiting for more of her manuscript:

> Pray do not think I have been spending my time idly. Since I saw you I have had a good deal of trouble and anxiety. That is over for the present, and whatever comes in the future, I trust it will not produce the same effect upon me. I tried hard to collect my thoughts to write, but I could not do much, and threw my pen down in despair. Last Monday I resumed it, and I hope nothing more will come to interrupt me for a while.

And Lucy ended about the manuscript 'I could have said more, but I fear not to be quite correct and as this is not fiction, it is better to write only of what I am quite sure.'

What writing of her travels Lucy had to draw on is ambiguous from her correspondence with John Murray for, in her first letter, she observes: 'In the style I have sent you I can write more letters, equally if not more interesting.' And yet she writes in her introduction that her work consists of 'letters written on the spot to friends ... with slight omissions and alterations'.

Lucy's book, republished a century later, in 1972, with an introduction by the historian A.G. Cross, has come into its own, partly as a result of Cross's careful research. He suggests of Thomas Atkinson's books, on the simple level of style, that they 'pale before the fresh and unpretentious work of his wife' (px) and that her account 'lacks none of the excitement of [his]; it only gains in comparison'.

Cross's opinion is interesting in another way for, as an academic male, he might be expected to prefer the more consciously literary and scholarly style of the man so anxiously seeking to establish himself in an age of writing about exploration.

Atkinson does more than fail to mention Lucy in his narrative: he concertinas time and fuses events, so that he only describes leaving Moscow once, in March 1847, when, in fact, he did so twice, again in February 1848 with Lucy. But the progress he describes from Moscow to Siberia includes incidents from both journeys. There is one incident in particular that makes that clear and says something about his treatment of Lucy which she could never spell out, perhaps because she did not expect it to be different.

They arrive at Nijni Novgorod (named Gorky from 1932 to 1991). In his narrative she is not with him; in truth she was hardly there either – but they can hardly be two separate occasions. Lucy writes:

> On arriving at the ancient town of Nijni Novogorod, I was pleased to find that we should pass the night there, as I had a great desire to see this place. We drove to an hotel in the lower town, dirty in the extreme, and were taken into a small room. I was horrified at finding that everything must be taken out of the sledge. I asked whether it would not be better to proceed at once. Such could not be, Mr Atkinson having promised to call on Prince Ourousoff, the governor of the town. After partaking of some refreshment, I gladly spread the bear-skins, and stretched my limbs, which felt a little stiff. (p8)

And Thomas's version:

> Having a letter to the governor, Prince Ouroussoff, I determined to stay a few hours and deliver it, also to stroll through this ancient city, ... Entering the lower town I was taken to a sort of inn on the banks of the Volga; but as my stay was to be short it mattered little what accommodation it afforded. All those travellers who expect to find a Russian host very attentive to his guest will be disappointed. My postillion led the way upstairs, and showed me a whole flat of pens or private boxes in a filthy condition, and with very little furniture; these were formed by dividing large rooms with inch and a half boards. My luggage was brought upstairs, as it could not be left with safety in the sledge. After a wash my man succeeded in getting (with some difficulty) breakfast. Having dispatched this meal I got into a sledge and paid my visit to the governor, who received me with much kindness, and insisted on my dining with him ... Having spent a few pleasant hours, I returned to my dirty room, intending to get, if possible, a good night's rest, and start at daylight. At this place they provided neither bed, mattress, pillows, nor sheets; a bedstead there was with a boarded bottom on it. I rolled myself up in my fur and prepared to sleep. (pp19–20)

The brevity and lack of colour in Lucy's account – normally bouncy and full of detail – tells the reader everything about her memories of that sordid inn and suggests much about their relationship – at least at that stage; they had recently been married. From Thomas's account one supposes that the squalidness of the place enhanced his feelings of being a stoic traveller. He ignores Lucy's obviously mild request – she does not complain to him of the filthy box-like room, but of the problems of bringing all the luggage up – to travel on because he has a letter of introduction to the governor. He leaves Lucy cold and tired after hours in a sledge over a pot-holed track to curl up in her furs, while he goes off to talk and dine with the governor.

There is only one other intimation of extraordinary behaviour on Thomas's part and extraordinary fortitude on Lucy's. Because she is writing chronologically and to some extent at the time (in detail if not as in the published version) a fine climax comes naturally. The scene is set by some remarks which suggest on the surface only an attitude of determination to keep up and not be a little woman, especially vis-a-vis their Cossack guide Alexae. There is a river to cross, one of many, this time only a stream during a stroll. Lucy tells how:

> I was standing, deliberating whether it was worth the dirtying of my boots, when I felt myself gently lifted over. I turned round, presuming it was my husband, but no! there was Alexae wandering off in another direction; I ungenerously felt a little indignant, for I had made the remark to my husband that he always treated me as a child, and this act was a confirmation of my impression. (p70)

A few pages later it was the end of that particular stretch of what was to be a five-year journey and Lucy writes of how Alexae said:

> ... with a look of pity, 'You must be very tired.' I said 'No, indeed I am not.' 'Well,' said he with astonishment, 'We are men and accustomed to riding, and you are not; there is not another lady could have done as you have done. And now that the journey is over, I have often wondered how you could go through all you have gone through.' This was sincere praise, and I can assure you I felt not a little proud to have merited it. (pp83–4)

A little later in that letter Lucy writes, 'I began this in October, and it is now the 14th November; you will naturally wonder what has prevented my finishing it; I am going to tell you' (p105). And so she does:

> You must understand that I was in expectation of a little stranger, whom I thought might arrive about the end of December or the beginning of January; expecting to return to civilisation, I had not thought of preparing anything for him, when, lo! and behold, on the 4th November ... he made his appearance. The young doctor here said he would not live more than seven days, but, thank Heaven, he is still alive and well ... the doctor says the premature birth was caused by excessive exercise on horseback.

If her son Alatau was due at the end of December, he was conceived at the beginning of April when they were already on the road. For the next seven months – he was two months premature – the journey was hardly one that a Victorian wife might have expected to undertake; even an early twenty-first-century one, who might go to the office full time until the day before delivery, might have baulked at it. Yet Thomas, if he suggested returning to Moscow or St Petersburg or even settling in Barnoul during Lucy's pregnancy, was turned down by this woman who, until then, had presumably led a rather sedentary life and who was having her first child far from family or competent doctors. She writes of the doctor available in Kopal, deep in the Southern Siberian mountains:

Doubtless, seeing I speak of the doctor, you imagine we have a competent one here. Far from it, he is but twenty-three years of age; theoretically he may be clever, practically certainly not. When my husband applied to him in my case, he declared he had not the slightest knowledge of anything of the kind. (p106)

Alatau Tamchiboulac Atkinson was the only baby born that winter in Kopal who survived.

Lucy's description of the journey that ended in Kopal not only gives some indication of what she went through; there are also hints in it of a relationship between her and her husband that had tenderness and important moments of laughter together. They had set out one morning with one of the guides saying that the distance to be covered before they could stop was 40 versts, the other 60 (approximately 26 miles and 40 miles). Lucy writes, 'I was quite capable of doing either'. But both estimates were completely false and she had to confess that at 2 o'clock in the morning – they had been travelling since seven the previous morning:

I said I could not go farther without rest; I was likewise so cold that I could scarcely hold the reins of my horse, as there was a cutting wind blowing from the snow mountains. I now dismounted, trembling with cold, having nothing on me but my dress, my warm jacket having been lost that day by coming unstrapped from my saddle; they gave me a bear's skin to lie down upon, and my husband's shube [fur coat] to cover over me. We had about a pint of rum, which we took with us as a medicine; my husband would insist upon my taking a little, when I drank about half a wine-glass full pure, without its taking the slightest effect upon me, further than I felt revived. He now sat down beside me; after sitting about half an hour I began to get warm, I then dozed off for a few moments, when our guide came to say we must go on or we should be all lost; without water the horses could not proceed after the sun rose. I got up, and felt so much refreshed, that I could go on again. My husband then fastened his shube around me with his belt, and got me with some difficulty stuck on to my horse, for the shube was such an unwieldy thing; then he tied a bear's skin round himself and away we went quite gaily, laughing at our singular costumes. Two hours more passed away, and then I found my strength begin to fail me. I dismounted and walked about a hundred paces; I again got on to my horse and another hour passed over, when I said, 'I cannot sit my horse longer,' and begged they would go on and leave me, and if they found water to return and bring me some. I once more descended and walked a little distance and again mounted. My husband now held me by the hand, in the other I kept the reins, but that was all, I had no power to guide my poor horse. We now saw a thin streak of light appear on the steppe, and knew that day was breaking. I heard the barking of several dogs; no music ever sounded so sweetly in my ears. I cheered up, grasped the reins of my horse and rode on quite briskly; and at five, or a little after, we got to an aoul [village] belonging to a poor Moolah. I was lifted off my horse by the women and actually carried into the yourt; they commenced rubbing my hands and feet, placed cushions and carpet for me to repose on. I asked for water, but Peter told me it was unfit to drink. (pp100–2)

One wonders if Thomas Atkinson can be entirely blamed for his wife's suffering. She does not seem to have possessed the attributes myth attaches either to Victorian ladies or put-upon governesses. Before the events just described, Lucy confesses that:

Some of the good ladies of the place ... entered, and advised, before completing our arrangements, that we should discuss the journey over a cup of tea feeling assured they would be able to show the impossibility of my continuing it; they had heard of the great horrors and miseries endured by some of the wives of the Cossacks who had but lately crossed the steppe with their families on their way to the new fortress. They were convinced I should die ere I reached the place. I laughed at their fears, and assured them that it would cause me much anxiety to be left behind, and, even though they told me that death would be my lot if I went, still I was firm to my purpose. You know I am not easily intimidated when once I have made up my mind. I started on this journey, with the intention of accompanying my husband wherever he went, and no idle fears shall turn me; if he is able to accomplish it, so shall I be. I give in to no one for endurance. (pp87–88)

By then, 9 July 1848, Lucy must at least have suspected she was pregnant. But had she told Thomas? Women play a large part in her narrative and their reaction to him suggests he was not totally thoughtless, for Lucy writes of the women among whom she moved just before the incident where she could take no more: 'What struck them most with astonishment was the attention paid me by Mr Atkinson, as our sex is looked upon by the Kirghis as so much inferior to the "lords of creation"' (p92).

Lucy was attuned to the position and treatment of women in Kirghis society and she wrote in her introduction:

My friends have so often importuned me to give them some account of what happened to me in countries where an English lady had never been seen before, and to describe the manners which characterise female society among the wild Kirghis, that I have bethought myself to collect some of the letters written on the spot to friends. (pvi)

She was true to her word but it is hardly plain description: she is not slow to add good strong comments that marry her own position with theirs. She describes how on one occasion her horse, Columbus, ran away with her, and when he had finally calmed down and their guide caught up with her; she writes:

... the man patted me on the back, and gave me to understand how proud he was of me; then he showed me what a Kirghis woman would have done under similar circumstances. First, he commenced screaming, and almost set my horse into another fright, and concluded by falling from his horse. He remounted, and again patted me with evident delight ... On reaching our party, I received so many congratulations at my safe return, as also for my bravery, that I verily believe, if we had stopped longer in the steppe, a woman would not have been looked upon as such a contemptible being as they consider her to be; for the men now began to notice me, a thing they had scarcely deigned to do before. (p191)

On another page she writes of Alatau:

How lucky it is that he is a boy, and not a girl; the latter are most insignificant articles of barter. I am scarcely ever looked at excepting by the poor women, but the boy is somebody ... he is to be envied, lucky boy! Why was I not born a boy instead of a girl? – still, had it been so, I should not have been the fortunate mortal I am now – that is, the wife of my husband and the mother of my boy. But, I pray you, do not make them acquainted with my feelings; they are both capable of taking advantage of the knowledge you would impart. (p153)

And again:

And a mother ...: as the hour of her accouchement draws nigh, it is stated she is possessed of the devil, and they beat her with sticks to drive him away; and as the moment approaches, they call on the evil spirit to leave her. Poor woman! her lot in a future existence, it is to be hoped, will be an easier one, as here she is a true slave to man, contributing to his pleasure in every way, supplying all his wants, attending to his cattle, saddling his horse, fixing the tents, and I have even seen the women helping these 'lords of the creation' into the saddle.

My husband says the Kirghis have opened his eyes to what is due to husbands, and he is half inclined to profit by the lesson; and even thinks of opening an institution to teach husbands how to manage their wives, and believes it might be made a profitable concern ...

Do fancy, for a moment, what a position a woman fills. A dog is even considered her superior. When a favourite one is going to have pups, carpets and cushions are given her to lie upon; it is stroked, caressed, and fed upon the best of everything. Women alone must toil, and they do so very patiently. One Kirghis, seeing me busy sewing (indeed I was occupied in making a coat for my husband), became so enamoured of my *fingers* that he asked Mr Atkinson whether he would be willing to sell me; he decidedly did not know the animal, or he would not have attempted to make the bargain. With me amongst them, there would shortly have been a rebellion in the camp. (pp154–5)

Lucy's humorous insertions concerning her own husband are an important commentary on her relationship with him – even if the whole of her account can also be seen as an Englishwoman noting gross abuse of women in traditional society and failing to appreciate her own position and that of other Englishwomen in their more 'civilised' setting. She, who has some consciousness of herself as a woman, is able to laugh rather than bridle. That suggests that, however much she devotes herself to him, and she does assiduously, he does see her as a person in her own right. Perhaps that is why he did not insist on mollycoddling her when she was so determined to go with him. That hypothesis is consistent with his attitude towards women in general, as it appears from his own account – though he does refer to women as 'the softer sex' (p114). He describes how, at the beginning of his first journey, before Lucy was with him, he sought shelter, communicating with a dictionary, with a Siberian family:

> I was placed at the head of the table, the good man at one side, and I naturally expected his amiable spouse would take a seat opposite to me, instead of which she walked to the end of the room and sat down; but, having refused to partake of their hospitality unless she would sit by us, the lady was induced to make one of the party, after which everything went on well ... Finally, as a finish to our repast, my host brought in a bottle of champagne, and *two* glasses on a tray, evidently intending that he and I should drink it alone; but here I was forced to disappoint him, for, as soon as he had filled a bumper for me, I could not help presenting it to his wife, evidently to her great surprise and pleasure. Another glass was brought for me, and we then very deliberately proceeded to finish the bottle. (p32)

Lucy's attempts to glean women's lore were not always successful; she writes of an occasion in Kopal:

> Colonel Keil (the officer in command of the Cossacks) called upon us and invited us to tea; he was a most gentlemanly man; we spent several hours with him; my husband gained, much information from him; but, unfortunately, I was the guest of the wife, and from her I would defy anyone to gain information upon any subject, excepting it might be dirt! and on this point I fancy her information would be original. (pp50–1)

And, of course, gleaning only women's lore had other drawbacks too:

> What rendered our little expedition here most agreeable was the presence of two or three ladies who had accompanied their husbands for the summer. Still it sometimes prevented me seeing all I should otherwise have seen, as without them I might have wandered about everywhere, and now I was obliged to associate with my sex, not that I was sorry to do so, but it debarred me from seeking novelty. (p233)

Some reasons for Lucy's travelling – and the ways in which she felt fulfilled by it – have been established: she had married, relatively late, an adventurous man and she was anxious to be with him; she liked to learn new things; she was interested in people and found the women where she travelled particularly fascinating; she loved nature. She writes, for example, of holding the party up while she picks wild flowers – though she regrets that she is not a botanist like Thomas who sprinkles Latin tags liberally. What also emerges is that she also had a dream of visiting Siberia. She and General Muravyev had discussed it long before there could be any question of her going there, for he had a distant family connection with the Decembrist revolutionaries of 1825.

Lucy's account of intentional meetings with exiles in Siberia is invaluable to the historian of that period and her detailed observation of them and their conditions and her compassion are more attractive than her husband's perfunctory comments.

Other small details show her to have contributed more to the five-year venture than her obstinacy and ability to endure. Early on, Thomas's retainer proved himself hopelessly unreliable and Lucy took over papers and money; she was now installed in 'my new office of "minister of finance"' (p6). It was she who had found the maps in St Petersburg with which Thomas had originally started out and it was she who procured fresh horses at the post stations when they were travelling by sledge. She took her turn in keeping watch at night when there was danger and she took part in the evening rifle and pistol practice. 'I hope, however,' she wrote, 'that I shall not be called upon to use any of my weapons in defence' (p21). Among the snippets of family lore that survive is that Lucy always carried a gun or pistol – one assumes only when travelling.

Later she gained kudos in front of a Kalmuk man for bringing down a squirrel; indeed, she was patted on the back for it. So elated was she at the renown she acquired that she resolved to shoot the bear that had been trespassing into the camp but the bear failed to oblige her. She was an excellent rider, admired even by the Kalmuks, riders par excellence, and she always looked after her own horse when there were dangerous passages on foot to traverse. Here is her description of other responsibilities that became hers:

> Remember, it was not as it was in Petersburg, where I had only my own 'traps' to attend to! I had, in the first place, to separate what would be necessary for us in the Steppe, from the clothing we should leave behind. Then there were dry provisions to think of and to purchase, as in the place we were going to there was nothing at all to be obtained, excepting sheep, and *they* not always; then all these were to be packed, and so contrived as to occupy the very smallest compass possible … (p49)

And when they were travelling there were her day-to-day duties:

> We rode for ten hours over burning sand without stopping; which, together with the intense heat of the sun, rendered me almost dead with headache.

The reflection affected Mr Atkinson's eyes very much. When we were encamped, I was so very ill that I became a little alarmed. How gladly would I have lain down! But it could not be. I had Alatau to wash and bathe, which I usually did whilst the tent was being got ready, and the camels unloaded; and this ended, I had the bed to make, – how I knelt down to it, I scarcely know. After this was done I fed the boy and put him to bed. We were exceedingly systematic in all our arrangements; each one had his allotted task; no one was idle; and there was no hurry or confusion. Having performed my duties, and seen my husband seated at his tea, I lay down on a bearskin, and thought never to rise again; but after a sound sleep I was all right, and ready for my breakfast a little after five, having fasted for twenty-four hours, and had a fatiguing day's ride. We never allowed Alatau to suffer if we could avoid it. (pp199–200)

There was more to Thomas's ill-health than eyes troubled by glare; it would be a mistake to think it was only Lucy who suffered from fatigue or sickness, through pregnancy or otherwise. There are numerous instances told by them both of him succumbing to fever or some injury. But they both had a strong streak of obstinacy that must have formed an important bridge in their relationship. She admits to '*a little streak of wilfulness* in my disposition' (my italics) (pp46–7) and says of him that 'my husband does not permit impossibilities without proving them to be so himself' (p162). But there was more to it than obstinacy for him. Early in his trip, before Lucy was with him, he writes of one occasion when 'At times I almost feared we must give in, but my English spirit said No, and on I went, determined not be beat by my woodsman' (p39).

Her driving force is a little different. At one moment of extreme danger she observes that Thomas 'started bidding me to lie down and keep quiet, but such was not my nature. If I were to be captured I was determined to see how it was managed ...' (p183).

Lucy was by no means all toughness and roughness. The sight of her son or a stricken deer or both with their heads on the same pillow in innocence, or wild flowers, inspire her to lyricism; and she had her moments of maidenly modesty, too; but she conquered them:

I have not told you of the many rapid streams we had to cross; some where we had all to ride together the one to bear the other up. The Kirghis, invariably placing me in the centre, and clutching my dress, seemed determined to take care of me. Some of the streams were broad and deep. When it was so, I used to retire behind the reeds or rocks, as the case might be, and, stripping, put on my bathing gown, with my belt round my waist; and tying my clothing into a bundle, boots and all, I jumped on to my horse – merely holding tight on to him with my legs, there being no saddle – and swam him across in the company of a Kirghis, he gallantly carrying my bundle for me; when I would again retire with my bundle to re-equip myself. These are the sort of things we have to do in travelling.

At first I used to feel (I will not say timid, but) my heart beat quicker; now I think nothing of it. I am vastly altered since leaving Petersburg. (p190)

Thomas writes on the same subject specifically rather than generally:

After this escape from wind we were soon on the bank of the Yeljin-saw-gash, a broad and deep stream, over which we must swim our horses. We undressed and took off our saddles; my clothing, and my sketches and fire-arms, were carried over on the heads of the Kirghis, some of whom swam their horses four and five times across the river. (p472)

No Lucy. And the pin-pointing of that occasion is misleading. It is virtually impossible to follow the way Thomas cuts his narrative about, the way he re-stitches not only chronology but the direction in which he is travelling. It would be tedious to devote space to the many details of that phenomenon but one example is necessary to give a feel of the problem and enough evidence to suggest a reason or reasons.

It is clear that occasionally Lucy was persuaded to stay behind; she admits it and always regrets it. She wrote of 1852:

I have been induced, through the very urgent entreaties of our friends, to allow my husband to go alone this summer to ascend the Bielouka. I consented the more readily, as I had visited the regions round about before; and, besides, Colonel Sokolovsky had intended joining him in this excursion ... He now tells me he regrets much that I did not go, as I have missed some fine scenery; and besides, he says, he missed his companion. He also missed the little arrangements I was able to make for our comfort; I always tried to do this, though scarcely able, at times, to move from fatigue ... All in Barnaoul had spoken of the terrors of a journey to Bielouka, but in his letter to me he says: 'It is only imaginary, and you have gone over places ten times more difficult.' ... I wept to think that I had, against my own inclination, yielded to the advice not to go with him; that storm, as he now describes it to me, I would have given some years of my existence to have witnessed. (p316)

Thomas, on the other hand, so far as one can work out his dates, describes an adventurous and original visit in 1852 to the Gobi desert, over the border into China, via a border town which he calls Tchoubachack (also known as Chougachak or Chuguchak). He says on page 469 of *Oriental and Western Siberia* that his party passed 'about ten versts to the north of Tchoubachack, a Chinese town, in which Russia has, since this period, established a consul ... we passed Chinese pickets about noon on the second day'. That is all he says, and the description of crossing the river just quoted comes a few pages later. He writes as if he has never been there before. And yet we know from Lucy, from an interesting two days which she describes in detail, that he was there with her in 1849.

She writes, 'On the 9th of August we arrived at a Chinese piquet close to Choubachack, or, as they called it, Chougachak. Falstaff [the nickname for a guide] tried to dissuade us from going on, as he had been told by a Tartar that the Chinese would make us prisoners; I laughed at his cowardice' (p193). They were not hindered; instead, they had a cordial meeting, at which sweetmeats and tea were served, with a group of Chinese officers. What is more, Thomas drew a picture of the occasion – reproduced in Lucy's book and at the beginning of this chapter – with him and Lucy on stools and Alatau in the arms of the senior officer.

Lucy writes, too, of an emissary that visited them the following day, 'They said we were the first English who had ever presented themselves in this part of China …' No permission being available to enter the town, Thomas was told that if he shaved his head and dressed like a Tartar merchant he could slip in 'but to this he would not consent, as an Englishman he would visit the place or not at all'.

Thomas mentions none of it, relating either to 1849 or 1852 when, given his tendencies to chop chronology, he could easily have inserted such an unusual sequence of events into his narrative, simply leaving out Lucy and his son. Soon after his brief mention of Chougachak, Thomas describes meeting and drawing Sultan Beck and his family (p475); but Lucy met them in 1849 (p205).

There may sometimes be some simple explanations for why they do not describe the same events – if one simply reads the book and speculates. First, he may not have intended at the beginning to take notes on which to base a book – he was, after all, primarily concerned with making sketches and providing a commentary on his work. Knowing that she was writing detailed letters, did he tend to leave out of his notes what she had covered? On the few occasions when she was not with him he mentions writing up his journal; the storm he wrote to her about is an example. Is it that he prefers to describe for his readers difficult journeys undertaken when he was alone, or did he make more copious notes when he was alone? Did he have more time to write up his journal when there were no domestic distractions?

But then there is Lucy's 26 June 1862 letter to her publisher John Murray: 'You bid me not to touch upon the subjects my husband had already written upon. I believe I have obeyed, at least I have tried to, to the letter.' One can sometimes come unstuck with biographical and literary speculation, even though, in spite of Lucy's efforts they do often enough write about the same events.

There are several possible answers to the mysteries of chronology, omission, inclusion and distortion in his book. (1) He had married Lucy bigamously (but that did not mean he had to distort the details of nearly every journey). (2) He was spying for the Tsar or for the British Government and wished for one reason or another to obscure his real routes. (3) He wished to show what an intrepid explorer he was – but, again, why the distortions which do not support that explanation? (4) His notes were such a jumble that he himself lost the true thread. (5) He rearranged the order for reasons of style, to make a good story. He was not always very successful if that was the reason.

It would be unfair and inaccurate to call Thomas Atkinson's *Oriental and Western Siberia* tedious – but there are patches of tedium. That tendency is even more marked in the second book which has been accused of plagiarism. The same applies to humour. He was not without it; the following anecdote shows that. He is spending the night with strangers in Siberia on his first journey; his hosts question him incessantly:

> They talked very fast, however, and I listened attentively, saying ('Dah!' 'Neate') Yes or No, in Russian as the case appeared to require. At length I got tired of this, and began an oration in English, speaking as fast as I could, by which I got the advantage, for they ceased immediately. But the moment I left off addressing the chair, one or other began to catechise me again. As a last resort, I was driven to try some snatches of poetry, which fairly silenced them. (p49)

But he does take himself seriously. The extract at the beginning of this chapter about their visit to Nijni Novgorod shows that. His writing tends to be impressionistic, while Lucy's is factual. He has a feeling for history, and progress; Lucy has a sense of the immediate. He is very conscious of style. He takes risks with pace sometimes which are probably necessary, given the density of his narration, but it can be disconcerting. He has the soul of a poet, or craves the soul of a poet, and carries it into his relationships with those he meets. Lucy tells of their guide Peter:

> I surnamed him the Great for he was one of the most consummate liars I have ever met with; my husband said not so! He was only a poet; his imagination was of a lively nature, he had an answer for everybody and a reason for everything. (p97)

Lucy stands no nonsense in her life or her writing. She tells her story straightforwardly, as it was, from her viewpoint. She is without pretension. She is prepared to say, 'I do not pretend to tell you …' (p186). And:

> The art of writing is a great boon to us, and I often bless the discoverer of it; as by our pens we are able to convey to those far from us some of our thoughts and feelings. Still, in comparison, how little it is we can say of all that happens to us …

He pretends, as we have seen. She seems to tell a good story naturally – though it is clear from her correspondence with her publisher that she reworked and polished; his working at it shows. She may even have been less guileless than it appears.

And what did they both get out of the journey? She says in a passage already quoted, 'I am vastly altered since leaving Petersburg.' Earlier she had written, 'Many a good lesson have I learnt on this journey … on our first arrival here I was dainty' (p123).

She was a surprising woman when she started out, and she did not have the usual rigidly ethnocentric Victorian attitudes to people in 'uncivilised' societies; she was able to establish relations with them which were a little maternal but trying to view them in their own terms. She describes a party of Kalmuks early on in the journey:

> They all commenced quarreling about a few ribbons and pieces of silk I had given to our men. They had tied strips of red around their necks; but I satisfied all parties, as I thought, by giving some to the new comers; it did appear very ridiculous to see these great strong men taking delight in things which would only have given pleasure to a child at home. And yet I do not know whether we ought to look upon their doing this with contempt; how many men in a civilised country take pride in adorning their persons with the view of looking fine, and these simple creatures were only doing the same, only in a ruder manner! Still the quarreling continued, and then it turned out that the fellows were drunk. We had much difficulty in getting rid of them, and not until near midnight did they take their departure.
>
> These poor men are hardly dealt with, having to pay tribute to two emperors, the Chinese as well as the Russian. They are extremely good-natured. Whenever they saw me attempting to climb the rocks in search of flowers or fruit, they would ascend most difficult places to procure them for me. (p68)

Much later in the trip, when the worst of it was over and they came to rest after months of travelling, latterly in bad weather, she writes a passage which can be linked to several other remarks that begin to conclude her account:

> Notwithstanding this little drawback, I have enjoyed my trip amazingly; and have returned, I hope, wiser and better, having learned how little is necessary to render us happy. (p256)
>
> ... I could almost wish I were a Kirghis, wandering forth like them, under a serene sky, in search of mountain pastures. Happy people! Free and unfettered by any customs of so called civilised life. In those beloved mountains, how many a wild idea has crossed my brain, how many a spot have we fixed upon to be our final resting-place in this world of care! It was usually under the shade of a tree, where the mountain rill could be heard which fancy led me to believe would sooth the spirit to rest. (p330)
>
> ... Whereas now I am in a warm room, and surrounded by every comfort. I should probably shock you did I say which I prefer. (p335)
>
> ... I now look back on all those scenes, and repeat what we have often and often said, that willingly would we face ten times more toil and difficulty rather than go down to mother earth without having beheld them. (p351)

And one of Thomas's final flourishes:

> With this view I shall take my leave of the Alatou and Mustou Mountains, among which I wandered for one hundred and twenty three days; visiting scenery of the most striking character, which contributed one hundred and nine sketches to my folio. In these regions I encountered many dangers; providence, however, preserved me. Once a Kirghis sent a ball from my own rifle, which struck the rocks three inches above my head ... I often experienced hunger, and when I departed from the neighbourhood it was almost without clothing and without a serviceable pair of boots. Notwithstanding which, as I rode away I looked back with regret upon the purple summits and snowy peaks, remembering only the happy days I had spent among their wonderful scenery. (p496)

They returned to England. He became famous, not only in London but also in his native Cawthorne where he was invited by the Spencer Stanhopes to Cannon Hall, and to speak in the village. But he died soon after publication of his second book, leaving a reputation that was later to tarnish. In the year of his lingering death, there was no sign of that. Lucy wrote to the Reverend Charles Spencer Stanhope on 6 May 1861:

> ... knowing the interest you have always taken in Mr Atkinson, I think you will be pleased to hear [?] that he has received another splendid ring from his Imperial Majesty, the Emperor of Russia. It is a large emerald set in diamonds. Being so unexpected it is exceedingly gratifying as it is a mark of his Imperial approbation of the volume on the Amoor.

She seems to have started her own book before Thomas's death in August. She was nursing him devotedly when she wrote to Stanhope and in that same May letter explained,

> As you so kindly enquire after my literary labours you may necessarily suppose that under these circumstances that an entire stop has been put to my plan. I sometimes doubt whether I shall ever have the courage to take them up again. (Wilkinson p361)

Following the discovery of Thomas's betrayal of her, of which she seems to have written nothing, Lucy published her book in 1863. But she was so short of money then, what with her failure to receive the government money owed to Thomas, that she had to draw on their connections for support. One of these, through her publishers, was the Literary Fund. Another fund, for their son Alatau's education, was set up by the Royal Geographical Society, probably at the instigation of its president, Sir Roderick Murchison. Galton and other friends contributed, enabling Lucy to send Alatau to Rugby. He later taught at Durham School, Murchison's old alma mater.

However much Lucy suffered financially and emotionally, she did not lose her verve nor, indeed, her status as an intrepid traveller in her own right. On 26 March 1863, she attended a dinner party and sat next to the magistrate Sir William Hardman who, in the memoirs entitled by his editor S.M. Ellis *A Mid-Victorian Pepys* (1923), describes her as 'a bright-eyed, intelligent woman, small in stature'. He summarises her Siberian adventures, particularly the premature birth of Alatau under inhospitable conditions, and continues with a delicious anecdote concerning a well-known poet and novelist:

> She polished Meredith off at dinner in glorious style. He was in high spirits, and talking fast and loud. The Surrey hills, the Hindhead, the Devil's Punchbowl were the subjects of conversation, and George Meredith asserted (I know not on what authority) that the view from the Hindhead was very like *Africa*. Mrs Atkinson pricked up her ears, and bending forward across the table asked in a clear but low voice, 'And pray, Sir, may I ask what part of Africa you have visited?' Alas! Poor Robin! He has never been further south than Venice. No one could be more amused at his own discomfiture than he was himself, and he gave a very vivid description of his sensations when he saw Mrs Atkinson preparing the inevitable inquiry. As he had talked about Africa without having been there, the great Siberian traveller was disposed evidently to hold him lightly; for, later in the dinner, the talk was of certain cannibals who are to be imported as the last sensation exhibition, and the question of feeding them was mooted. 'Oh!' says Meredith, 'there will be no difficulty about that, we shall feed them on the disagreeable people, and those we don't like.' I was amused at the notion, and turning to Mrs Atkinson ... I said, 'I wonder how many persons would survive if every one disposed in that fashion of those he did not like!' 'Yes, indeed,' said the mother of Alatan [sic] Tamchiboulac, 'there would be very few, if any, and that gentleman (meaning Meredith) would be one of the first to go!'

Francis Galton's last word on Lucy is that she returned to Russia. Of course she had contacts there, but that was hardly reason enough. A clue to what took her back lies in Alatau's 1906 obituary in Hawaii, where he had a successful career as a journalist and educationalist. It says that he visited Russia in 1867 as secretary to the Turko-Russia Boundary Commission. Did Lucy, then aged 50, accompany him for old times' sake, and even to provide him with connections and to interpret for him? Murchison, too, was much involved in Russia, visiting it three times as a geologist, in 1839, 1840 and 1844, before the 1845 publication of his finds. Was he behind Alatau's visit there, and did he even speak up for Thomas 20 years earlier, together with an introduction to Humboldt in Berlin? Murchison returned to St Petersburg to present the Tsar with a copy of his book and receive honours from him in late 1845, and Thomas arrived there in March 1846. Murchison and his geologist wife, Charlotte, were childless and he is known to have taken intellectual 'sons' under his wing.

In the years following Lucy's later visit to Russia, she may even have travelled elsewhere. Her mother, widowed in 1847, had emigrated to Australia with her three youngest children, and later been joined by four others. Alatau, his wife and seven children made their life in Hawaii, his elder son 'Jack', a lawyer, not only going into politics but, as Immigration Secretary, travelling to Russia to bring back much-needed Russian labourers for Hawaii's sugar plantations (an unsuccessful venture).

Unfortunately, neither the descendants of the emigration to Australia, nor those of Alatau, have any evidence that Lucy visited her family in either place, and she may well not have been able to afford it. I know from the family, though, that she sent a fabric length to each of Alatau's daughters for their first ball.

There is at least one other late sighting of Lucy. According to family history, she was 'housekeeper' to the family of Sergeant-at-Law Benjamin Coulson Robinson at 43 Mecklenburgh Square, Bloomsbury, London. The 1881 census confirms that she lived there, together with Robinson's wife, Hannah, and it calls Lucy a cousin. It seems likely, therefore, that a 'poor relation' was taken in, as would have been commonplace then. Certainly Robinson had given a substantial contribution to Alatau's 1860s school fund. But Robinson died in 1890. In the 1891 census, Lucy was listed with the family of another relative, Thomas Sampson, in Stepney – where her parents had been married.

Lucy died of bronchitis, aged 76, on 13 November 1893 at 45 Mecklenburgh Square. That much is certain, recorded on her death certificate; more speculative is the suggestion that the owner of that house was Edward J. Conder, coffee roaster and dealer for the East India Company, who died two days later. Conder's mother was an Elizabeth Robinson. That is a common enough surname, but is it possible that Lucy moved next-door-but-one to another relative and that, in a final irony, she and Conder (aged 45) died in the Russian influenza pandemic that swept Western Europe from 1889–94? She and Benjamin Robinson were buried near each other in Stepney.

As for the rings given to Thomas by the Tsar, the emerald, at least, remains in the family.

2 – The Saving Grace of Humour

M. Whitecross Paton, *Letters and Sketches from the New Hebrides* (1896; 1994)
John G. Paton, *Missionary to the New Hebrides* (1889; 1994)

2.1   The Paton family, circa 1887
(from Paton, *Letters and Sketches from the New Hebrides*)

'The quality of endurance in the diaries and letters of a Victorian missionary wife makes hard reading', writes Joanna Trollope in *Britannia's Daughters*. Mary Anne Robson, first wife of John Paton (1824–1907), led that sort of life: she died from tropical fever in March 1859, a few days after the birth of their first child, who also died. She was the only white woman on Tanna, an island in the South Seas, in the chain of islands that now make up Vanuatu, what was the New Hebrides. She was 19 years old, had been married for less than a year and on Tanna for only three months. Three years later Paton himself fled for his life after a missionary couple had been murdered on nearby Erromanga.

MELANESIA

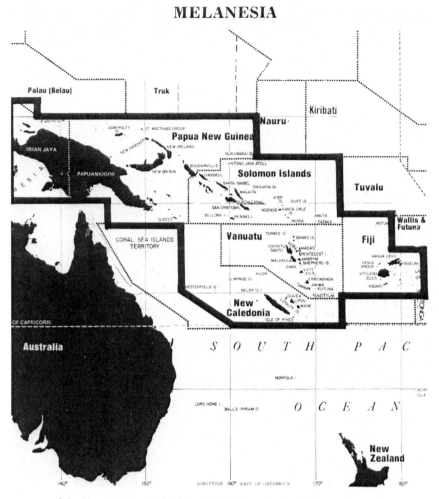

2.2   Vanuatu (New Hebrides) within Melanesia; tiny Aniwa to the south
(from Crocombe, *Politics in Melanesia*)

But the 15-year stay of John Paton's second wife, Maggie Whitecross (1841–1905), on Aniwa island in the same chain gives a rather different impression.

It is not that Maggie did not endure; it is more that she does not make it hard reading; and that was partly a question of personality. Look at Maggie when the mission church had just been built and they had managed to tempt a few Aniwa people through its portals for the first service. Like most missionaries in warm lands where people had previously not worn much, the Patons insisted on modest clothing. But access to drapery on Aniwa in 1862 was limited, so that first morning formal attire was a somewhat scratch affair.

Paton, 'Missi' as he was called, a bearded patriarchal figure, a covenanter of the Reformed Presbyterian church, welcomed them with relief and gratitude. It was that which Maggie found so difficult:

The effort at self-control was fast becoming unendurable, when the worthy Missi unintentionally proved 'the last straw'. His face was a picture of adoring thankfulness, and his prophetic soul – unconscious of anything grotesque – saw them already on the way to glory. He whispered, 'Oh Maggie, shouldn't we be grateful to God to see them all coming out to Church, so nicely dressed!' He was adding something about 'jewels' and 'trophies', but I was already half-way out of the Church, under cover of a convenient fit of violent coughing, and just managed to slip round a corner before going into prolonged convulsions! Pray forgive me; I loved them none the less; but that phrase – so nicely dressed – was rather more than my woman's soul could withstand. (p36)

Maggie is not very good at controlling what she calls her 'risibles'; indeed, having once failed to stifle her mirth in public, she lost her reputation and wrote home, 'I have rued that day ever since, as they have made it impossible to reform' (p116). But then, as she says, 'I wish I were a wise woman of, say, thirty, instead of an inexperienced girl' (p64). She was 23 years old when she married the 40-year-old widower in Scotland in 1865, and they sailed for the South Pacific a year later.

2.3 The mission house on Aniwa
(from Paton, *Letters and Sketches from the New Hebrides*)

John Paton was of similar background and endeavour to Thomas Atkinson, though his vocation was different. He was born into a peasant family of stocking makers, one of eleven children, and he entered the trade at eleven.

Soon thereafter he started to support and educate himself – working as a farm labourer and then attending Dumfries Academy for a few weeks when he could afford to. His first mission was ten years in a neglected part of Glasgow where he created a school.

At 33, in 1857, he was licensed as a preacher and a few months later ordained.

Maggie's life had been rather more comfortable until they met, though it had started to prepare her to be Paton's wife: her father was author of *Whitecross's Anecdotes*, 'illustrative of the shorter catechism and of the Holy scriptures'; her brother had died in mission harness and one of her sisters was married to a minister in Adelaide.

After 15 years on Aniwa, Maggie was still laughing, though it had not all been a laughing matter. As John Paton writes of one year in his autobiography,

> During the hurricanes from January to April 1873 when the Dayspring [the island mission ship] was wrecked, we lost a darling child by death, my dear wife had a protracted illness, and I was brought very low with severe rheumatic fever ... (p383)

But Maggie always bounces back in the end and one can begin to picture her, reading the odd clue here and there, even after childbirth – she had four children there, and arrived in the islands with a five-week-old baby – and fever: 'It is no use now for me to pretend I'm delicate, as appearances so tell against me' (p322).

It was not just her bubbly temperament; it was not all laughter; Maggie was a spirited lass, too. The following extract shows that, as well as giving some idea of her contribution to the enterprise on Aniwa:

> It will be so nice when the building is all complete; and I am trying my very best to make it the prettiest and most inviting Home I know – as refined, as civilised, and as nearly what we have been accustomed to as our limited resources will permit. We must not let ourselves 'down' because we are among savages, but rather try to lift them up to our Christian level in all things. One's Home has so much influence on one's work, and on life and character; and it is due to our two wee Boys to make it a bright one. We should do our life-work all the better, for having a Home in harmony with our tastes. At least it is no part of my creed to believe that there can be any religion in ugly surroundings, or that everything pleasant is sinful; though one old witch, a regular Mrs Grundy, did tell me, before leaving Australia, that Missionaries' wives were expected to live and dress in the most primitive way, and to set an example of great gravity and solemnity, else they would get to be talked about. The old Adam in me felt like choking such insolence; but I controlled myself to retort, that in my Bible there was no separate code of rules for Missionaries' wives, any more than for other Christian gentlewomen. (p61)

She does not compromise with John's flock either. Rangi, in a confrontation with Missi, threatened 'to go to Hell'. Maggie writes:

> John rebuked him and appealed to him. But I, not being the missionary exactly, felt free to express my mind, hinting pretty broadly that that was the place for him, that he would find suitable company there, and that it need not affect us whether he went upstairs or down! Whereupon he turned in amazement, and asked, 'If it doesn't make any difference to you then, for what did you leave your own land and come to us?' (p110)

That was the whole dichotomy of Maggie's life for, as she wrote in an open letter to be distributed to Australian children in a fund-raising effort for the *Dayspring*,

> If you came to be missionaries, you would find it uphill work indeed to be sacrificing your whole life merely for the sake of those who could not understand your motives, and who know not what it cost you to give up home and friends. (p102)

And one of her brightest moments is when one of her protégés, Litsi, says, 'Missi, I never knew what you had given up to come to our Dark Land!' (p120)

Maggie recognised the dichotomy herself but she had the character as well as the personality to withstand the dreadful tugs such as sending her children away to Australia. At a time when John was very ill and had to face decisions, she wrote home in her usual frank way:

> You will be apt to say, it serves him right after all your repeated advice to him about leaving the Mission and doing a parent's duty to his Children; but I must vindicate my old man even to his relatives, and most emphatically deny that it is mere obstinacy that makes him stick to Mission life. You know his whole spirit is saturated with it; and it's just as impossible to take the missionary spirit out of a man as it is to put it into him. Besides he does not feel that God has given him a direct call to leave it; and until that is the case, you may be sure he will not make the first move! Even I, who have never indulged in missionary sentiment (believing that John had enough for the pair of us!) would not leave one hour sooner, even for my children than God would have us; but if He does give the call, won't I spring with alacrity to obey! (p249)

She does not always accept that John is right about the sacrifices when it is between them, rather than defending him to his relatives:

> I find that those very noble women whom [John] holds up as examples to me, in devoting all their sons from infancy to be Missionaries, and whose only regret is that they have not another dozen to dedicate, have never been in the mission field themselves. (p301)

But John knows how to handle her, as well as she does him. The mission soon
has an adopted family of young rejects from their own families and aspiring
converts – a large burden on Maggie's shoulders. The day comes when yet
another lad dumps himself on their hospitality and it is too much:

> John was all for receiving him; but I was at crying point, and declared I
> could not feed more Natives or make food go further than other people.
> John said, 'Then am I to send him away?' Well, no! I was hardly prepared
> to do that either; so, after talking over it a few minutes, we felt sure the
> Lord had sent him; and though I did not feel particularly grateful at the
> time, I have often thanked Him since. (p254)

The relationship between Maggie and John Paton comes through warmly
from her account; he is more restrained, for obvious reasons: he is writing
the serious autobiography of a particularly important missionary. She is a
woman without pretensions writing gossipy letters home. There are, however,
asides from time to time that hint at her consequence in his ministry: phrases
such as 'accompanied generally by my dear wife' (p329) and 'at Mrs Paton's
advice ...' (p332). And we can see from her account that he was not the
humourless, self-important man that he seems from his own version. What is
more, he is able to put her own joking self-importance down with humour, as
she recounts when he falls ill soon after their return from a period in Australia:

> I felt myself a very important member of Society – keeping Schools going,
> giving out medicine to the Natives etc., besides housekeeping – and I asked
> John triumphantly what he would have done without his nurse, had I stayed
> in Melbourne, as he insisted? To which he rather profanely retorted, that he
> would just have died and got a far better rest in Heaven, while I would have
> been comforted among kind friends and had my Bairns around me! (p247)

On another occasion she shows that in spite of the sacrifices he expects of
her, he cares deeply:

> It is bad taste to praise one's own, and I wouldn't indulge in it for the world;
> only, I must say, I have had some rare chances to die, if John had been less
> lovingly vigilant. (p349)

How important Maggie Paton was in the mission work is confirmed by one
small incident from two descriptions of how it came about. It is worth noting
that John Paton's account is not unlively, and he is generous in giving his
wife a credit she does not take for herself. Nor, when we look at Maggie's
particular interest in the Aniwa women, should his ability to describe them
be overlooked. He writes:

> Next after God's own Word, perhaps the power of Music was most
> amazingly blessed in opening up our way. Amongst many other illustrations,

I may mention how Namakei's wife was won. The old lady positively shuddered at coming near the Mission House, and dreaded being taught anything. One day she was induced to draw near the door, and fixing a hand on either post, and gazing inwards, she exclaimed, 'Awai, Missi! Kai, Missi!' – the Native cry for unspeakable wonder. Mrs Paton began to play on the harmonium, and sing a simple hymn in the old woman's language. Manifestly charmed, she drew nearer and nearer, and drank in the music, as it were, at every pore of her being. At last she ran off, and we thought it was with fright, but it was to call together all the women and girls from her village 'to hear the bokis sing!' (Having no x, the word box is pronounced thus.) She returned with them all at her heels. They listened with dancing eyes. And ever after the sound of a hymn, and the song of the bokis, made them flock freely to class or meeting.

Being myself as nearly as possible destitute of the power of singing, all my work would have been impaired and sadly hindered, and the joyous side of the Worship and Service of Jehovah could not have been presented to the Natives, but for the gift bestowed by the Lord on my dear wife. She led our songs of praise, both in the Family and in the Church, and that was the first avenue by which the New Religion winged its way into the heart of Cannibal and Savage. (pp362–3)

Maggie writes:

The Natives, indeed, are extremely fond of singing and of music of any kind. I was most amused to see the power it had one day over a poor superstitious woman. She had ventured to come and look round the place with her little boy; but nothing would induce her to come near the door. She always drew back, saying she was frightened; and, when I patted her little boy on the shoulder, she drew him quickly away. I thought to try what effect music would have, and, slipping into the parlour, I began to play very softly the Tyrolese Evening Hymn. In a moment or two she came gliding in, all her superstitious fears forgotten, with a wistful and eager expression in her large black eyes, and she sat down by my side. When I finished, she lifted both hands imploringly, crying in her own language, 'O Missi, make it sing more!'

I have such a fine large Class of women and girls; and I never expected it could be such delightful work to teach them – they are so amiable and pleasant and willing to learn. There are about fifty of them; and you can imagine that it is no light work preparing seams for them all, especially as they are so fond of sewing. But I shall soon be able to vary the occupation, by teaching them reading, for Mr Paton has finished printing our first Aniwan book, greatly to the delight of the Natives! I hope my women will learn to read, and will like it as they do the sewing and singing; for, at present, after sitting for two hours and a half, they would like to go on still longer. Some of the Mothers bring their Babies, and sew and nurse alternately. It is a fine sight to see them all, some of the old ones with their spectacles, sitting in rows round the parlour floor, the spectacles having given them 'new eyes' and a new lease of life. (pp56–7)

The accounts of the music incident are interesting to compare. John is clear that it was Nameki's wife, an older woman; Maggie writes that it was a woman (presumably young) with a child. John goes on to recount how he helped Nameki's wife to read by giving her spectacles, leading one to suspect that he is running two stories together, irrespective of the real character, in order to make a neat and better single story, a characteristic, as we have seen, more male than female. But then Maggie tells the same story to another correspondent and that time it is her husband who patted the little boy on the shoulder, not her, as above, suggesting that it is a question of memory not contrivance.

Any inconsistencies there are trivial; it should be noted, however, that Jeremy MacClancy writes in *To Kill a Bird With Two Stones: A Short History of Vanuatu* (1980) that in spite of John Paton's 'good story ... It is a pity that so little of it can be believed ... there is no doubt that he embellished the truth' (p50). That is a serious charge and, since the history concerned is a brief one and only touches on Paton in passing, it is unsubstantiated. Because it tends to provide support for a line emerging in this study, it would have been remiss not to seek a second opinion. The Pacific historian, Sione Latukefu, replied to my query in the exemplary way I expected of him:

> Paton was not a trained historian. Like most of his fellow missionaries – as well as many of us – he had his biases and his strong convictions and the world view of his day. He did not have the benefit of the accumulated knowledge available to us today – a century after his time. (16 December 1987)

Maggie adds some revealing words about her relations with Aniwa women to her second account of the hymn incident. Very often when our women travellers are discussing the women they observe there is inevitably a feeling of *de haut en bas*, the civilised looking kindly but with condescension on the uncivilised. With Maggie there is reason for there to be a slight difference:

> I never dreamt it would be really such a delightful work teaching them, but my heart was drawn to them for the kindly way they behaved to me, when I landed among them, timid, and rather frightened at feeling myself the only white woman on these lonely shores. (pp77–8)

Earlier, she had written in detail of her arrival in a letter to her sister, particularly of Kanathie, the wife of one of the two Christian 'native' teachers:

> I am sure Kanathie can never know what a thrill of comfort and hope her presence gave me, that day we landed on Aniwa! I was eager enough to step out of the Dayspring into the little boat that was to carry us ashore;

but as we neared it, and saw black creatures (for really they hardly looked like human beings) peering at us from among the reefs, with not the flicker of a smile of welcome on their faces, I really began to tremble with a sort of dread, and wondered if they were thirsting for our blood ... I scarcely ever felt such a clinging to any one in all my life as to that poor woman; and I began to walk with a firmer tread ...

How anxiously did I watch for a smile from any of the women that day; and really they were very kind and civil, and did not refuse to shake hands, although I rather think I am the first white woman that has landed among them. Indeed, they would certainly have taken my heart by storm with their bright smiles, had I not been already sufficiently inclined to love them. (pp32–3)

The relationship established from the beginning ripened as the years went by and the women continued to show concern for Maggie, including during her confinements, though not necessarily for reasons that she appreciated. She was lying quietly soon after giving birth one year when she heard a persistent rustling:

It turned out to be two dear elderly Native women, creeping on their hands and knees, determined to get close to me by fair means or foul, in order to console me in what they thought my misery! They seized my hand sympathetically, and said, 'O Missi, Missi, you are young, and will live to forget this day! ... You must not fret about having only a Girl this time; you know you have had two Sons already, and will have many more before you die. We all have to bear the same disappointment. We cannot always have Sons!' I used the most forcible language which I knew, in their vocabulary, to make it very clear to them that their sympathy was entirely wasted. I made them exclaim with delight at the fat dimpled face and hands; and they left the room comforting themselves that they had seen 'a real white little Woman of Aniwa'. (pp107–8)

Sometimes Maggie's consciousness of herself as a woman in a man's society has humorous overtones, such as her description of their cook:

By the way, he is quite a character, that Cook of ours; knows a few words of English, which he is fond of airing, and say, 'Yes, Sir,' and 'No, Sir,' to me. I can't feel in my heart to bring him down from his pedestal of politeness, by correcting his mistake, and John won't, pleading that the fellow shows great penetration and knows exactly who rules the roast! (p129)

Sometimes Maggie's feelings about her own society are tongue in cheek, in a way that suggests that Victorian women put up with men's attitudes about their own superiority, even though the women knew better. Of earthquakes, which are a constant feature of the region, she writes: 'I think the greatest damage done is to the nerves of the poor Missionaries' wives (the Missionaries themselves would be indignant if you accused them of having any!)' On another level she writes of the occasions when the missionary couples living alone on the various islands got together for a few days for work and recreation – an annual and much enjoyed event: 'We four wives had then a most delightful time; and there was no gossip, no small scandal talk, which our lords and masters ungallantly predicted there would be' (p186).

It is not all good humour and laughter, however, when Maggie looks at the treatment of women by men, particularly Aniwa women. Then there are signs of bitterness in Maggie not seen elsewhere. Take Litsi, for example. She married a personable young man who turned out to be mad. Maggie writes:

> It seemed strange that Litsi, who so longed for death, should survive so much ill usage, for I could not pen a fiftieth part of the cruelty – the refinement of cruelty – with which he treated her. One instance will suffice. We missed him from Church one Sabbath, and found that he had spent the time skinning the lower part of her face and pinching little bits of flesh out of her chest from shoulder to shoulder, threatening her with his club if she dared to cry out. You will wonder that the Natives did not interfere. We began to lose all patience with them … I … have had to live twelve years on Aniwa to learn how exclusively a man's wife is regarded as his own peculiar property – that is to be used exactly as he likes. They would as soon think of interfering with a man's conduct to his wife, as we would if in Civilization a man chose to burn his own carpet or smash his own timepiece. They would break out in the most amused smile, when John was begging them to protect her, and say, 'But, Missi, it's his own wife!' (pp274–5)

John Paton has, so far, by his own writing, shown himself to be lively and concerned with the women of his flock. His writing is not, however, always so vivid and usually that concern was expressed in generalisation, theory, analysis; he has an anthropological approach, and, of course, an overtly religious one. It is not that he does not care about the particular woman; Maggie shows how he struggled on Litsi's behalf, more than is indicated from the extract. But from Maggie's description of Litsi's persecution one can see that for her it was a personal thing – a woman friend was suffering and she writes about it from the heart; one senses that she identifies with Litsi in a way that one cannot expect of John. He appears more comfortable writing in the following style:

> … we found that the Heathen practices were apparently more destructive to women than to men; so that in one Island, with a total population of three hundred and fifty, I found that there were twelve adult men over and above the number of women. As a rule, for every man that has two or more wives, the same number of men have no wives and can get none; and polygamy is therefore the prolific cause of hatreds and murders innumerable …
>
> While they remain Heathen, and have many wives to manage, the condition of most of the women is worse than slavery. On remonstrating

with a Chief, who was savagely beating one of his wives, he indignantly assured me, 'We must beat them, or they would never obey us. When they quarrel, and become bad to manage, we have to kill one, and feast on her! Then all the other wives of the whole tribe are quiet and obedient for a long time to come.'

I knew one Chief, who had many wives, always jealous of each other and violently quarrelling amongst themselves.

When he was off at war, along with his men, the favourite wife, a tall and powerful woman, armed herself with an axe, and murdered all the others. On his return he made peace with her, and, either in terror or for other motives, promised to forgo and protect her against all attempts at revenge. One has to live among the Papuans, or the Malays, in order to understand how much Woman is indebted to Christ! (pp405–6)

John's description of the ferocious favourite, for all its detachment, is important in building up a picture of the attitude of 'native' women towards polygamy – a state, it is often argued, that women not only put up with but valued.

Maggie is rewarded for her concern for the women of Aniwa. In 1881 she was very ill for a long time; she writes of an incident after her recovery:

... months after, when I was taking myself to task for my over-keen appreciation of the discomforts of the sick-room, instead of counting my blessings – the kindest Husband in the world, and three darling Children round me, etc. – Hushti, the Girl I had had most trouble with on the island, came into my room, burst into tears, and cried passionately: 'My heart is breaking for you, Missi! I can't think of you lying there, month after month, with not a white woman to look after you. We can't turn ourselves into white people, or cook things to make you eat; but keep up, Missi; you don't know how much we love you, and we are all praying for you ...'

How overwhelmingly sweet was such sympathy! I told Hushti, that it was worth being ill to get it, and that I felt strong now to bear anything. (p348)

And when Maggie and John went back to visit Aniwa in 1889, after leaving in 1881 because of ill-health, an old woman told her:

'Missi, you did not think we felt like you. You never told us your troubles. You used to smile, when you spoke of your Children in the far-off land, when we knew your heart was crying out for them. We knew the language of your heart, Missi, though you tried to hide it from us; and we Mothers often cried about you!' (p279)

So Maggie never gave herself completely to Aniwa women, in spite of spending hours in their company. They were not her sisters in the way the other missionary wives – whom she rarely saw – were; indeed, she refers to the latter as her 'sisters' and to their 'sisterhood' (p91). There always had to be a final reserve, the missionary front, the white front, however much she sympathised with the women among whom she lived.

Her first letters home show that her instinctive, or perhaps we should say conditioned, racial prejudice was quite marked, particularly towards Melanesian men. She writes, for example, of an occasion during the journey round the islands before they settled on Aniwa:

> It was [on Maré], if I remember rightly, that I first saw a real savage. I recollect so well, standing at the head of the Cabin stair with Baby, amusing myself watching the buying and selling going on a-deck, when Baby gave such a crow of surprise that I wheeled to see what was attracting him. A naked Savage was grinning over my shoulder, with scarlet and white paint stuck on his forehead and cheeks, and long white hair streaming down his back! Instinctively, I rushed half-way down the stair; but, recalling that I must come into contact with such creatures, I returned, and rather liked the poor soul before I had done with him ... (p13)

And she is entrenched in the same ethnocentric value system of most nineteenth-century travellers – one which can best be described by Oscar Wilde's dictum, '[he] knew the price of everything and the value of nothing'. She writes:

> They have not the slightest idea of what we call value. They simply take violent fancies for certain things, and, like children, can be pleased with nothing else. On Aneityum, for instance, the Officers of the Curacao were highly amused by the Natives there taking a penny in preference to a sovereign or crown, offered for a pig which was sold to their ship! (p15)

But then we see the making of a woman, for she writes some years later of an occasion that shows the Aniwa man and the white woman at their best and best able to communicate. She hears of a confrontation between an Aniwa man, Taia, and one from Erromanga. She knows that it will lead very quickly to violence but is loath to wake John whom she suspects is about to be ill. She decides to put a stop to it herself:

> They subsided for a few moments, when it was whispered the Missi was there; but on finding that it was only the Missi-finé, they went at it with renewed vigour. I took no notice of the Erromangan, knowing my only chance was with Taia; so I went over to him, and implored him not to utter another word, whatever provocation he might receive; and though reluctant at first, he behaved nobly and stood what I think few white men would have done in the circumstances. I kept close beside him all the time; and though for three quarters of an hour that villain stood heaping insults upon him, and at last in his rage cut down his bananas and fences before his eyes, he never spoke though his muscles twitched and he clutched at his great club sometimes – one that I knew had done good (?) service in Heathen days under the great brawny arms that wielded it, for Taia is a

perfect Hercules, and such a contrast to the little treacherous sharp-nosed Erromangan who was dying for an excuse to get a shot at him. When I thought Taia was going to give way I put my cold white paw (it did feel so cold) on his black arm, and every time I did so he turned and looked down at me with a grim smile, saying, 'Don't fear, Missi; I'll not speak.' Now I maintain that though John sometimes fears Taia's Christianity is not of the highest type, yet he is undoubtedly a perfect gentleman, or he would not have stood there, the greatest living orator on Aniwa, silent at the bidding of any woman. (pp229–31)

And Litsi, visiting Australia for the first time, opens Maggie's eyes to another way of looking at things:

In truth, Litsi's remarks about Civilization showed more wide-awake intelligence, than did as a rule the White folks' remarks about Heathendom. She once asked me if the Adelaideans had all quarrelled, as hardly any of them alofa-ed each other in passing; and when told that they had to wait for 'introductions' before speaking, said 'Was it not enough that they knew each other as Christians?'
… How instinctively she at once detected the difference between an intelligent interest in her, and that of those who petted her like a favourite pup that can appreciate nothing but food! (pp120–3)

In spite of their progress, both Maggie and John are certain that level of 'civilisation' is connected with 'age'. He writes, 'They were but children and full of superstition; and we had to win them by kindly patience' (p318). And she confirms his, and a common white, view:

Our Natives are very amusing in many of their ways; and, though often provoking and disappointing we do not lose heart, as we might do with white people, remembering that in these respects they are only children after all. (p130)

Sometimes intelligent children, of course; in the same letter Maggie writes:

You can have no idea how companionable the Natives are, when once you can talk to them freely. Their faces light up with such intelligence; and they are eager both to hear and to communicate … but they don't by any means take everything on trust. They must be convinced, before believing all you say. Once I described to a lot of women how water got so cold in Britain that it froze, and became so solid and hard that the people ran about on the top of it. I saw perfectly in their looks that they did not believe it, though too respectful to say so. It so happened that the Dayspring called the very next day; and what should Dr Geddie bring on shore, but a huge block of ice! … What crowds came to examine it! They touched it; they howled wildly over their first experience of real freezing cold; and they eagerly yet sorrowfully marked it melting away. I made the women confess their unbelief of the Evening before; but they added, with pawky grace worthy of a Scot, 'We did not believe you would lie, Missi! We just thought that somebody else had told you crooked.' (p138)

Maggie Paton was a child of her time – she died in 1905 – and one must be careful to judge views that may grate on us by the standards of her time, while at the same time marking any changes in women travellers who came after her. And she saw many things from a perspective that gives us insights her husband's account does not allow.

Her editor, James Paton, John's brother, tells us in his preface how fragments of Maggie's letters appearing in John's autobiography had whetted the appetite of readers. Maggie was persuaded that such family letters as had not been lost should be gathered together and published. James Paton sums up their worth:

> None of them were originally intended for other eyes than those of our Inner Circle. Hence the spontaneousness, the life-like look and feeling, which distinguish these Letters, and make them, in my judgment, worthy of being preserved and published. Their literary grace is of the unconscious kind – the rarest grace of all ... they [also] present another picture of Mission life and experiences in the New Hebrides from that portrayed in the now famous Autobiography of her Husband. No feature will be found in the one contradictory to the features in the other; but many lovely and thrilling scenes of a supplementary and illuminative kind. Here we have the Woman's delicate touch; we see with the Woman's eye; and, above all, we have what has been called 'the saving grace of humour' ... (ppv–vi)

The Patons settled in Melbourne after 1881. He was appointed mission agent of the Presbyterian Church of Victoria; Maggie was the founder of the Presbyterian Women's Missionary Union. Following her death, the organisation built a church at Vila, today's capital of Vanuatu, and a hospital in Korea in her memory. Of the Patons' two daughters and eight sons, one daughter and two sons died in infancy. But the link with the New Hebrides remained: one daughter married a missionary, and two sons became missionaries there.

3 – Equally Fearless and Feminine

Morning Star: Florence Baker's Diary of an Expedition to Put Down the Slave Trade on the Nile 1870–1873 (ed. Anne Baker, 1972)
Samuel Baker, *The Albert N'yanza* (1866); *Ismailia* (1874; **1895**; 2011)

3.1 and 3.2 Two faces of Florence Baker, 1865, after the first Nile expedition
(from Baker, *Morning Star*, and Hall, *Lovers on the Nile*)

Of all the travelling companions, undoubtedly the most intrepid, in the true sense of the word, were Samuel and Florence Baker who explored the Nile area between 1861 and 1865, and 1869 and 1873. The two journeys took them through today's Egypt and Sudan, ending in Uganda. Of all the women, Florence endured most with conspicuously active courage and lack of fuss. Sam ends his first book about Africa, *The Albert N'yanza* (1866):

> Had I really come from the Nile sources? It was no dream. A witness sat before me, a face still young, but bronzed like an Arab with years of exposure to a burning sun; haggard and worn with toil and sickness and shaded with cares, happily now passed; the devoted companion of my pilgrimage to whom I owed success and life – my wife. (p339)

But of all the women's accounts, that of Florence is the most disappointing. The diary and letter extracts contained in *Morning Star* (1972) give little feeling of a woman who must have been truly outstanding, and the deficiency

3.3   Samuel Baker dressed for the first Nile expedition
(from Hall, *Lovers On the Nile*)

is emphasised by Sam's books for he, unlike Florence, wrote as he travelled, with exuberance, humour and style.

It is not entirely surprising that Florence's account of 'The Expedition to Put Down the Slave Trade on the Nile 1870–1873' lacks lustre: she did not start learning to write English until she was 24, on her return from the Nile expedition in 1865, and then she was taught by a Victorian miss – her 18-year-old stepdaughter, Edith, who had early been deprived of her widowed father's unconventional presence and style. He might have leavened the effect his straight-laced sister Min (Mary) had on his daughter's upbringing.

Florence's editor, Anne Baker, wife of one of Sam's descendants, uses the term 'understatement' (p71) to describe her subject's style. But British understatement is something specific and can be effective in describing events the reality of which might seem exaggerated. It is not an appropriate description for the passage in question, written when Sam discovered a Nile boat full of hidden slaves, at a time when he was trying to eliminate the slave trade. Florence writes:

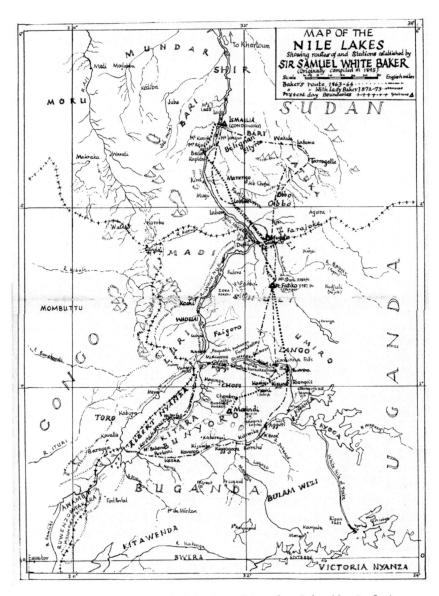

3.4   Nile Lakes, showing the Bakers' expeditions (from Baker, *Morning Star*)

Poor things, they were concealed in every way, some of them were nailed down with planks, others were put in mats, two or three were put into the sail, and a great many were hidden with elephant tusks. Of course Sam had the Captain of the two vakeels put immediately into irons and had all the poor slaves taken out of the boat. They seemed quite happy to get on shore again. (p71)

That is not understatement for style; instead, Florence's diary and letters, broken up by editorial linking and comment, and written originally in what Richard Hall describes in *Lovers on the Nile* (1980) as a 'large copperplate hand, strikingly different from the style in which she wrote German' (p184), usually appear stilted, trite and superficial. Some people can write and some can't. Sam wrote brilliantly, Florence did not.

What a life Florence had, and *Morning Star* is all the published record of it left showing her point of view; one has to read his books and use one's imagination, then Florence comes alive.

Queen Victoria refused to receive Florence, even though she had knighted Sam. It was not known about at the time – Florence and Sam appeared to, and did, lead a glittering public life on their return from Africa the first time. It was only in the 1980s that Victoria's behaviour and the possible reason for it became common knowledge, largely through Richard Hall's study.

The story is that Sam bought Florence in a Bulgarian slave market in January 1859 when she was about 17 and he was 38. He lived with her in Eastern Europe for a couple of years and travelled in Africa with her for another four and did not marry her in a Church of England ceremony until their return to England in 1865. The family believes there was an earlier marriage, perhaps in 1860 in Bucharest. Queen Victoria must have received an inkling of irregularity – perhaps from a jealous explorer who resented Sam's success.

Florence Barbara Mary Finnian von Sass (Szás) (?1841–1916) came to be in Widdin, in the Ottoman Empire a hundred miles from the Hungarian border, because of the revolution in the Hapsburg Empire in 1848. Her father and brothers, it is said – Florence never wrote about it – were killed before her eyes when she was six; she was rescued by her nanny.

Samuel Baker (1821–1893) was in Widdin in 1858–59, accompanying a young Maharajah on a European tour. He had been married before – in 1843 – but his wife died of typhus in 1855, leaving him with four daughters (three other children had died). Devastated though he was by his wife's death, Sam did not have the capacity to stay in England and be mother and father to their offspring. He had already proved himself a traveller, sportsman and writer; he did not have to earn his living and he did need adventure. He saw Florence in the barbaric setting of a Turkish slave auction; impulsively he bid for her. She belonged to him and that is certainly how she felt about it thereafter. In later years she would write, 'I owe everything to Sam' (Hall p29). That and nothing more.

The American historian Pat Shipman, conscious of gaps in Florence's life, has sought to remedy this in her biography *The Stolen Woman: Florence Baker's Extraordinary Life from the Harem to the Heart of Africa* (2004). You need to know, however, that she reconstructs Florence's early life mostly from general sources (detailed in endnotes), ones not specific to Florence. She also constructs conversations throughout the book. The chronology of events she provides is useful though, because of her general research into the harem and slavery in the Ottoman Empire of the time, she suggests that Florence was younger when she was sold than other sources do. I have used the more usual birth date, the one on the Baker family tree.

It was ironic that Sam and Florence should end up attempting to put down the slave trade of Egypt. Florence wrote of slave traders on 14 April 1870, after an incident when some of Sam's officers were caught buying women slaves, 'I really hate the sight of them, whenever I see one of them it reminds me of olden times' (p61). Anne Baker comments, 'Here Florence must have meant the first expedition to Lake Albert when she and Sam had been forced to travel with Ibrahim the notorious slave trader.' But might it not have been to her own past that she referred?

Sam married Florence formally immediately on their return to England – whatever her previous status had been – and he was knighted in 1866. They were soon appearing on public platforms together. On one of these, Sir Roderick Murchison, president of the Royal Geographical Society, after whom Sam had recently named the falls, talked of 'What the wife of a gallant explorer can accomplish in duty to her husband' (Hall p161). It went down very well.

Colonel Christopher Rigby complained to Nile explorer James Grant about 'Baker putting his wife forward'; and they knew what she had once been. Sam was doing just that, but it was sour grapes because Sam and Florence had been magnificently successful and his book was a tour de force.

By the time the second journey started in 1871 to put down the slave trade, Sir Samuel and Lady Baker were eminently respectable in most people's eyes. But had Florence become what she appears from her account – not his – of the next two and a half years? In her society image, perhaps, but it seems fair to assume that it was partly an image. If one places side by side, as at the beginning of this chapter, the two photographs of Florence taken at about the same time, at the end of their first African journey in 1865, one can see two versions of her: one a conventional Victorian Englishwoman, the other foreign, unfathomable, strong.

Some aspects were common to both images. When it seemed in 1873 that the Bakers had been killed by hostile natives or slave traders, *The Times* obituary described a Florence 'Who first shared Baker's adventures as a girl bride, equally fearless and feminine' (Hall p205). Florence would undoubtedly have been pleased with that. At the end of *Ismailia* (1874) Sam wrote:

Lastly I must acknowledge the able assistance that I have received, in common with every person connected with the inland expedition, from my wife ... In moments of doubt and anxiety she was always a thoughtful and wise counsellor, and much of my success through nine long years passed in Africa is due to my devoted companion. (p471)

But Florence describes the retreat from Masindi in terms that make her seem hardly more than a little woman who had to be protected. Sam, in his capacity as a Major General in the Ottoman army, Pasha of Equatorial Egypt, finds himself in unexpectedly hostile native territory. Through the treachery or incompetence of one of his officers, he has only a hundred soldiers with him. The local chief, Kabba Rega, has already proved himself vicious and well able to organise his thousands of followers. Florence writes in a letter to her stepdaughter Agnes which arrived long after all in England thought the Bakers dead:

> We started on the 14th of June, at 10 a.m. after we had set fire to the station and effects – I must say that my heart was very heavy to see all my beautiful things burn … Papa had made capital arrangements for marching.
>
> Abdel-Kader, the Colonel, marched in advance with a guard of fifteen Snider rifles and a bugler – Then Papa followed with Julian [his nephew] and two more Sniders and a bugler. I walked close to Papa with some ammunition for a large rifle. Whenever Papa fired that large rifle into the grass, we heard the natives groan. I also carried two bottles of brandy and two drinking cups, and two umbrellas and my pistol in my belt, and a heap of other little things. (pp156–7)

Baker's accounts, both *Albert N'yanza* and *Ismailia*, give countless examples of her courage, restraint and flair for taking action that made all the difference. For one thing, as Sam put it, 'Mrs Baker was not a screamer' (*Albert N'yanza*, p70).

Their position at Masindi was extraordinarily fraught with danger. Undoubtedly it was Sam's leadership that brought most of his party to safety but Florence tilted many a situation in their favour that had been in the balance. Most of those incidents are not mentioned in her published diaries or letters.

The party of a hundred or so left Masindi having burnt everything but what they could carry to protect and cater for themselves on the retreat. One of the bones of contention with Kabba Rega had been his refusal to give Baker and his troops more than one day's food at a time – a calculated form of insult and control. How then would they manage for food during the retreat? Sam explains:

> At this critical moment, when every man of the expedition felt the fatal truth, my wife confided her secret, that she had hitherto concealed, lest the knowledge of a hidden store should have made the men extravagant. She now informed them that in past days of plenty, when flour had been abundant, she had, from time to time, secreted a quantity, and she had now *six large iron boxes full* (about twelve bushels). This private store she had laid by in the event of some sudden emergency. (*Ismailia*, p377)

That was consistent with Florence's role all along as overseer of food supplies. Rather surprisingly at first, her diary constantly shows what animals were shot each day; it was a record of food supply. She also supervised the kitchens, kept daily meteorological records (which are shown in a table at the back of Sam's book); and collected botanical specimens which were eventually handed over to the authorities in Cairo. Sam called her not just his 'devoted companion' but 'my little colonel' (Hall p188). Elsewhere he calls her the 'commanding officer' of the domestic corps (*Ismailia*, p220).

That duty extended in all directions. At the beginning of the battle of Fatiko, when Sam was surprised by hostile slave traders and their hangers on, he noted, 'My wife, who was always ready in any emergency, rushed out of her hut with my rifle and belt' (p413). Later he discovered that, 'My wife had placed sentries on the high rocks which commanded a view of the entire country. She also had the cattle driven within the fence; and had secured the prisoners ... in two large huts, over which she had placed a guard' (p414). And then, 'With her usual forethought, my wife had ordered the cook to have breakfast ready' (p415). But an entry about food supplies shows Florence at her most 'Victorian miss' style:

> 25 February 1870. At 10 a.m. when we stopped, I called directly to the cook, and ordered him to kill one of the beautiful fat sheep which the governor of Fashoda kept for us, but to my disgust the horrid cook informed me that both of them were killed and already eaten too, it really did annoy me very much, I must say. (p54)

It should be noted, at the same time, that wherever Sam halted for any length of time with his forces, he had them digging vegetable gardens. He explains why in a way which only the grand imperialist could contrive:

> I arranged that the sailors should cultivate a piece of ground with corn, while the soldiers should be employed in a similar manner in another position. The sailors were all Nubians, or the natives of Dongola, Berber, and the countries bordering the Nile in the Soudan. These people were of the same class as the slave-hunter companies, men who hated work and preferred a life of indolence, lounging sleepily about their vessel. I quickly got these fellows into order by dividing them into gangs, over which I placed separate headmen, the captains of vessels; one superior officer commanded, and was responsible for the whole.
>
> They only worked six hours daily, but by this simple organization I soon had thirty acres of land cleared. The grass and roots were burnt in piles, the ashes spread, and the entire field was dug over and sown with barley, wheat, and dhurra. There is a civilizing influence in cultivation, and nothing is so cheering in a wild country as the sight of well-arranged green fields that are flourishing in the centre of the neglected wilderness. (p65)

Sam's imperial cadences roll full of energy and courage, paragraph after paragraph, in a way that the Victorians found irresistible; indeed, he and his like established the Victorian imperial ethic; and even today one cannot help but admire the man, if only for his grandeur.

Occasionally Florence's spare entry shows to advantage. She wrote on 17 March 1870:

The hippo Sam shot last night was floating early this morning, to everybody's delight, as all the people are very short of meat. Sam ordered the small boats directly and some ropes to haul the old hippo close to the diahbeeah. All the troops came running with their knives in their hands, and they looked quite happy to see such a large beast lying before them. Sam shot him in the ear with a shell. ... We are going to have our dinner of hippo today; one of his feet and a piece of lip are going to be made into soup, and also some roasted meat which we shall call roast beef, but I am sorry to say he is not very young. (p57)

While Sam observed, in a detail that would be numbing but for his enthusiastic expertise:

I was anxious to observe the effects of the explosive shell, as it was an invention of my own that had been manufactured by Mr. Reilly, the gunmaker of London. This shell was composed of iron, covered with lead. The interior was a cast-iron bottle (similar in shape to a stoneware Selzer water bottle); the neck formed a nipple to receive a percussion-cap. The entire bottle was concealed by a leaden coating, which was cast in a mould to fit a No. 8, or two-ounce rifle. The iron bottle contained three drachms of the strongest gunpowder, and a simple cap pressed down upon the nipple prepared the shell for service. On examination of the head of the hippopotamus, I found that the shell had struck exactly beneath the eye, where the bone plate is thin. It had traversed the skull, and had apparently exploded in the brain, as it had entirely carried away the massive bone that formed the back of the skull. The velocity of the projectile had carried the fragments of the shell onwards after the explosion, and had formed a sort of tunnel which was blackened with burnt powder for a considerable distance along the flesh of the neck. I was quite satisfied with my explosive shell. (p27)

For once their two accounts complement each other attractively, in a way that it is obvious they were able constantly to do in their functions and their relationship. But it must be to Sam, despite his often uncontrolled prolixity, that one turns to receive any sort of sensitive account of events. Florence writes of the drowning of a member of Sam's elite 'Forty Thieves' force:

It would be shocking to see any man drowned so close to the diahbeeah, when every help was there! but he was such a very nice man, and everybody was very fond of him, he was so good and cheerful, and always at his work. We halted directly the poor man was drowned, for the night, and all the people looked exceedingly distressed that their jolly friend and companion was gone for ever. (p101)

She might have been describing anything; while Sam allows the reader to see the whole scene and to mourn with him:

Ali Nedjar was, as usual, revelling in strength and activity, and was now foremost in the work of towing the diahbeeah.

A sudden bend in the river had caused a small sand-bank. It was necessary to descend from the high shore to tow the vessel round the promontory.

Men, women, and children, jumped down and waded along the edge of the bank.

As the diahbeeah turned the sharp point, I noticed that the water was exceedingly deep close to the sand-bank, and the stream was running like a mill race. Fearing some accident to the children, I ordered all who could not swim to come on board the diahbeeah. At that time the bow of the vessel was actually touching the sand, but the stern, having swung out in the stream, might have been about fifteen feet from the edge of the bank in very deep water.

When the order was given to come on board, many of the people, in the ebullition of spirits, leapt heedlessly into the water amidships, instead of boarding the vessel by the fore part, which touched the sand. These were dragged on board with considerable difficulty.

The boy Saat would have drowned had not Monsoor saved him. In the confusion when several were struggling in the water, I noticed Ali Nedgar, who could not swim, battling frantically with his hands in such a manner that I saw the poor fellow had lost his head. He was not three feet from the vessel's side.

My four life-buoys were hung on open hooks at the four corners of the poop-deck; thus, without one moment's delay, I dropped a buoy almost into his hands. This he immediately seized with both arms, and I, of course, thought he was safe: the buoy naturally canted up as he clutched at it, and, instead of holding on, to my astonishment he relinquished his grasp!

The next moment the strong current had hurried the buoyant safeguard far away. A red Tarboosh followed the life buoy, floating near it on the surface ... Ali Nedjar was gone! – drowned! he never rose again ... I was dreadfully shocked at the loss of my good soldier – he had been much beloved by us all. We could hardly believe that he was really gone for ever. Who would now lead the song in the moonlight nights? Or be the first in every race? (pp222–3)

One thinks, of course, Florence was writing a diary entry, probably on a day when she had a lot to do, or a day or two later, in a language that was not her own. But her account lacks even immediacy. Sam was writing at leisure, for effect. He achieves it.

But that entry of Florence's niggles. The editor introduces it with the suggestion that there were other events that day recorded by Florence. Wondering how the original entry had read, I wrote to Anne Baker. She replied by return, a warm and helpful letter (25 October 1987). And she had copied out for me by hand the original entry:

The 24 Wednesday – Ther 6 a.m. 80° Noon 92°

It is very sad but a poor fellow, one of our *best* men of the forty thieves, was drowned yesterday afternoon only about 18 inches from the diahbeeah. It was a fearful thing to witness, we were quite in shallow water, and the diahbeeah appeared to be on a mudbank, so the Reis called all the people on board to cross over to the west side; as they were all in the water, soldiers, boys and girls, to tow the boat ahead, but when they heard that they were able to come on board, they made a rush together to see who would be the first. But the torrent was so strong that it carried the people into the deep water, and these unfortunate black soldiers cannot swim, and of course got dreadfully frightened and confused, and I saw directly that this poor man would be drowned, as he lost his head entirely; but Sam in an instant threw a lifebuoy over board, but the man was too far gone because he caught hold of the lifebuoy, but let it go immediately and down he went just like a stone, and never appeared again. It would be shocking to see any man drowned so close to the diahbeeah, when every help was there! but he was such a very nice man, and everybody was very fond of him, he was so good and cheerful, and always at his work. We halted directly the poor man was drowned, for the night, and all the people looked exceedingly distressed that their jolly friend and companion was gone for ever.

In her letter Anne Baker writes 'I did not find her writing at all disappointing but very very interesting and thrilling.' And of her editing policy, she explained,

> Florence noted the weather *every* day in her diary (as I have written at the top of the extract). My publisher and I agreed to leave this out, also some of the long monotonous days of the expedition – However, *some* fascinating moments may have been left out, and for this of course I am only too sorry, but the book could not be too long, so could not quite contain *everything*.

It would be impossible to describe Florence as lacking in sensitivity. Sam's record shows her antennae were amazingly acute. She had her own spy network among the troops who always seemed to be on the verge of mutiny. It helped that she could speak Arabic and she was constantly 'adopting' children caught up in the civil strife of the slave trade and adding them to her variegated household. One or two of them were in a position to listen to the men and report back to her. Her own eyes were everywhere so that once from her sickbed she saw what was going on and ran out at the psychological moment, pushing her way through the crowd, making those about to attack Sam pause, and giving him long enough to react. It was not only her eyes and ears: she had an intuition about which Sam wrote: 'My wife, upon whose cool judgement I could always depend, described vividly her apprehensions of treachery ...' (p352). And on another occasion, just after the drowning incident, Sam notes:

Although great numbers of natives thronged the country, and came down to the vessels, there was *not one woman or child*. The absence of women and children is a sure sign of evil intentions. My wife, whose experience was equal to my own, at once expressed her suspicions. Had the natives been honest and sincere, their women would assuredly have come to visit her from simple curiosity. (p225)

But, of the same occasion, Florence writes somewhat petulantly, as if she had had no insight into the culture of the people they were dealing with:

After all the beautiful things that Sam gave that miserable Sheikh he told Sam yesterday morning about 11 a.m. that his people would not carry the luggage. It is really quite dreadful to have anything to do with these wretched brutes of Baris! (p102)

The Baris attacked that night but Sam was ready for them.

Florence had plenty of opportunity to observe different kinds of women but she does not appear to be as helpful as she might be in providing access to women's lore. When the boatload of slaves was released that has already been mentioned, Florence took two of the women into her service and she was pleased to see how happy they were to settle down with her. 'I had a long talk with them', writes Florence, and the reader becomes all interested:

Of course I could not speak to them myself, but we have a very nice girl on the diahbeeah who makes Kisris [pancakes] for the sailors and she knows these girls' language so she spoke for me, and I never heard such dreadful accounts as these girls gave me of what goes on in these horrid zareebas [campsites] of the traders, the brutality and cruelty in every way is disgusting. I am sure nobody could imagine what goes on in some parts of the world. (p73)

Was it that Florence had no time to report what they said, or did Victorian modesty prevent her? I have checked that details were not edited from the end of that extract. Later she notes:

The King's wives spent the day with me while he went with Sam to superintend his people at the wreck. I gave the women each a pretty handkerchief for their heads, they were very pleased with them, also I gave them something to eat which made them perfectly happy. (p84)

It was not that Florence could not communicate with them; she spoke fluent Arabic and, as has been seen, had access to interpreters for other languages.

The entry of 9 April 1872 reads: 'Eddrees's wife came to see me with her children today – she was not much changed, she is still very good looking, and her children are very pretty little things' (p131). There are no details of the woman's life, no comment of substance. And, of her sisterly sympathy with women? She noted on 30 November 1872:

> Little Mahomet had a quarrel with both his wives today! And they came to me to say they are not going back again to him, but I made it up with them all. I do not know how long it will last. (p179)

On 20 December she jots down another episode in the saga:

> Mahomet again had a quarrel with one of his women, who ran away from him. This time, I am not going to take the trouble to make it up – they can do whatever they please! (p181)

And eight days later:

> I have nearly every day some bother with a woman or two who have quarrels with their husbands. Formerly they said that if I should force them to go back to their homes, they should run into the grass and die there. But now that the ditch is completed, they are going to throw themselves into it, rather than return to their men. Certainly my people do not run away, but it is the custom among all the boys and girls and women in these countries, that immediately they are corrected and punished, they run away. They do not know how often gentlemen's sons get punished at school and little girls at home for doing wrong. I have told them very often about it. I know that the people in this camp are not really cruel to their servants, because they are looked after. (p182)

And on 30 December: 'This morning Wat-el-Kereem was discovered in the act of sending her lover some sweet boiled potatoes, yet she is quite aware that lovers are not allowed in my establishment' (p182).

It would be a mistake to assume that Florence's scathing remarks about servants are purely racial – though she and Sam are often critical about the shortcomings of 'natives'. They may only have concerned class or even her own standards of behaviour and endurance. She had taken with her from England a lady's maid, Margaret, who was unhappy with the rather unusual conditions and decided to leave at the first real staging post up the Nile, one that had taken a year of struggle to reach. Florence wrote on 25 May:

> She says she did not know that it would be quite so difficult as it is. I have not seen any very great difficulties she has gone through as she has a *very* comfortable cabin in our diahbeeah and eats exactly what we do, also she has a very large and comfortable tent, neither has she suffered from any very bad illness. (p73)

Florence, of course, had nearly died on more than one occasion from heatstroke or fever, and her other feats of endurance have already been touched upon.

With Margaret gone, Florence made do with local help. Old Karka had been with them on their previous African journey and joined them again; indeed, they almost took her back to England but Florence notes, 'We have quite given up the idea of taking old Karka home, as she is too great a savage for Europe! She would be perfectly miserable to be among civilised people' (p177).

Florence writes only cursorily of Karka; Sam makes the old woman come alive:

> The girls were under old Karka, who had been with us throughout our former journey. This old woman was very proud because I had given £12 to purchase her freedom in Khartoum. She was a good old soul, but wonderfully fond of fine clothes; and on great occasions she always turned out in clouds of snowy muslin with red edges and fringe, like a young Abyssinian beauty. It was amusing to see her emerge from her hut in full costume, her broad, flat face beaming with smiles in happy consciousness of universal admiration.
>
> Old Karka was the sort of duenna to watch over the morals of the younger girls, and to see that they did not become too 'fast'; but I believe that even the heart of Karka beat high when a certain corporal of the gallant 'Forty Thieves' passed by. Old Karka was actually accused of sending presents of food, carefully cooked by her own hands, to the house of this same corporal, Abdullah, thus appealing to his stomach, which is the direct road to the heart, in African courtship. The younger girls and the boys of the establishment exclaimed, 'Mashallah! Old Karka! Who would have believed it?' (pp173–4)

Did Karka and Wat-el-Kereem have the same propensity? Or did Sam confuse two stories Florence told him? Or was he slightly distorting the facts to make a good story?

The contrast between Sam's ability to describe local women and Florence's apparent lack of empathy is marked, too, when the Shillock king and his retinue arrive for talks. Florence observes:

> We had a very large carpet spread for the King and his wives; they all arrived with their large pipes in their mouths; they sat down and began to spit upon our carpet. The King did not speak a word as he thought himself too grand to speak with his own mouth – he had a chief to speak for him, also the chief never said anything unless all the women were asked first if it were the right thing to say and if they gave their consent, then the chief interpreted what the King wished him to say. (p66)

Sam notes of the king's means of communication:

> Instead of replying, he conferred with one of his wives, a woman of about sixty, who appeared to act as prime minister and adviser. This old lady immediately took up the discourse, and very deliberately related the

intrigues of the Koordi governor of Fashoda, which had ended in the ruin of her husband ...

... I had heard this story a few days before, and I was much struck with the clear and forcible manner in which the old wife described the history. (p50)

Later Sam had a similar experience with the Baris when an 'exceedingly clever' sister of the sheikh carried out negotiations. The Fatiko women had their own methods. They counted on Sam for their protection but he would insist on going hunting with their menfolk for wild and dangerous animals. They decided, as he recounts, that he should be kept in camp:

> This declaration of the ladies of Fatiko could hardly be called *petticoat* government, as their total independence of attire precluded any reference to such a garment; but it was a distinct assertion of women's rights to protect the person who protected them. (p445)

Some of Sam's passages about women are models of Victorian male writing, as progressive as could be expected. Of course, when it came to how independent women could affect his own plans, Sam's reaction was rather different, or did he grow mellower with the years? One would like to think that it was Florence's influence, but the evidence is not there.

In 1862, during their first visit to Africa, Sam and Florence were stuck in Khartoum, unable to find the finance to take them upstream. Alexine Tinne and her rich widowed mother, Harriet, had no such inhibitions and Sam wrote furiously in a letter to his brother (he was more circumspect in his published writing):

> There are three Dutch ladies travelling without any gentlemen. They are very rich and have hired the only steamer here for £1,000. They are bent upon discovering the source of the Nile. They must be demented! A young lady alone with the Dinka tribe ... All the natives are as naked as the day they were born. (Gladstone p106)

Florence has been described as 'fearless and feminine'. On their first African journey she had dressed in trousers and bush jacket, like Sam – both sets of clothes made by herself – and she had often been mistaken for Sam's son. One of the most appealing revelations of *Morning Star* is Florence's letter to Edith – written during the second trip, when she obviously became much more of a memsahib – about her clothing requirements:

> Will you be good enough to send me out ...
> 6 pair of the best brown gauntlet gloves
> 6 pair of different colour gloves
> 1 pair of best rather short French stays with 6 pair of silk long stay laces.

2 pair of yellow gloves for Papa, I think they are number 7½ but they must be the best you can get.
6 pair of best steels for stays ... the stays to be 23½ inches.
12 good fine handkerchiefs 6 for dear Papa. We are getting very short of handkerchiefs – in fact we are getting short of everything. (p90)

It would be a mistake, though, to think that it was only Florence who was interested in appearance and appearances, that it was a female frivolity; Sam was just as concerned:

I distinguished 'The Forty' from the line regiment by a scarlet uniform; this was a simple red flannel shirt, worn outside their Zouave trousers, and secured by a belt, with ammunition-pouches round the waist. The uniform, with linen gaiters, and with a head-dress of a scarlet fez, bound by a turban of cobalt blue, looked remarkably well. (p145)

And elsewhere he noted:

... A hut having been swept out, I entered to change my dress, as I wished to inspect the troops. I never wore a uniform in this country, except upon state occasions; but a simple Norfolk shirt of thick white cotton, and trousers of the same material. This, with an Egyptian silk coffeeah arranged over my own old helmet hat, was sufficient for Central Africa. (p411)

Sam Baker comes through from both their accounts as the person one feels he must have been. The only question one has to ask is how much he exaggerates to make a good story concerning Florence?

Richard Hall finds that in the first draft of the first part of *The Albert N'yanza* Florence remained totally unmentioned. Indeed, she is scarcely mentioned – and then only cryptically – in Sam's unpublished diary either, and that, together with other research, led Hall to suggest that Sam did not intend to take her back to England with him in 1865. The truth of their private relationship at that time will probably never be known, nor Florence's true background.

The family, in the shape of Anne Baker, dismisses Hall's theory. In Sam's published version Florence is given not only space but depicted as a paragon of bravery, initiative and competence. This image was carried onto the public platform. Sam wanted women as well as men to read his book and he wanted the women to identify with Florence. 'Should anything offend the sensitive mind,' he wrote, 'I beseech my fair readers to reflect that the Pilgrim's wife followed him, weary and footsore through all his difficulties, led not by choice but devotion' (*Albert N'yanza*, p2). He led his readers to accept, through an impressive sleight of hand, that Florence was not only his wife, then, but also English!

Florence, who started out speaking only German with Sam and, indeed, retained a German accent, left no record of 1861–65. Looking at *Morning*

Star, the only public record we have from Florence of 1870–73, and *Ismailia*, Sam's version of the second African expedition, one cannot resist the question, were some of Sam's plaudits undeserved or did Florence downplay her key role in her diary? It may simply not have been important enough to mention – a matter of course. Her entry about her maid Margaret wanting to return home through lack of moral fibre may be an important clue, and her remark, 'certainly my people do not run away' (p182).

Whatever Florence's true role in Africa, she had had enough. For years after their return from Africa in 1873 Sam was approached to return. He wrote to Henry Stanley who had just come back from the Congo, 'If my wife were not too valuable to risk again in those parts, I would go myself ...' (Hall p220).

That is not to say they did not travel; they did. But they were travellers, tourists even, not explorers. Florence, whose traits of 'grande dame' show in her writing, side by side with the 'Victorian miss', was settled at last in a beautiful mansion in Devon with all the comfort and luxury that she had missed in her childhood and early womanhood. It was enough that their summer house was built in the style of an African palaver house, and that they were surrounded by memorabilia (some of which are now in the Newton Abbot Museum).

As for her inability to express herself in writing – so frustrating to the reader – it may have had something to do with what happened to her between the age of six and 17. On the positive side, Pat Shipman suggests that she would have been well-educated in preparation for being sold. There is no suggestion that Edith taught her to read and write, only to write in English. An explanation for her reticence is that she saw and experienced things in those eleven or so years that inhibited her from articulating any real emotion though, as we have seen, her original account of the sailor drowning shows rather more involvement than the published version suggests. She expressed herself instead in her fearlessness, her femininity and her devotion to Sam.

Whatever the image Florence conveys in her writing, her strength of character and humour seem to have remained intact until the end. Sam's great-nephew, Robin Bailey, tells of a visit he made to Florence in 1914, two years before she died aged 75 and when Sam had been dead 21 years:

> Aunt Florence enjoyed having parties, and looked charming in her black velvet with snow white arms and neck ... She took little part in the conversation, but made everybody else feel at ease, and she smiled and laughed at anything that tickled her. For instance, she allotted me a pretty girl to take in to dinner, and asked me across the table, in Arabic, what I thought of her, and I answered in Arabic, 'Allah will reward you, oh my Aunt, the girl is lovely' – and she shook with interior laughter. (*Morning Star*, p227)

4 – A Small and Very Feminine Woman

Anna Forbes, *Insulinde: Experience of a Naturalist's Wife in the Eastern Archipelago* (1887), later published as *Unbeaten Tracks in Islands of the Far East: Experiences of a Naturalist's Wife in the 1880s*) (1987)
Henry O. Forbes *A Naturalist's Wanderings in the Eastern Archipelago* (1885; 1989)

4.1   Anna Forbes' honey-eater (*Myzomela Annabellae*) (from Forbes, *A Naturalist's Wanderings in the Eastern Archipelago*)

'I have simply been the voluntary companion of an ardent lover of Nature, the reflex of whose happiness I could not avoid sharing', wrote Anna Forbes on the last page of her book, so providing her own text for this chapter. And Henry Forbes responds, tailor-made, in his introduction, 'I cannot close without adding one word of recognition of the companion of my travels whose constant encouragement and valued aid lighten all my labours' (pvii).

Annabella and Henry Forbes were another couple whose life was to travel; he for his passion, natural history and everything he could cram under that umbrella – ethnology, anthropology, geography, geology, botany,

61

ornithology, zoology, entomology – she to be with him. Information about them, particularly her, is scanty, but one can deduce that they met on home ground – they both came from Aberdeenshire – perhaps during the vacations while he was at Aberdeen or Edinburgh universities – he attended both. He started by reading medicine but lost an eye in an accident and, after curtailing his studies, took to travel to pursue his interests. Between 1875 and 1877 it was biological and geological investigations in Portugal.

4.2   Anna and Henry Forbes' voyage round the Dutch East Indies 1882–83
(from Barlow, 'Anna Forbes')

He was 27 when he left for the Eastern Archipelago – today's Indonesia – then part of the Netherlands East Indies, known to them as Insulinde. By then he must have had an understanding with Annabella Keith, for half-way through his account of Indonesian travels that last from 1878 to 1883 he writes:

> At the end of March [1882] the future companion of my travels arrived from Europe, to whom I was married on 5 April, and henceforth the record of those wanderings must pass from the singular to the plural pronoun, while the observations hereunder recorded are those sometimes of the one, sometimes of the other of us. (p282)

He does not appear to have expected her to write her own book. But when they got home in August 1883 and Henry's book was published, Anna's sister Carrie obviously said to her, 'Don't you think you should turn the letters you wrote to us and your journal into a book of your own?' By then Henry seems to have left for New Guinea, while Anna stayed to recuperate from their previous trip. In the middle of her rewriting Henry sent for her to join him and off she went again, leaving Carrie and a friend to complete the work of getting her book to the publisher.

In a fascinating chapter 'The Holy Land of Victorian Science: Anna Forbes, with Henry Forbes and Alfred Russel Wallace in the Eastern Archipelago' (in *Places Matter*, 1996), Susan Morgan explains the significance of Anna's original title, *Insulinde*, and the post-colonial politics of the change for the 1987 reprint.

Anna makes two important remarks in her preface, one putting herself, her writing and her observations into the perspective she thought appropriate, the other discussing the virtues of distancing herself from her subject – an especially important factor in her case because, as she also says in her preface, 'I was never one single fortnight free of fever after entering the tropics.' She manages to a large extent to remove from her narrative the patina of sickness. She continues:

> After I joined [my husband] we shared for the most part the same experiences; but we looked upon them from an entirely different standpoint. Many of my own sex who might turn from 'A Naturalists Wanderings' because of the admixture of scientific matter, may find some interest in reading my simpler account ... I consider it an advantage to write when time has removed the exaggerations with which the mood of the moment might have distorted facts or influenced feelings; while I have also had opportunity for maturer consideration of, and authentic information on, many points. (ppvii–viii)

The fact that Anna, in her published account, consciously distanced herself from her immediate account is most useful. It is what most of the men did, consciously or unconsciously, and few of the women. What is more, it is possible to compare Anna's two accounts – the immediate and the considered – because Henry uses occasional extracts from the former in his book. Susan Morgan suggests the opposite, that Anna copied from Henry; it would be reasonable to accept that they both did it.

The most relevant borrowing, for me, comes towards the end of their travels in Indonesia. They were now on Timor and had moved from the capital, which they call Dilly (more usually, Dili), to a small shack which Henry had had built high above the town of Fatunaba. Anna joined him when it was nearly finished and some time later, when they were settled there, he left her to go further into the interior. She was happy enough to stay but she became very ill – probably malaria picked up in low-lying Dili where most Europeans were stricken.

The first discrepancies are slight but indicative of the difference between private and public, immediate and considered. Just how much cosmetic tidying up did go on in travel accounts? And how much did it distort the more immediate impression? In her published version, writing as if to Carrie, slightly in retrospect: 'I lay everything at hand which I shall need during the fever, and put dry garments within reach. The perspiration which follows is surprisingly profuse' (p290).

In the journal that Henry quotes from she wrote, 'For some days I must have been delirious; during the nights I tossed in my sweat-soaked garments, sometimes able to reach out for dry ones, sometimes not' (p484). Obviously a Victorian woman, lady, in public, perspires; she does not sweat. Interesting, though, that in private she does sweat. And a Victorian lady could not have lain, even in perspiration, without changing her sodden clothes; she must be prepared, so as to prevent that, however ill.

The next two passages occur during the same illness. She wrote in her journal again (the square brackets are Henry's):

> A passing lad – whom I sighted through the bamboo slits of the hut – I called to me, bribing him by coin after coin to carry a note to the Palace begging for medicine and aid. Just as he at last consented, after much dubitation, and the most urgent entreaty on my part, it began to rain [rain is always abhorred by the natives], which made him hesitate in his purpose – a terrible moment for me; but, espying my open parasol in a corner, he seized it and marched off … (p484)

Her rewritten account reads:

> By good fortune a lad from a neighbouring valley, whose open intelligent countenance had attracted us before, came past that afternoon. I explained to him that I wished a letter carried to the town, and would reward him well. 'No; he would not go among the white people; he was a hill-man, and was shy.' I tempted him with coin after coin: he did not know their value. He consented, he refused, he wavered; he little knew that he held me on the rack – that I was almost stifled with eagerness – I was really bargaining for my life. At last he gave in so far: he would go to the town and drop the letter in the street, but he would not go to the Palazzio. Off he ran, and I lay back thankful and exhausted. But in three minutes he was back again; rain had commenced to fall, and with a native's dread of wetting, he would not face it. My parasol lay in a corner. I pointed to it; he seized it and ran off. (p298)

Apart from the fact that she has refined the writing and elaborated the account, including the addition of ethnographic detail, there are two changes here that are particularly striking. In the rewritten version she already knew the lad; in the journal she did not appear to. In the latter she talks of the lad 'espying' her umbrella and 'seizing' it. In the rewritten one, 'I pointed to it; he seized it'. In the private version she accosted a stranger who took the umbrella uninvited; in the published version she hailed a known boy and, as it were, gave him her umbrella.

That distinction can be interpreted thus: if a woman accosts a stranger, she takes a risk. Can a Victorian lady admit to having been so indiscreet, even on her bed of fever? And note how the strange boy was 'bribed' in desperation; the known boy was 'tempted', after she understands the ethnological reasons for his reluctance.

Were those changes important even after the 'cruder' version had been published in Henry's book? Women, ladies rather, would be reading her book; she has already said they might find his a bit difficult intellectually, so they were more likely to read hers. Of course, one must not carry such an analysis too far; Anna's published book is vigorous enough; it is by no means a stream of lady-like euphemism – in word or action. But then, again, the best conditioning is the most subtle.

The next comparison is stranger because two of Henry's accounts come into it, and bring no enlightenment. Anna writes in her published account (in the same letter home of 14 April already quoted from) of the receipt of a letter from Henry brought from the interior by some of his companions who had come to collect more supplies:

> H. is delighted and full of the interest of his work, if he could be sure that all is well with me. That he may pursue his course with an easy mind, I have carefully hid from him the true state of matters. What would he say if he knew a band of thieves made a raid on me the other night, and lifted everything that was readily portable? (p286)

In the extract from her journal quoted by Henry in his book, Anna writes, and the square brackets are Henry's:

> My nights quite sleepless, I lie and listen for the return of the thieves [who had entered and robbed the house, and had a second time in the middle of the night returned, decamping, however, on A's calling out, and who, had she dared to oppose them, would not have scrupled to put it beyond her power to turn informant. When writing to me in the interior, with rare self-denial she restrained from telling me the state of affairs at Fatunaba]. (p483)

All neat enough – one assumes he does not mean rare self-denial on Anna's past record, but rare in the sense of commendable – but 20 pages earlier Henry had written in his own account of receiving supplies from Anna then, among which he:

> found a note with the evil and disquieting tidings that our house had been attacked in the night and plundered of nearly all the stock of trade goods and other valuables that it contained by treacherous hill-men, who had taken advantage of her defenceless condition ... (p460)

She says she spared him the news; he says she spared him the news; and yet he writes of receiving the news from her. How does the reader interpret such inconsistencies? What is certainly true is that the Forbes were protective of each other and careful of, or locked into, their gender roles, to the extent that their bouts of illness even complemented that of the other! Henry was unattractive to mosquitoes – often a male advantage in the tropics; but he was not immune to all fever. In the Tenimber Islands (Timor-laut) they stayed in a village, Ritabel, that had a rival, and hostilities intensified during a period of fever suffered by them both. First Henry describes a night of climax:

A____, wretchedly weak and reduced from weeks of almost continuous fever, was assisting me to get up after a bad day of the same about the hour the village was going to rest for the night. A terrific shot from a native gun – always charged to the very muzzle – startled the whole community. Shouts of 'Kaleobar' resounded everywhere. Like a disturbed ant's nest the villagers, every man with his arrow on the string or a sheaf of javelins in his hand, one of them ready poised, clustered out round the barricades shouting and gesticulating. We were alone – the Postholder and our men not having returned from Molu – except for one servant, useless in such a case. After barricading the door and sliding an explosive shell into my Martini, with a cheery word to my companion who held ready a handful of cartridges, and a hasty look to see if the boat which, unknown to her, I had purchased expressly for perhaps such an emergency was still riding by its line to the pillar of the house, to serve as a last means of escape, I stood ready at the open window for what might follow. (pp330–1)

She wrote of the same occasion:

Towards sundown one day, while [the men of our household] were still absent, H. was getting up from a very bad attack of fever. Rolled in all the clothes he had, he had just sunk into his chair, when a terrific shot startled us and the whole community. Shouts of 'Kaleobar!' resounded everywhere, and the villagers, every man with his arrows and javelins ready, ran swifly to the barricades in wild excitement. It was like nothing but a disturbed ants' nest. The post-holder's wife came to our window and cried, 'Master! master! come!' but master was already disburdened of his heavy clothing, and busy with rapid arrangements for defence. I called Kobenz, but afterwards it was remarked that no one caught a glimpse of him during the alarm. I think he must have burrowed in the sand or climbed a tree. H. very highly praises my self-command on this occasion, but I am bound to confess that the latter resource would have been mine could I have scaled these smooth-stemmed trees, and could I have had the heart to leave H., so weak that he could scarcely stand. After one moment the feeling of fear passes, and the excitement of the emergency lifts one above any thought of self. (p197)

Their accounts are in many ways similar but Anna's shows that she was neither a Lucy Atkinson nor a Florence Baker. She herself writes on another occasion, 'You must remember that I am only a small and very feminine woman and no masculine woman with top-boots and a fowling piece' (p281). Nevertheless, with her husband ill, she found the reserves of courage to stand her ground, and reached that plane where the adrenalin flows strongly enough for bravery to be self-generating. Of course, her initial courage, that of will rather than adrenalin, is the higher form.

That incident was a false alarm but the whole period was one of danger and Anna writes of it in retrospect in terms that suggest Henry was wise to keep the possibilities of attack from her.

The protestation that she was only a small and very feminine woman came in connection with a herd of buffalo. These Anna was afraid of encountering on the long trek down from Fatunaba to Dili which she made by herself when Henry was away. More frightening was the experience she had with a single man 'with a fatuous leer, and an expression of hideous cunning which made my heart utterly fail' (p282). He probably only wanted to touch the strange white woman. But he kept his eye on her locket, and kept stroking her as they walked, but graciously:

> And I, remembering H.'s injunction never to show fear, reciprocated by gently patting his greasy back. But I kept a firm grasp of my parasol handle, and never relaxed my unflinching stare, while with most self-possessed manner and easy nods I indicated that he must precede me. There was little use in getting angry: he had a large knife against my parasol handle. The only way was to divert him until we reached the confines of civilised life. For two hours I drove that man before me; but when we came in sight of the monastery of Lahany I got imperious, and commanded him to leave me. Then I sat down and gave vent to my pent-up feelings, for I had passed through the severest trial of my courage yet required of me. (p283)

One wonders what she would have done if she had not remembered Henry's injunction! But, as we have seen, she had her own brand of courage. On the occasion that follows it is expressed in retrospect, when she rewrote her account. In her original journals she merely noted of the time of her illness, 'I shuddered to think how H. would find me if I should die before he returned or help should come' (p484). Her published version reads:

> What sustained me was the determination not to die. The thought of H.'s agony should he come in some day and find only what of me the rats had left, inspire me to struggle for life. I seemed to exist in a dual state: one side would have sought pity and sympathy, the other scorned and scouted and imperiously forbade any such weakness, or the luxury of giving in to it. (p296)

And in local terms Anna was a heroine for even contemplating staying at Fatunaba without Henry. When he went off into the interior, he was accompanied by a military escort and notes, denying Anna's Scottishness:

> The officer expressed the greatest astonishment at all absence of timidity on A.'s part on being left alone; but, on being reminded that she was an 'English

Senhora', he appeared satisfied that the fact was sufficient to explain the phenomenon. (p427)

Nor should it be thought that Henry was unresponsive to Anna's plight. He was anxious about leaving her in the first place and when – as a result of her note – she was rescued from her hilltop and a message sent to Henry. 'He never left the saddle for three days and three nights', Anna recorded. (p300) He describes his 'forced march': ten hours march with 30 minutes' break, very little food, great heat (110 °F in the sun, 92 °F in the shade). And he writes of reaching her at last:

> I was thankful to find A. amid our kind friends much recovered, but showing in her emaciated figure how severe her sufferings had been. When the trying strain she was exposed to and her terrible position and privations are realised, it is surprising not that she at last broke down, but that she bore up so long and so bravely. (p482)

And now he realised that he must take her home to Scotland.

Henry Forbes must have known what he was letting Anna in for when he sent for her to be his wife. He could not have known how her health would stand up to the conditions of the Eastern Archipelago but he must have had some idea of what sort of woman she was. It is probably fair to assume, therefore, that some of Anna's 'little woman act' is an act, for the sake of her readers; or is she simply honest about fear that was perfectly natural? Henry never mentions being afraid; but he wouldn't, would he!

What sort of woman was Anna? With few facts to go on, much has to be surmised. The 1987 reprint of her book is without an introduction; his biographical details give the date of her death as 1922. Henry Barlow's 'Anna Forbes: A Naturalist's Companion in the Far East' (1995) found that she was born in 1855, so she was 27 when she arrived in Batavia to marry Henry Forbes and leave for Timor-laut ten days later. The date of their marriage is given as 5 April 1881 but Henry's book clearly says it was 1882.

Anna's father was a granite merchant – a master of polished granite and slate works employing 43 men. She was the eldest child of three daughters, and a son who went to a grammar school. Anna herself was not uneducated – that shows in her writing. She also spoke French and German. She started learning Malay as soon as she arrived in the East but she is tentative and self-deprecating about it in a way that was natural under the circumstances, though she expresses it in a way one would not expect of her husband when she writes, 'My ignorance of Eastern ways and of Malay prevents my taking any but a very submissive part in our impromptu *menage*' (p70).

Henry went about it in a different way when he arrived. He could not work without Malay and he was alone; indeed he isolated himself completely 'from all European-speaking people for the purpose of acquiring, with the aid of a few books and chiefly with my native servants, the Malay language as soon as possible' (p51).

Anna gains confidence, however, by the time she arrives in the Tenimber Islands, for she writes, 'We soon learnt to converse with the natives' (p162).

As for Anna's administration of their affairs, she was not always successful. She writes of their supplies in Ritabel:

About the middle of our stay our coffee went done. We gave it to the men when down with fever, knowing ourselves the advantage of a hot drink during the terrible ague. Then we were thrown entirely on tea. Alas! that failed us too. Being so often sick, I did not have the same care of things as I should otherwise have had, and neglected to put it in the sun to prevent it spoiling in the tropical moisture. If we had been wise we should have had it in sealed tins; but it is H.'s way to be absolutely indifferent to personal comfort, and I was too inexperienced then in the housewifery of a tropical climate to be on the outlook. (pp192–3)

Nor had Anna come as a professional naturalist, but she was anxious to learn and help; she writes:

I am beginning to enter into the joys of a naturalist, and have grown quite learned in long names of birds and insects, and can help H. in labelling and arranging. The later hours of every afternoon are looked forward to by both of us as the most pleasant of the day, when the hunters' spoils are displayed for our admiration. The gay parrots and beautiful kingfishers, the curious maleos, whose terra-cotta eggs are a table luxury, and those wonderfully plumaged pigeons, give us special delight. Strolling along the bay, on whose beach the east wind has been throwing a wealth of sponges, hydroids, and shells, we spend many hours examining them and watching the fields of shore-crabs, with their richly coloured pincer limbs, and the curious fishes which come up out of the water and hop along the shore in their odd way.

When H. goes with the men to the forest, I accompany as far as I am able. (pp89–90)

In Henry's account of the same pleasures, we can see what Anna meant by her 'simpler account'.

The later hours of every afternoon have been looked forward to by us both as the most pleasant of the day, when the hunters' spoils were displayed to be admired, examined and labelled. Among the butterflies we have I added a few more of the fine *Ornithoptera* found at Paso, numbers of 'swallow-tails', chief among them the deep blue *Papilio ulysses*, species of *Hebomoia* and *Pieris*, *Charaxes eyryolus*, and many 'Blues'; among beetles we have added to our collection many species of all the finest families, Longicorns, Rose-chafers, Tiger-beetles and golden *Buprestidae*; among the birds may be mentioned the beautiful racquet-tailed Kingfishers of the genus *Tanysiptera*, which I was rather surprised to find in large chattering corrobories in the tops of high trees ... (p295)

Henry Forbes was no dilettante naturalist. He starts one of his chapters on Timor-laut 'Of the natural history of Timor-laut, about which almost nothing was known before our visit, I have been able, to a considerable extent, to fill up the blanks in our knowledge' (p334).

Anna was a novice, but she learnt: 'I am serving my apprenticeship as a naturalist and have made such progress that I can net a bee without getting stung, and I now know the proper way to grasp a beetle' (p269).

Apart from the dangers and the beauties, there were periods of intense activity which Anna fully shared:

H. being anxious to despatch the most important of his collecting to Europe by this, the first opportunity, we laboured incessantly at labelling and packing, the task occupying the greater part of the nights as well as the days – a great strain while so weakened by fever. (p209)

They are a team, too, when it comes to his writing:

H. has been writing an account of the journey through Bourou, accomplished before we came to Timor. We relieved each other, writing and dictating from the sketch-sheets alternately, and the humbler duties of fire-making and cooking were no unwelcome change to tired eyes and cramped fingers. (p267)

There is a slight ambiguity there as to who experienced that not unwelcome change, though she does go on to refer to 'we'.

Sometimes Anna was left to get on with the less exciting parts of being a naturalist; Henry notes in his diary: 'Lopes and Peter as usual out hunting for birds, while I went to the forest to botanise; Anna labelling the insects and birds at home' (p291).

She was given her reward for her baptism of fire as a naturalist (illustrated at the beginning of this chapter); Henry describes how he thanked her:

Besides these, another lovely new species of the same family of the Honey-eaters, belonging to the genus *Myzomela*, which has been named after the devoted companion of my travels (*Myzomela annabellae*) was obtained. (p338)

It was in Ritabel that Anna began to make her individual mark for, as Henry observes, 'Through A____, who had become a great favourite with the people, caressed and affectionately patted by them in her wanderings about the village, we got to know much of their inner life' (p306).

Anna's capacity allows us, more than a hundred years later, to learn about the women of Ritabel. It is often clear from both their accounts of life there that they were drawing in their published books from one original account. One can assume that the basic observations are mostly Anna's, the more ethnological touches Henry's. So married are their accounts that the following can occur:

> They allowed me to climb up the trap-stair to see a newly-born infant, who was lying in a rude cradle (called in the Tenimber language a *siwela*) of rattan wickerwork, with only a palm spathe beneath its back, and quite naked but for a tiny rag on its stomach. But it was kept warm, as well as defended from tormenting mosquitoes, by being swung over a fire, on this occasion in a smoke so dense that I was amazed it was not suffocated. (p156)

One might have expected Anna, as the woman and the one who had already been accepted enough to hold babies, to be invited; and she does suggest she was by herself. But Henry was not to be left out and wrote in his account:

> Strolling through the village one evening we were beckoned into a hut to see a newly born infant. It was lying quite naked, with only a hard palm-spathe beneath its back and a square inch or so of cloth on its stomach, in a rude cradle or *Siwela*, a rough rattan basket suspended so as to rock over a fire in a smoke so dense that we were amazed that it was not suffocated. (p316)

A composite of paragraphs from Anna's book gives evidence of how much time she spent simply watching the women, first an individual and then women in general:

> The post-holder is a dreamy sort of man, but his wife is a wonderful little woman, full of energy and tact. I always stood by her to learn as she bartered for the day's supplies. The natives pressed round with fish, fowls, yams, Indian corn, bananas, melons; and though I could not imitate her ways, I admired how well she kept order in the unruly crowd, with loud good-natured scolding, a push, a hearty slap, or a kindly pat ...

> ... The women, if not treated with a great show of affection, and though left to perform all the harder duties of life, are not subjected to restraint, and have a free and happy air about them. It is they who go to the distant forest to cultivate on the poor soil covering the coral rocks the sweet-potatoes, manioc, sugar-cane, Indian corn, cotton, and tobacco which are needful in their daily life. It is they who stamp the Indian corn into meal; all day long, somewhere in the village, the dull thud of the stamping-pole in the large *tidacna* shell is heard. They must have good muscles; they lift the heavy pole as if it were a bamboo ...

> ... Here and there a woman is to be seen sitting close under the eaves of her house weaving cloth. Her loom is indeed an heirloom, and the simple contrivance is often elaborately carved, it being the pastime of lovers of successive generations to make fresh carving on the fair one's loom. The

buckle of her waistband is also his work; I am not quite sure but that it is a token of betrothal when a girl wears the buckle her suitor has made ...

I have stood hours watching her lift the threads, and form – with, to me, deft and bewildering swiftness, as well as surpassing patience – the favourite Tenimber pattern which borders all the garments they make ... The result is a pretty and very soft cloth, and it is worn by the women when the evening chill comes on, but too often it is taken in loan by the men ...

A fashionable toilet would be quite lost on them. One of the ship's company who landed with us when we came, left with the post-holder a sheet from a French fashion journal, which was hung on his wall ... as far as I observed, – and I noted their manner carefully, – they saw no resemblance to human being in these figures; they were as triangles or squares to them. Ah! may advancing civilisation keep such monstrosities far from the graceful Tenimber women. With head erect and chest expanded, how easy, graceful, healthy, happy they looked! Untrammelled in limb, free of foot, it was worth while to watch their every motion ...

In budding womanhood some of them look sweet ... but later they get thin, and the skin becomes shrunken. They do not dye the hair as the men do, and give little time to its arrangement. I never heard a woman sing. They may, but I did not hear even the 'li-li-la-a-a-a,' which is the spontaneous expression of exuberance and content with the man, who also frequently bursts into wild happy song. They laugh often, however, with true Papuan heartiness. And they can scold too! I once saw a woman rating her husband soundly; he, however, took it very coolly, and went on quietly baling water from a prahu with a cocoa-nut, wisely letting her expend her wrath without a word. (pp147;165;166;168;169)

Anna is as observant of the men; but a couple of sentences will suffice here:

The men have the advantage of the women in looks; they give more time to personal decoration, and they do not toil. They are undoubtedly lazy fellows, and seem to work only when in the mood. (p172)

It would be a mistake to suggest that Henry fails to describe the women of Ritabel for his readers but his comments lack the element of involvement and spontaneity which are part of the appeal of Anna's writing and suggest that he has written up his notes from her journal, with some scholarly flourishes, later. He writes, for example:

The women wear a short sarong (Malay petticoat), artistically woven by themselves out of the fibres of the Aloan-palm (*Borassus flabelliformis*), suspended by a borad belt made from the stem of its leaf and fastened by an elaborately carved buckle of wood which frequently in married women has been the gift of her husband at the time when her purchase-money was agreed on, possibly a sort of engagement token. (p313)

But Anna, as we have seen, recorded that Henry wrote up his notes of his Bouru trip with her soon after his return from there. That seems to make a difference, to provide a quality which his writing, and that of other travellers, particularly men, often lack. You feel he was there when he writes of receiving hospitality from a village:

> To accommodate me with a seat to listen to the musical 'function' a large stone had to be brought in. The performers, who were of both sexes, disposed themselves in the passage on stones and logs. The men sang an improvised song to their own vigorous accompaniment on the native *tifa*, or drum, to which the women, sitting on their heels, languidly supporting their heads on their arms, which rested on their knees, contributed an unchanging refrain at the end of every few words of song. The men seemed to enjoy themselves, often laughing heartily at their own improvised conceits, but the women might have been absolute automata; for not a single expression of pleasure, interest, or enjoyment ever passed over their impassive features. The exhibition was one of the saddest possible pictures of the miserable position among the Alefurus of the women, who, though not treated with cruelty or harshness, live in abject uncomplaining slavery – as if for the man alone all things, woman especially, were created. (pp400–1)

That passage of Henry's is quoted in order to be as objective as possible – to show that Henry, especially on his own when he obviously had to keep his own detailed records, was interested and could glean women's lore, had a progressive approach to women and could write with a certain immediacy. There is, though, a contradiction in suggesting the women were not treated with harshness or cruelty, and yet lived in abject slavery – that covers my definition of harshness and cruelty.

The following two passages, one from each of them, show that there is still a subtle distinction that gives the woman traveller's record an edge. They arrive by boat, for a very brief stop to let off passengers and cargo, in Macluer Bay, New Guinea. They are met by a group of villagers. Henry writes:

> We were surrounded at once by a crowd of tall, erect, frizzy-headed, well-disposed men and women, who found us most curious objects apparently. It was evident that they had but seldom seen white faces, for our colour interested them very much. They examined our legs, arms, and faces, rubbing them gently and looking at their fingers to see whether the colour came off or not; others, taking off the scanty head-cloth they wore, took our hands within its folds in a most reverential attitude. A____, probably the only white lady that has ever trod this northern part, was, however, the object of curiosity. After looking at her very intently for some time a thought suddenly seemed to strike two of their number, who, dashing

away towards one of the houses, returned in a little leading between them an Albino woman with fair skin and yellowish hair, and placing her side by side us, burst into a hearty laugh, as much as to say, 'We know now why your skins are white.' (p300)

While Anna adds that extra personal element:

Greetings and salaams over, the Rajah's wife ran forward, and, a fold of her garment over each hand, took mine between, and dragged me, still running, into her dwelling. Here others joined us, and in similar fashion took my hand between their covered hands, which they then drew slowly over their faces, meanwhile bowing low. For a moment I was afraid, they pressed so close and were so excited; but I could soon see that they meant only kindness. I took time to look round their dwelling, in which there was no attempt at furniture. A few rude vessels lay on the floor; and some ashes in a corner showed that they made fire, and were thus far above the brute creation.

When they had duly examined me, I got out of the hut ...

... the crowd had gathered, and I found myself so hedged in that I could not move farther. With a certain diffidence, looking first to see if I would allow it, they gently pushed back my hat to look at my hair, drew back my sleeves, lifted my skirts, and laughed immoderately at my boots. Presently, with shrieks of excitement, the crowd parted, and, with no regard for her evident shyness, a tall albino woman was dragged forward by two others and shown to me as a sister! She was the only one who wore a white garment (at least it had once been white), and was a marked contrast to the others, not only from her fair skin, but from her unusual height, and especially from her coiffure, which was quite remarkable. The hair was very fair, golden-tinged, and had the appearance of being carefully dressed, though it was nature which laid those rows of soft curls so neatly on her head. Her skin was as ugly as her hair was pretty, being of a reddish-yellow hue, as if raw from the sun; and her teeth, quite blackened, and filed almost to the gums, gave her anything but a prepossessing look. (pp123–5)

What is not so clear from those passages, but is from earlier ones, including his description of the Alefurus women, is that even there Henry tends to generalise; Anna much more often writes about individual people with identities, undoubtedly a factor in creating immediacy. She writes about people because that is what happened; those individuals are who she met; it is enough in itself. Henry explains why, for him, writing about people is as important as the discovery of a new butterfly; he builds on what has already been quoted from Anna about intrusion from the outside world, but in a general way:

The ideas as well as the manufactures of Western lands are beginning to be felt and seen in the huts of the rudest tribes, and among the people the most distant from civilisation. It is therefore more incumbent than ever on all travellers to record with the utmost fidelity every minutiae of the customs and ideas of the rude peoples they encounter, for with the disappearance of their untainted legends, words and thoughts, will die out a chapter of the far-past history that can never be recovered again on the globe. (p401)

It is for that reason that Anna's acceptance among the women of Ritabel is so important. It is interesting to note, however, that there is no resentment expressed by her towards the situation of the Ritabel women, exploited as they were, even though she was conscious of the significance of details such as their failure to sing.

The way Anna and Henry recorded their impressions is often complementary – allowing the reader to see more than one facet; the way they lived together, the way they saw their roles, was also complementary. But, as I have already suggested, how they saw things and the perspective from where they saw them was highly individual. Thus they reacted in a different way emotionally; there was a difference in the way they were prepared to put up with things. Anna writes of the postholder's geese, for example:

I was lying in greatest prostration, after the delirium of fever had abated, in acute physical agony from rheumatic pain in every part of the body, and with every nerve on the stretch, the shrill *skraik, skraik, skraik* of these birds used to cause me to jump quite out of bed from the start and sudden fright. I bore it as best I could, though I felt sometimes as if it would make me mad, for I could understand what a disappointment it would be to the post-holder's wife to disturb the fowl when it had set ... H., however, was much engaged in calculations from observations with his sextant ... and when thinking deeply, the disturbance of these creatures was more than he could bear. (pp195–6)

It was not only because of his work: Henry had nerves too! He writes of one of the results of fear of the Kaleobar:

Extra guards were placed, who danced, as is their custom on such like occasions, round the village god night and day with a hideous howling chant accompanied by beating of drums which was equally incessant, and to our fever-strained nerves execrable and unbearable during the day, but perfectly maddening at night. How we longed and looked for the steamer! (p338)

Their different reactions are even more marked where passages from their books are identical except for the odd word. She writes (emphasis added): 'Arriving about midnight, we were *perplexed* to find the door of our old quarters unopened' (p104), while he writes, 'Arriving about midnight utterly worn out, we were *much annoyed* to find the door of our old quarters unopened' (p296). She goes on philosophically to observe:

The little furniture that was in the house had been removed during our absence of a month; but we found a boatsail in a corner of one of the rooms, which, spread on the stone floor, had to serve that night for a resting place. (p105)

Either she was resigned to suffering, or she wished to save Henry's 'face' vis-a-vis her family. Or, was it because Henry was so cross that she was calm! For he fulminates:

Finding a boat-sail in one of the rooms, we were glad to throw ourselves upon it on the stone floor – a wretched night even for me, but worse for my companion, hardly yet inured to roughing it, and for whose sake I bitterly grudged such hardship in a town so civilised as Amboina. (p297)

How quickly had Anna changed? It was only a month since they had first arrived in Amboina. Then the authorities had refused them permission to follow Henry's plans; they were stranded.

H. proposed that we should camp in a field, or by the road-side. Fresh from European ways, I stoutly objected. One does not mind setting up a tent on a savage shore, but in a civilised town like Amboina, I simply could not bear the idea. (p68)

She appeared to arrive in the Eastern Archipelago, too, with other European ideas, otherwise known as the prejudices of whites against non-whites. But how far is it useful to discuss them when she writes of the Ritabel people, 'Their appreciation of beauty is characteristic of them, which, absolutely wanting in the Malay people, I was surprised to find among a less advanced race' (p178).

And on page 317 he writes exactly the same. Whose opinion is it? There is no doubt that what Anna experienced herself must, therefore, be considered the important part of her book; and the same can equally be said of his. Not surprisingly, at a time of constantly changing impressions and assaults on her preconceptions, her judgements about such things are often inconsistent. An example is her shifting views on what can be called 'the watcher watched'. She writes:

They walked about examining everything with the interest and ways of children, and especially honoured us by their close attention – a liberty we could not well resent, since we were equally busy discussing them from top to toe. (p130)

But she does not see the incongruity of writing later, 'We were rather pestered by their perpetual presence in our dwelling, for, like all untutored races, their inquisitiveness knows no bounds' (p163). And three pages later she records how 'I have stood hours watching [a weaver] lift the threads ...' (p166).

But it is surely an advance when she can write of the lads with whom she runs races at Ritabel, 'I could then talk with them, and they seemed to enjoy the fun as much as I. How near of kin is the whole world' (p180).

After three months on Tenimber she writes of it as,

> An experience which neither of us would willingly repeat, but which, nevertheless, neither would have foregone. Our sickness, privations, anxieties, and labours we felt not worthy of name beside the beautiful pictures both on the face of nature and in her creatures, the recollection of our pleasant relations with our savage friends, and the interest of our pursuits, which would henceforth furnish food for many a reverie. (p208)

And he ends his book with a description of 14 August 1883:

> We arrived in London, transported in seventy five days from the make shifts, discomforts, and rough contrivances of a rude hut among half-naked savages, to all the elegances of a great London hotel, with its fashionable crowd, a contrast – to me certainly – too great to be comfortable or pleasant for some time at least. I realised that I was more than half a barbarian, to whom the restraints of civilisation had become irksome, and who would have rejoiced to have been at once spirited back again to his swarthy friends in the Eastern Archipelago. (p488)

One wonders if Henry Forbes was ever again fulfilled as he was in those years, although he had a varied career throughout the world as a naturalist and museum director, as far as can be assumed taking Anna with him. We have seen from her introduction that he called her to join him in 1886 in New Guinea where, his entry in *Who Was Who* notes, he led two expeditions to Mount Owen Stanley and was an acting deputy commissioner. But Papua New Guinean sources do not suggest he was successful or appreciated in either venture, rather the contrary.

And of Anna, all that was noted of her was 'While in New Guinea he was accompanied by his wife Annabella and Mrs Forbes' presence in Port Moresby doubled the population of European women' (Dutton p164). What is more, Anna was little wanted for she had to stay with Hugh Hastings Romilly, an administrator of a part of a very large, hitherto unexplored island that had been British territory for only two years, 'as there was no other place she could stay in', and he was forced 'to put her up and brace [sic] whatever scandal' came of it (p164). She must have longed for some good healthy savagery.

Anna accompanied Henry to New Zealand, where he was director of the Canterbury Museum from 1890 to 1893, which inspired her to write the not-readily available novel *Helena* (1905). Henry Barlow describes it as 'very mediocre'. I think that is unfair – naïve, perhaps, and of its time, but well-meaning in its attempt to tackle Maori-colonist relations and the burgeoning suffragette movement in New Zealand. Some novels are better-appreciated by women readers.

Anna appears as co-author, with Henry, of *British Birds' Eggs and Nests* (n.d.). Barlow, whose list of sources for his chapter on the couple is extensive, writes of later years when Henry travelled widely for his research that Anna is unlikely to have accompanied him and suggests, without giving the evidence, that 'Anna can have seen little of him and it is hard to imagine that as the childless couple approached late middle age their marriage was much more than an empty shell.' Perhaps Barlow got carried away by bird metaphors.

5 – Hurrah for Wanderlust

Ella Sykes, *Through Persia on a Side Saddle* (1898; **1901**)
Percy Molesworth Sykes, *Ten Thousand Miles in Persia* (1902)

5.1   Ella Sykes and Percy Sykes on their way to Kerman
(courtesy of the family)

Ella and Percy Sykes, who travelled together in Persia between 1894 and 1897, were sister and brother, rather than wife and husband, giving a different slant to travelling companions. Also, unlike her four predecessors, Ella came from an upper-middle-class background.

Percy Sykes (1867–1945) is perhaps best known as the first English historian of Persia – though he was also a successful soldier, administrator and intelligence officer. He came to know Persia very well between 1893 and 1918. His first book, which includes his version of the journey with Ella, covers eight of those years and his account had, therefore, been well-considered by the time it came finally to be written up. Much of it – perhaps too much – is a dummy-run for his later history, for he has a tendency to write such introductions to an area he is visiting as, 'after this brief description of the province I now propose to discuss its history' (p48). And, 'To avoid plunging *in medias res*, I will give a very brief account of the state of Europe and Asia at that time' (p260).

What Ella Sykes (1863–1939) wrote of her two-and-a-half-year journey was published only the year after her return from Persia but it is a less obviously

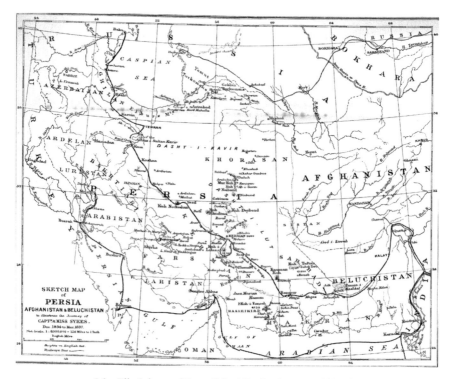

5.2   Ella Sykes and Percy Sykes' Persian journeys 1894–97
(from Sykes, *Through Persia on a Side Saddle*)

spontaneous document than that of many of our women. In spite of the fact that she wrote her account in a considered narrative form and that she has a stronger sense of the proportions of history and travel that might appeal than her brother, her preface shows the same tentativeness that is increasingly recognizable from the women who travelled in tandem:

> This book has no pretensions to be either historical, scientific, or political, being merely the record of a very happy period of my existence which I have, in a way, re-lived by writing about it. My information, however, may claim to be correct as far as it goes, my brother, Major Sykes, who has travelled for several years in Persia on Government service, having revised my manuscript. As I believe that I am the first European woman who has visited Kerman and Persian Baluchistan, my experiences may perhaps interest other women who feel the 'Wanderlust' but are unable to gratify their longing for adventure.

It was certainly not lack of formal education that made Ella use that self-deprecating tone. She was the first of our women travellers who we know went to university – she was up at Oxford, at Lady Margaret Hall, between 1881 and 1883. Although in those earliest days women were not allowed to attend lectures nor take the exams of the university, and the subjects and exams they could take were limited, Ella undoubtedly gained intellectual confidence – a confidence she built on in Persia, enabling her afterwards to establish a career.

She did not marry, possibly from choice. Sir Patrick O'Reilly, Percy's son-in-law, suggested to Percy's biographer, Antony Wyn, that men found Ella 'intimidating' and she found those in her circle 'dull'; the family even wondered if Ella wasn't 'Lebanese' (p31) – perhaps more of a commentary on their confusion about sexual orientation than on Ella's unmarried state. Whatever the reason for not marrying she remained available to her brother when he needed a travelling companion. Although he married in 1902, it was Ella, not his wife Evelyn Seton (mother of his six children), who accompanied him to Kashgar (Chinese Turkestan) in 1915 when he temporarily relieved Sir George Macartney at the Consulate General there. Percy was knighted that year and he and Ella wrote a joint account of their Kashgar stay, *Through Deserts and Oases of Central Asia* (1920) – she writing the descriptive part and he the chapters dealing with 'geography, history, customs and other subjects'. Ella published her second book on Persia in 1910 – *Persia and its People*.

A year later, concerned to read of a 1 million surplus of women in England – unmarried and unemployed and thus looking for work – she travelled to Canada under the auspices of the Colonial Intelligence League, to study conditions available there for educated women. She returned to England having worked as a home help for a while to get a real feeling of the situation, and published *A Home Help in Canada* (1912) – not an account of her time there but a guide to opportunities for Englishwomen.

Ella did responsible war work in hospitals during which, in 1916, she was elected to the council of the Royal Central Asian Society of which she had been a founder member. She was also elected a fellow of the Royal Geographical Society and was awarded a silver medal by the Royal Society of Arts. Between 1920 and 1926, she was secretary of the Royal Asiatic Society, and on the governing body of the Church of England Council of Empire Settlement 1927–1937. She died in 1939, six years before Percy.

It helps to see Ella in her later life – a stalwart Englishwoman with a sense of duty and empire and her own worth – in order to picture the woman who travelled to Persia in 1894 aged 31, four years Percy's senior.

There is a significance in the title of Ella's book *Through Persia on a Side Saddle*. It says most obviously that the book is by a woman but it is probably fair to assume that there is also a hint of rebellion in it. Ella was seldom nervous or ill and she soon got used to riding for hours on end across desert. The only thing, really, throughout the book, that she complains about is her side saddle. She wrote first:

> … the more I rode the more I saw the disadvantages of the saddle to which I was condemned … Some of my lady friends at Tehran always rode on a man's saddle when they went among the hills, modifying their habits to the altered position, which they all assured me was preferable in every way to that which custom obliged them to conform. (p248)

On a later occasion Ella had to ride a donkey; it was almost the only time she felt nervous of anything and the reason was not hard to find:

> ... and as stirrups and bridles were entirely lacking, I confess I felt somewhat nervous as to how I should stick on ... I would have given much to have dispensed with ceremony and sat astride, which I should most certainly have done had I been alone with my brother, but as things were I was obliged to cling on to the curved front of my insecure perch, having near escapes of falling off when my donkey stumbled in the middle of its rough gallop on one occasion, and one of the riders collided with me on another. (p261)

Ella and her side saddle put the English woman traveller in a new context. Did Lucy Atkinson ride side saddle? The only clue we have is when she crosses a river and writes of 'merely holding tight on to him with my legs, there being no saddle' (p190). But how about when there was a saddle? Such apparently small details are not usually mentioned, though Isabella Bird discusses the clothes she had made to accommodate riding astride, a release she discovered in Hawaii in 1875. Ella, although so commonsensical, did not make the final break in Persia. Even 20 years later when she wrote about her time in Kashgar she was still using a side saddle part of the time.

She was otherwise a well-balanced and self-possessed woman. Her good health and lack of nerves are quite marked and in contrast to, for example, Anna Forbes; and she comments on them herself. Of her well-being in Tehran – where they spent seven weeks after the journey into Persia, and three months on the way out – she writes:

> I took to Persia and things Persian at once, and never felt better in my life than at Tehran. The climate seemed to exhilarate me in the most delightful way, and to one accustomed to English winters it was a treat that never palled to wake up morning after morning to a world bathed in brilliant sunshine, with perhaps a covering of crisp white snow on the ground. (p16)

And of Kerman, where Percy set up a new consulate and Ella set up home for a year, she wrote, 'Throughout our entire stay at Kerman, neither of us had a touch of illness, but were invariably in the best of health and spirits' (p115).

Some of Ella's hardiness must have come from her upbringing: not only was her father a military chaplain but she tells us that to prepare them for the long journey when they left Kerman and rode for 600 miles in 40 days towards the Indian border, Percy, educated at an English public school and Sandhurst, 'thought it would be wiser to forswear fires altogether, fearing that if we got accustomed to them we should probably get ill when our tent life began' (p186).

Indeed, when one of them did get ill, when they travelled along the Persian Gulf, it was Percy who let the side down and was very ill for some time in temperatures which reached 118 °F. While Ella notes, 'The entire lack of exercise told on me a good deal … as, however, I never succumbed to the effects of the climate, I feel that I have no legitimate complaint against it' (p282) .

That she survived so well – even the less demanding desert conditions between Kerman and India – was something of a miracle for their friend, the Farman Farma, a local governor, 'strongly objected to my accompanying my brother on this journey, affirming that even if I survived the sun, I should re-appear in civilised life with my skin burnt to the colour of that of a negress' (p219). And he was right, for Ella writes of 'arriving at camp about 8 a.m., in broiling sunshine which scorched me considerably, in spite of my huge pith hat, two gossamer veils and a cosmetic for my face' (p245).

She took it all in her stride, accommodating herself to everything new and potentially disturbing. Right from the start – a rather awkward ride from the shores of the Caspian Sea where they landed after a boat trip from Russia – Ella makes remarks such as:

> The experiences of the day before had quite hardened me by this time, and I was positively surprised at finding that I was able to ride down places never imagined even in my wildest dreams with scarcely a tremor. (p9)

Awakened at night at Kerman to find a jackal prowling round her room, she writes, 'I soon got used to such harmless visitors' (p106). And she and Percy started to make a collection of insects for an entomologist friend in England. She notes, 'My most exciting find was a large tarantula', admitting that, 'I began my hunt with considerable trepidation' (p103). But when later on a journey she came across a snake, 'I seized my riding whip to despatch it' (p232). Not a screamer, Ella. The only time she was in danger from people, as opposed to conditions or nature, she did not have to prove herself in the way that Florence Baker or Anna Forbes did.

Ella was generally adaptable and unflappable – good to have on a journey from that point of view; but how capable was she? What contribution did she make in her own right? Their personal staff from Tehran to Kerman consisted of nine servants and by the time they reached Kerman she writes, 'I had sufficiently mastered Persian to be able to housekeep on my own account' (p32). Once they reached Kerman it was all go, as Ella explains in her inimitable way:

> We settled into a routine as time went on, my housekeeping occupying a good part of the morning … My first act every morning was to inspect each cooking vessel, and it took a considerable amount of energy to get the remains of one meal emptied out of the saucepans before a fresh dish was commenced in them, and soon I found that I must explore the recesses of the large cooking-boxes, as my cook had an unpleasant habit of hiding vegetables cooked a day or two before, so as to save himself the trouble of preparing a fresh lot for each meal. To fine Abu ten *shahis* (2½d.) for each dirty vessel was the only way of appealing to his feelings, although it was an unpleasant method to resort to, as it made him sulky, and covertly insolent

to boot. He would tell me lie after lie, with such admirable self-possession, looking me straight in the face with such guileless eyes the while, that he often fairly staggered me. However, his perversions of the truth were not consistent, and this betrayed him. Thereupon I would say, 'That is not true,' and when he perceived that he was found out, he would answer cheerfully and without a trace of shame, 'Yes, *Khanum*, it was a lie'!

From the kitchen I went to the store-room, cook and kitchen-boy carrying a regiment of pots and pans behind me, and here fresh trials of patience awaited the housekeeper. All Persian servants try to get as much out of their master as they possibly can by fair means or foul. They look upon it as a sort of sport, do not think it wrong, and set more store on the chance of perquisites than on the rate of their wages. In Persian houses the servants are fed, and are paid little, if anything, in coin; but Europeans give good wages, and expect their dependents to cater for themselves.

Abu was a thorough thief, rapacious to a degree, and I confess I was by no means a match for him at first, but I soon got into the habit of considering that I was playing a game with my cook and the other servants. At first they won all round, but after a while I began to score myself, and felt considerably elated when Sultan Sukru informed me one day that all the servants were blaming him, and saying that he had told the *Khanum* so much that they could hardly cheat at all now! (pp75–7)

That is typical of Ella's housewifely duties in Kerman and one can see how the traditional image of the white memsahib arriving to disturb the tranquillity of a masculine household came about: a clash of cultures that it is hard entirely to blame Ella for.

When it came to travelling, the problems were similar because, as Ella says, 'The helplessness of our Persian servants makes the supervision of every detail indispensable' (p128). And when they finally left Kerman for good to ride East for Percy to take part in the commission that would settle the boundary between Persian and British (Indian) Baluchistan they were given very little advance notice. Percy wrote, 'Thanks to my sister, everything was accomplished the day after the arrival of the gholám from Tehrán with the written instructions' (p213).

Although Ella was sad to be leaving Kerman, where she had been very happy, and the journey was likely to be arduous, she was her usual irrepressible self:

Perhaps what distracted my thoughts more than anything else was the fact that I was riding a new horse for the first time – a horse that had never had a lady on its back before, or a side saddle and English bridle; and to me there are few things more interesting than to get the mastery over a spirited animal, and to establish that delightful sympathy which makes the rider and his steed as one. So hurrah for the road again! hurrah for nomadic existence! and hurrah for the *wanderlust* that lurks in each man's blood, and drives our English race so far from home and kindred over the face of the globe. (p191)

Ella and Percy Sykes are a pronounced example of what being English (more accurately, British) was about at the height of Empire. It manifests itself at all levels of conduct and relations; it is expressed overtly and it pervades. Ella illustrates it most simply when an Englishman has been injured in the Persian Gulf: 'My brother and Mr Parry did all that could be done, and his heroism and pluck were something wonderful making us prouder than ever of the name of Englishman!' (p273).

Percy appears to travel for his own satisfaction when he writes of climbing a mountain:

> ... 'toiling, rejoicing, sorrowing,' we floundered on, and at noon reached the foot of the cone, at an elevation of 10,000 feet. Then came the last long climb, in which I was somewhat at a disadvantage, as I was reduced to an old pair of tennis shoes as footgear. The guides had had enough and so had I, but, led by Brazier Creagh, we gained yard after yard, and at last received our reward in having scaled another virgin peak. (p140)

His penchant for finding the new and, in particular, for altering received wisdom, often at the expense of proving former travellers wrong, also seems at first sight personal: 'Grant had reported that the drainage flowed away from the Bampur river and on this point we were enabled to prove him mistaken, unless, as is probable, it was due to a slip of the pen' (p121). Or, 'I believe that I may claim to be the first European who has crossed this section of the Lut, although, until I studied the question, I believed myself to be travelling in the footsteps of Marco Polo' (p34). And, 'I was delighted to see a map full of blanks in that direction, which I determined to fill in to the best of my ability' (p72). And yet, his preface suggests by its tone that it is more than his own identity and satisfaction that are at stake:

> I can claim, without fear of contradiction, that in the present generation no Englishman, and indeed no European, has travelled more extensively in Eastern and Southern Persia than myself, while my official position has given me exceptional opportunities, such as are rarely if ever enjoyed by unofficial travellers, of meeting the better classes of natives, and thereby of obtaining accurate information. (ppix–x)

It is, ultimately, British prestige that has been enhanced. And his mode of travel, eccentric and individualistic, is not only recognisable from the writing of other English male travellers, but was also recognised by foreigners as essentially English. Sykes writes of the start of his travels – when he reaches the Caucasus in 1893 on his way to join his regiment in India:

> Subsequently I was considered rather a suspicious character, at least I was shadowed, until I demonstrated my harmlessness and the absurdity of their suspicion by asking the shadower to carry my water proof. This, as

I afterwards heard, elicited the remark of 'only a mad Englishman,' and I was left in peace! (p3)

The English mode continued into Persia where, having clashed with an alien culture, Percy Sykes is also able to manipulate it to his own advantage:

> From enquiries which I made, it appeared that the Persian Deputy-Governor would not favour my going alone among the Turkoman, and, as I could not afford the expense of a large escort, it seemed best to keep my plans to myself until all our arrangements were completed, and then march off without applying to the authorities for assistance. (p11)

Later the administrator said of that ruse:

> I was sure to be killed or robbed, in which case he would be held responsible by the Persian government. This objection was defeated by my giving him a letter to the effect that he had warned me of the risk, and that I absolved him of all responsibility. However, matters remained at a deadlock, as Musa did not see why I wished to run risks instead of keeping to the main road, and when I tried to explain that I was anxious to explore for the Royal Geographical Society, his contempt for a body which existed for such a purpose was not concealed! ... When I played my last card and said that his reputation in Europe for hospitality would suffer, he yielded to this dire threat. (p14)

The eccentric English mode, apparently so individualistic on the personal level is also seen as part of a bigger whole when it comes to the official one:

> I think that our officials are somewhat apt to forget how great a power display still is in the East. In Baluchistán a traveller's status is partly determined by the number of his loads, in Persia by his servants and his general turn-out, while everywhere, as far as my experience goes, the greater the show, the greater the effect. Travellers on more than one occasion have told me that they had only brought rough shooting clothes with them; all such I would refer to Lord Curzon's work, where it is laid down that a dress suit is the most essential article of outfit, even for those who would attempt to reach Lhassa. (p292)

No wonder Ella rode side saddle in public, as an English lady was expected to!
  An incident concerned with appearance – his clothes – while confirming Ella's ability to keep up no matter what, provides the only glimpse beneath the surface of their equable companionship – a glimpse one has to conjecture for oneself. The countryside through which they were travelling was flooded and the muleteers wanted to go back to the village they had left. Percy was determined to push on; 'They were ordered to cross at once', Ella wrote, and continued:

> The first three streams were the worst. It was a horrible sensation to feel my horse slipping and floundering under me, and I got ready to spring off if he came to grief. However, though he nearly 'sat down' three or four times, and I got quite dizzy with the water swirling round me, and the curious feeling that my steed was making no way at all, yet we both stumbled through our six miles of flood in safety, and reached Dafa some time after sunset, our horses taking three hours to do this short distance, and the mules seven … The only box the contents of which were seriously damaged was the one containing my brother's uniform, part of which, unluckily, was quite ruined, but we could not complain, as we felt that we had really been most fortunate in getting the greater part of our baggage safe and sound. (p62)

One imagines that she did initially demur but then kept quiet when the muleteers made a fuss. There was obviously, however, a certain satisfaction about the state of his uniform – a feeling shared by Ella Maillart in similar circumstances. Percy mentions nothing at all of the ordeal except:

> After passing Kushkuh on the following day, we found our caravan in difficulties, owing to the flooded state of the road. The two leading mules had fallen, with the result that my uniform, packed in a so-called air-tight case, was partially ruined … (p184)

It is unlikely that they quarrelled much and her companionship was vital to him for, as he remarked at the end of his first long journey in Persia, alone except for his servants, 'I yearned for the sight of an English face after such a spell of loneliness' (p23). Who could be more ideal than Ella: she allowed him to do what he wanted to do, while usually getting credit for doing what he felt she would prefer and, what is more, she had English practicality and English moral fibre. When the instructions came through at the last moment to march through the desert to the boundary commission, he wrote:

> My sister was very kindly offered a temporary home by Lady Durand, but in the true traveller's spirit she preferred to face all fatigue and discomfort, and immediately set to work to empty our store-room of its very mixed contents, and to insure that the supply department, at any rate, should be thoroughly well organised. (p212)

As Ella wrote of another occasion, 'It was a wonderful achievement of English energy over Oriental obstructiveness' (p15). One cannot say that she does not understand part of the reason for this orientalism; it was not only laziness, duplicity and venality. As she explains, 'Persian servants [have] a great respect for the Feringhee Sahib and very little for the Khanum [Mistress] unless she has a man to back up her authority' (pp26–7).

And 20 years later in Kashgar, another Islamic society, things had changed little. Ella wrote:

To counterbalance my lack of tongues I had a fair knowledge of cooking and a good deal of energy, a quality useful in dealing with the slackness of the Oriental, particularly in Mohamedan countries, where a woman is obliged to hold her own, as her sex is of so little account. (p40)

It was hard to avoid the issue of Islam and women and Percy himself did not do so, though he saw it more as a political matter in general and, on the personal level, one affecting his sister's enjoyment of her life at Kerman when he wrote of the Governor General of Kerman province:

His Excellency was most friendly, and asked particularly that when he returned my visit it might be regarded as private and informal, so that he might see my sister.

This disposed of another question, many Europeans not permitting Persians to meet their families, on the ground that the jealous *anderun* [women's quarters] is closed to Europeans of the male sex. There is indeed much to be said for this opinion, but I thought that its observance would only widen the gulf between East and West, a gulf that I was anxious, even in a very small way, to bridge over; and we finally found that by judiciously choosing our guests, and always inviting one or two who had been to Tehrán, there was nothing disagreeable for my sister, who preferred these arrangements to almost entire isolation, as she did not know enough Persian to mix with the wives of my friends. (pp202–3)

Ella does not pick up on the issue on that occasion and her Persian improved enough to get by. Even if it had not, she confirms it is possible to communicate, at a certain level, without fluent language, when she describes a meeting with hill women outside Kerman. Her account, compared with Percy's, gives an illustration of how much would have been missed if he alone had written about their travels. He records:

While halting, some nomad ladies came to call, headed by a very determined old party. After presenting us with some cheese, a demand was made for medicine, but our tabloids were not at all favourably received, the idea that anything so small could be potent being rejected with scorn. In fact, so much was this the case that our visitors were not mollified until a bottle of some decoction, mainly water, was mixed for their edification. The whole business reminded me of a Cape doctor, who said that if you gave a Boer less than a quart of medicine, he would decline to pay the fee! (pp210–11)

(Percy had just come back from fighting in the Boer War when he wrote his book; it is almost his only joke.) Ella elaborates:

One day when here we had a visit from seven nomad women, the principal ladies of their tribe, who brought us offerings of cheese and *mast*. They refused to take money in return, saying that they intended to see the

Khanum, and would sit near our camp until I had interviewed them, even if I kept them waiting for days. So they were all ushered into the tent where we were sitting, fine looking women for the most part with fresh complexions and beautiful eyes and teeth. They left their shoes at the door, and an old lady in white cotton garments, wearing many bead and amber bracelets and several turquoise rings, entered first, and sat, or rather squatted, well to the front. This personage demanded medicine for her eyes, which were inflamed, and accordingly I gave her lotion for them; but she was not content with this, and pulled at my skirt and she begged in the most insinuating manner for any and every kind of remedy, until my brother, yielding to her passion for drugs, gave her a few drops of chlorodyne on a lump of sugar to assuage her *dar-i-dil*, the only complaint she could muster, being in remarkably robust health. She retired at last with some Elliman's Embrocation to rub into an imaginary stiff shoulder, grumbling bitterly, saying that we had given her nothing at all, and beseeching us, up to the end, to be more liberal with the contents of our medicine-chest. (pp146–7)

In Kerman itself Ella is thrown more into the company of Persian men because, if educated, they were likely to speak French. But the men had their drawbacks:

I must confess that after a time their company became somewhat wearisome. To find fresh subjects of discussion was my great difficulty. One could not (at least I could not) talk for ever about sport and horses, and it would have been contrary to all laws of Eastern etiquette to question them about their womankind, in whom I was deeply interested ... As they got to know me by degrees, some of them spoke bitterly about the need of education for their women, comparing these latter with me, to whom they did the honour of saying that I could understand whatever they said! They complained that their wives could talk nothing but gossip picked up at the weekly bath, and that as their religion forbade the men seeing their womenkind, save in the house, they had very few interests in common. I always told them that they alone were to blame, and when I explained to them how I had been educated, they were quite aghast, and one of them exclaimed indignantly, 'It is all the fault of our accursed religion, that binds us in chains as well as our poor women!' (p151)

Ella did manage to talk at a deeper level with women as her Persian improved. She came to learn quite a lot about her women friends and acquaintances and formed strong views about their position; the traffic was not one way:

They all professed to be sorry for my solitary condition, evidently not understanding that my brother and I could be companions in any way, and were incredulous of my assurances that I was perfectly happy, which assurances I reiterated with fervour, as I dreaded offers of a three or four days visit from my guests ... and amused me by warning me earnestly not to enter into the state of wedlock with a Persian, as their marriage customs were *khaili kharab* (very bad).

I was always afraid of allowing my female friends to compare their secluded lives with my free one, as it only made them discontented with their lot, and as I could do nothing to help them, I felt it was cruel to stir up vain longings for existences less like those of prisoners ... Persian ladies, to our ideas, have rather a dull time, though they probably get more fun out of life than is apparent to English ladies ... (p168)

Ella describes details of their lives, and then goes on to marriage customs, continuing:

When the couple settle down to a humdrum married existence the Persian theory is that a man has linked himself to a being inferior to him in every way, who must submit to his sovereign will in all things. From his extreme youth he has been taught by the priests to pay no attention to the counsels of his wife, and they have strongly impressed upon him that if a woman advises him to any course of action he had better do the exact contrary.

I remember on one occasion calling on a lady when her husband was present, and the latter at once asked me whether I thought his wife pretty, in much the same way as if she were a horse or a dog. He also bade me remark how ill at ease she was in his presence, adding with pride that if they were at table together she would have trembled in every limb from fear of her lord and master, and it was impossible to make him understand my indignation at this state of things. (pp171–2)

In spite of her strong opinions, not just on the treatment of women, Ella does try to be objective. She may not have heard of the word 'ethnocentric' but she senses it when she writes:

... I feel that perhaps I am too severe. Most of the gentlemen with whom I was brought in contact never appeared to me to do anything much beyond sleeping, talking and eating, never reading a book on any pretence whatever, and not even throwing themselves heartily into sport.

Yet, of course, the Oriental point of view is not the European one, and probably they looked upon us as lunatics for our ceaseless energy, our love of exercise, and our habit of filling up every spare moment with some occupation or other.

'*Kismet!*' ('It is fate!') is sufficient explanation for an Oriental to give when he is ill, or when things go wrong, even from his own fault; and this fatalism is too alien to my Western mind to permit me, I fear, to be quite fair when writing of my Persian acquaintances. (p180)

Ella makes no attempt to analyse her own position; and why should she?, she had a marvellous time in Persia. One wonders if she failed to notice the patronising attitude of Major-General Sir Frederic Goldsmid when he introduced her book. He wrote, '"Of course, the Oriental point of view is not the European one" is one of the naively but forcibly expressed truths in the volume under consideration.' He goes on, 'This cannot be too frequently inculcated on statesmen, secretaries, and others in any way responsible for our relations with Persia – and vice versa, ...' One has to ask, if it is so necessary to emphasise it because people who should know better fail to realise it, why is it naïve on Ella's part to spell it out?

Goldsmid also writes, 'The *couleur de rose* apparent in her descriptions does not detract from their reality; it is the reflection of her own good nature, for which allowance has to be made, such as readers are accustomed to make for the idiosyncrasies of authors.' There are two points here. Ella is even-tempered, not necessarily good-natured – as her dealings with her servants and her opinions of Persian men show. As for *couleur de rose*, she points that out herself when she shows the reader exactly why she went to Persia and what she got out of it. She writes pages of continuous panegyric, of which only a flavour is needed here:

> The 'Gorgeous East' has always possessed a strong fascination for me, and after reading *Eothen*, ... the indescribable attraction of the Orient became, if possible stronger than ever before ...
>
> ... I had been civilised all my days, and now I felt a sense of freedom and expansion which quickened the blood and made the pulse beat high. The glamour of the east penetrated me from the first moment of landing on its enchanted shores, and although many a time I encountered hard facts, quite sufficient to destroy the romantic illusions of most folk, yet they struck against mine powerlessly.
>
> I was under a spell throughout my stay in Persia – a spell that endowed me with rose-coloured spectacles, and that, even as I write, fills me with a strange yearning for the country which became a much loved home to me, and where I spent the happiest years of my existence ... (pp1–3)

Is she naïve? She certainly writes simply and directly, for she is writing from the heart, of the effect on her, as an individual of what she saw and felt; that is a valid aspect of a traveller's observation. What is more noteworthy is that the down-to-earth Englishwoman, a spinster at a time when such a condition was inhibiting, is able to take flight; two and a half years in Persia have released in her a lyrical streak probably previously unsuspected. It is a bit presumptuous, without knowing more about Ella's life in England before she travelled, to suggest that it was limited – after all, her education and its surroundings had been fairly unusual for her time and gender; nevertheless, it is likely. It would seem that Persia began to break that down so that later she concerned herself with wider issues, particularly those affecting women, if not on an overtly feminist level, at least with consciousness, in a way that she might otherwise not have done. And even 20 years later she was able to summon up the indignation which fuelled that consciousness. In 1915 she visited a Chinese household in predominantly Muslim Kashgar and wrote:

My entire ignorance of the language prevented me from enjoying this glimpse of a Chinese home in the way I might otherwise have done, and my thoughts centred on the neat little 'hoofs' shod in black satin which served our hostesses for feet. I had heard Mrs Archibald Little lecture on this fashion, and her account of the tortures inflicted on so many thousands of tiny girls to bring about the repulsive mutilation which the Chinese euphemistically call 'golden lilies' had filled me with an abiding indignation. And yet a recent traveller in China says that these crippled feet possess for him a 'quite extraordinary exotic charm,' and he exhausts himself in conjecture as to which mistress of an Emperor's heart introduced a custom that 'entailed a new charm on her sex.' I have no theory to offer as to the origin of the custom, but from the position of women in China it seemed to me that some man must have been responsible for a plan that would firmly tether his womankind to their homes, just as the veiling of Mohamedan women was a masculine device. (p75)

Part II
Twentieth Century

6 – A Travelling Wife

Eleanor Holgate Lattimore, *Turkistan Reunion* (**1934**; 1975; 1994)
Owen Lattimore, *High Tartary* (**1930**; 1975; 1994)

6.1   Eleanor Holgate Lattimore in Chinese Turkestan
(from Lattimore, *Turkistan Reunion*)

'For a wedding journey Chinese Turkistan seemed to us, and still seems, a most desirable land', wrote Eleanor Lattimore of 1926. And she continued, 'for it is far away from our familiar world not only in space but in time' (p15).

For how many travelling couples was their honeymoon, their period of learning to live together, a long, gruelling period in foreign climes? Lucy and Thomas Atkinson, Maggie and John Paton, Anna and Henry Forbes, and now, Eleanor and Owen Lattimore.

Perhaps Eleanor's sentiments provide a clue to the success of those enterprises: being so far away from all that is familiar breeds a team spirit essential if the couple is to survive. They always say, that if you can travel together you can manage anything else together.

6.2   Owen Lattimore and Moses in Chinese Turkestan
(from Lattimore, *High Tartary*)

If the Lattimores' journey has something in common, then, with those that
have gone before, it also has some differences. Ways of travelling and writing
about what you saw seem to have changed, if the Lattimores are anything
to go by, with the changing century – more likely with the upheavals of the
First World War. Or was it that they were American, not constrained by
expected forms of expression like the British. Take the subject of sex. No one
has mentioned it before. The Lattimores do. Indeed, simply talking about a
'wedding journey' is rather new; the others do admit to having been married
as they started their journey but otherwise they got on with the travel as if
that were newly married life for everyone.

The second difference is the conditions under which the couples travel.
Those who have gone before have faced real physical danger from humans, as
well as from disease. That is, of course, those that travelled to proper foreign
places, not the Londonderrys visiting St Petersburg in 1836, or the Ruskins
in Venice in 1849. The Lattimores in 1927 go to areas not far from those
visited by the Atkinsons 75 years before, but the worst the former have to

6.3   Eleanor and Owen Lattimore's journeys in Chinese Turkestan
(from Lattimore, *Turkistan Reunion*)

endure is the freezing cold and cramped conditions and, later, altitude sickness crossing the Karakorams. They were by no means tourists but neither were they explorers in the sense that their predecessors were. Owen Lattimore is rather conscious of that; is he also a bit too cynical?

It is a sad thing. Central Asia may be a little bit woolly about the edges, but it is not wild. Nor, so far as I can see, has it been wild within the last thirty years, or maybe fifty, except for a few irregular episodes, like the irruption of the White armies ejected from Russia, and their subsequent collapse. When I became a vagabond, I lost a last illusion, of the Adventurousness of Travel – the Great Traveler's Bluff. I weep for this loss ...
   ... I wonder how nine travelers out of ten who have proclaimed their prowess, supported only by assiduous retainers and alleviated only by supplies from home, would stand six months of the life, diet, and exercise of an English farm laborer. (pp28–9)

This fresh look needs a firmer context. Eleanor Holgate (1894–1970) and Owen Lattimore (1900–1989) both knew China before they came together. He was born in Washington DC but spent his early childhood in China. He was educated in England at St Bees but was back in China again at the age of 19. There he engaged in research, journalism and business. He spoke Chinese and the Tientsin (Tianjin) dialect fluently, to an extent that must have enhanced his journey and certainly enhances his writing. On one occasion he is trying, unsuccessfully, to unload his luggage from a public cart in unendurable cold and needs help. He is an unwelcome stranger when he goes into the nearby inn:

> When I came in I heard a Tientsin voice that said, in effect, 'Another damned Oross! [Russian]. Wonder what the hell he wants?' Then, as I began speaking: 'Why, it can talk!' Chinese, of the ignorant classes, are apt to regard foreign languages, not as human speech, but as collections of animal noises. Only men who can speak Chinese deserve consideration as human men.
>
> I spoke directly toward the corner from which the voice came. 'Yes', I said, 'I can talk; and what is more, I have come a long way, from Tientsin, and my talk is Tientsin talk. You are a Tientsin man, for I have heard you talk. Now, I am being *ch' i-fu* – harassed – by the people of these parts,' – and I threw in a word about their young sisters, for all to hear, to show that I had the Tientsin swearing, – 'and if the good fame of all Tientsin men is not to be eternally ruptured, you've got to lend a hand.'
>
> 'Why, of course,' he said, sitting up; 'what's to do?' (p19)

Eleanor Holgate was born six years earlier than Owen, into an academic family of Canadian origin in Illinois. She graduated in Liberal Arts from Northwestern in 1915 and became a teacher. During the First World War, she worked for the YWCA at army bases persuading 'camp followers' – young girls smitten with the uniform – to return to their families, and was later co-founder of the YWCA in Estonia. In so doing, she hoped to be able to get a Soviet visa permitting her to travel on the Trans-Siberian to China, so that she could write. She travelled to China with her parents in 1921, did postgraduate work at Columbia and then returned to the Orient again teaching in Chinese schools from 1924 and then becoming secretary of the Peking Institute of Fine Arts; Peking (Beijing) is where the Lattimores met.

When Eleanor and Owen decided to marry, they planned an unusual start to their married life. She was to accompany him to the Mongolian border and see him off on the sort of journey which she describes as 'impossible for a woman' (p17). Certainly from his account in *The Desert Road to Turkestan* (1928) and the beginning of *High Tartary* her presence would have cramped his style, not so much because of the physical difficulties but because of the male camaraderie he enjoyed travelling with the camel pullers, as one of them.

But, as Eleanor so tellingly puts it in *Turkestan Reunion*, 'There are bound to be hitches in any projects as ambitious as travelling half across Asia' (p17). Thus it was that the camels that Owen and his companions – including Moses, his family's retainer – were to use for the journey were commandeered by participants in the Chinese civil war and he had to return to base after a few hours. He and Eleanor spent the next six months waiting there together for another opportunity for him to leave. She sums it up briefly, 'I had brought clothes for a week and stayed for six months' (p17).

Finally Owen set off across Mongolia. She went back to Peking and waited for him to let her know he was nearing the end of his journey and that she should leave Peking, travel on the Trans-Siberian Express and meet him at Semipalatinsk in Soviet Siberia or in Chuguchak, just inside Chinese Turkestan – the place, you may remember, visited by Lucy and Thomas Atkinson 75 years earlier.

Eleanor had been on the Trans-Siberian before; she was not a complete novice in that part of the world but they had planned for her journey to be in summer; the delay meant that it was winter. She left Peking in early February 1927. What is more, because the United States Government had made difficulties for the Soviet ambassador, Alexandra Kollontai, to reach Mexico, her government refused to let Owen travel from Chuguchak to meet his wife in Semipalatinsk. Until then things had gone so smoothly for Eleanor that she wrote home:

A woman can travel alone more easily than a man. A man is expected to look after himself and do things for himself, and besides he is often darkly suspected of being a spy or some sort of subterranean agent, and is in consequence cross-questioned and harried, examined and watched, until he begins to wonder himself if he has any right to be there. Whereas a woman alone, whether she wants it so or not, seems always to be an object of public concern and beneficence. In fact it seems probable that she could travel to any iniquitous city or barbarous country in the world and be convinced that it was full of kindly people. For everywhere there are some who take pleasure in good deeds and she is their involuntary target. To officials she can completely explain her 'profession' by the innocuous term of 'housewife,' and the 'purpose of her journey,' 'to join her husband.' These anyone can understand and warm to. Her existence is explained, her journey justified.

And now I feel as if this journey of mine were going to prove or disprove my theory for ever, for I am sure that nothing could be much more difficult for a woman alone than to set out across the snow wastes of Siberia in the dead of winter toward a vague spot in Central Asia with the ridiculous name of Chuguchak. (p23)

She was right in what she wrote; Owen confirms it:

The next morning Moses and I regarded each other in the loneliness of Chuguchak. ... The situation stood thus: my wife had been able to get a Russian visé to travel through Siberia, but I was not sure of a visé to enter Siberia to meet her at railhead. For one thing, the sort of human nature from which not even officials are exempt makes it seem somehow easier to grant permits for a woman to travel through 'political' territories to join her husband than to grant the husband permission to cross cherished boundaries to fetch his wife. The Consul-General at Urumchi, again, though I think he was reasonably assured that I was not a bundle of 'secrets' rolling through

Central Asia acquiring more 'secrets,' might well fail to persuade Moscow of the accuracy of his observation. (p85)

There Eleanor was in Semipalatinsk, with too much luggage, too much snow and no Owen. She writes:

I must confess that when I reached here I felt somewhat as if I had come to a blank wall across my way, and that a rendezvous with one's husband at Semipalatinsk or Chuguchak seemed almost as impossible as everyone in Peking had told us it was. For Owen wasn't here, and I discovered that in spite of my firm resolution I had counted quite a lot on finding him waiting on the snowy station platform when I tumbled wearily out of the train at the end of the line. But when I arrived, after thirty three hours' 'hard', and climbed out of the dim car into a glittering world of snow, there wasn't any husband, but only a forlorn wooden railway station in the midst of a vast white plain, far across which I could see the roofs and onion-shaped church towers of the city. (p34)

What choice did she have?

I will have to get to Chuguchak some way or other. It must be possible. Chuguchak is on the map, and other people go there. But it is four hundred miles away, across desolate wastes of snow. The road, they tell me, is well-nigh impossible and the cold terrific. To get there I must hire a sleigh and, if possible, I must find a travelling companion, as the sleigh drivers are unreliable and there are Kirghiz bandits on the road. And I'm sure I don't know how to accomplish all this. The people here seem horrified at the idea of my attempting it. (p39)

She attaches herself to a train of sledges carrying matches from Semipalatinsk to Chuguchak in the company of a courier from the Chinese consulate called Kitaiski (Chinese). The conditions are very cramped, the weather freezing, their nightly stopping places crude in the extreme.

It is on that 17-day journey that Eleanor is forced, delicately, to regale her family with the sexual mores of Turkestan's inhabitants and how they affect her:

The men have been teasing my driver about some escapade of his last night, the fine points of which I miss in spite of Kitaiski's noblest efforts to explain, which explanation, in order to maintain my reputation as a perfect lady, I feign not to understand at all. It seems that in the small hours of the morning he attempted to seduce the young daughter of the Kazak household, offering her five kopecks for her services. Whereupon she got the giggles and squealed loudly, 'You can't love *me* for five kopecks. Half a rouble is my price,' thereby waking everybody in the house. The poor driver will never hear the end of it. They are already calling him 'Five Kopecks' ... (pp52–3)

Sometimes Eleanor herself is more directly implicated:

> The most attractive Kazak woman I have seen yet climbed out of bed to make us tea. She made the usual coy remarks about Kitaiski and me and offered us her bed. How did I dare travel without my husband with another man? Kitaiski explained that it was because we were both 'educated', which was a little beyond her comprehension.
>
> I get awfully annoyed at not being able to talk. There are so many things I want to know. Of course, travelling with six men, not being able to talk with them has been in a way a protection, especially against a good many embarrassing conversations. They are pretty crude animals and the Kazak women in the huts where we have stopped are certainly not much in the way of chaperons. They seem to be completely unmoral creatures. I had heard of travellers being embarrassed by the hospitality of Kazak households which pressed upon them the services of their women and were offended if they were not accepted, and that almost any Kazak woman was considered to be at the disposal of the passing traveller, and from bits I did understand of the conversations of the drivers I can well believe this to be true. While we were drinking tea at two in the morning, just before our start, Kitaiski asked me if I had heard this woman chattering to him in the night. It seemed that he, the protector of my virtue, had suggested getting into bed with her but that she had refused to let him, saying at first that it was the fast of Ramazan and it was against her religion. He had tried to persuade her that it wouldn't matter as her man was away and wouldn't know she had broken the fast, but much to his surprise she still refused to have him. Finally she confessed that she was feeling hurt because he had said that I was 'educated' and then was treating her as if she weren't. But later she melted and said that if he would wait till after I had gone it wouldn't matter. Kitaiski says that everyone knows that any Kazak woman will take any traveller to bed with her and he was amazed at this woman's spirit. (pp66–7)

Owen, at this leg of Eleanor's travels, is waiting for her in Chuguchak, having no idea where she is or if she has got any of his messages; she hasn't. But, during his previous months of travel, he has had the opportunity of doing his own research into sexual mores:

> Throughout this province the brothels, which add so much to the adventurous restlessness of night life in most Chinese cities, are positively discouraged by officialdom; but no amount of suppression could prevent the existence of a few houses of resort in such a city as this [Ku Ch'eng-tze], at the end of such a caravan route. In Ku Ch'eng-tze, however, prices are so high and results so meagre that most men are content with the more easy society and less exorbitant demands of Turki or Mongol women, whose idea

of the bosom of the family is very cordial. Yet Chinese women are so scarce that, in the natural tendency to make them go round, the rigid Chinese standard of decorum for married women suffers, among the lower and even middle classes. Many a caravan owner talks knowingly of the matron he has *hung-lo* – played – when he was in town and her husband was not. Sometimes when a Chinese gives himself over to a really thoroughgoing passion he cannot halt this side of tragedy. Out in the desert I had met a caravan which was taking home a cousin of the House of Chou, who had come a cropper over a woman. He had sold his more than a hundred camels, run through the money, and was at the charge of his friends for a passage home. Again, at a God-forgotten military post I was told of a broken opium sot who had once been wealthy and was now servant to soldiers for the scrapings of their pipes. He had not only sold his camels, but mortgaged land and property in Kuei-hua, so that his wife continued to live there comfortably and bring up his children respectably, while he wore out the butt end of his life on the desert fringe of the Golden West.

But, as I have said, most of the camel pullers were shy of town women. After talking for the whole journey of the streets, restaurants, women, and shops of Ku Ch'eng-tze, they ducked uneasily through the bustle for two or three days. Then they sighed and went back to the wind of the open and the smoke of the tents. As for wenching, 'So-and-so,' they said, 'and Such-an-one, who talk so much of their exploits, they don't really have more fun than we do, who can spend the whole night in a Mongol yurt for one paper tael, which is forty cents of silver money. With the Mongols – dogs defile them – when the light is out no one minds anyone.' (p11)

Eleanor is meeting similar men on her journey though she is treated at a different level from Owen:

The drivers and Kitaiski are very nice to me. They are crude, of course, and have a lot of vulgar jokes at my expense, but they don't know that I understand them at all and are always polite and respectful to me. They tease Kitaiski about me, but he takes it good-naturedly … (p55)

… They had been reluctant in the first place to take a woman along, but, having accepted me, they treated me as one of them. I liked that and would not for worlds have been a poor sport about it. They did do little extra things to make me comfortable and always gave me the best place to sleep, but nevertheless it was a communistic group and I could picture their scorn if I tried to put on any extra airs like face washing … (p57)

… I have had a queer kind of pleasure out of suffering from the filth and squalor and discomfort of this trip. It is so awful that it's funny. And in a way it's rather glorious. I like knowing I can have a grand time in spite of it. And it's glorious because it's real and human. It's all 'experience.' I can't explain it exactly, but it seems a great experience to me. And I think

I'll never be squeamish about anything again. I'm sure a good many of our 'sensibilities' are very artificial. (p59)

Owen, too, had revelled in his separate journey:

Alas and alas, that the good caravan life should be over and done with! I don't suppose I shall ever again think and dream in a language not my own, as I did during those full months: not the Chinese of phrase-book and cultivated teacher, but the inimitable vernacular of the merry, vagabond, rascally classes ... (p27)

... I wished that I might go on in this noble progress, without count of time, seeing all Asia unroll before me. (p59)

Now they prepare to meet; Eleanor draws nearer to Chuguchak:

Perhaps the journey's end will be an anti-climax after all, and my pot-of-gold husband not arrived. So I'm trying not to be excited. But it is exciting.

... It is silly how I always think of Chuguchak as my 'journey's end' when really it is only the beginning. But all the difficulties of the little-travelled roads through Turkistan and across the Himalayas, and even the trips we are planning that no white woman has done before, seem so simple when I'll be no longer a 'woman travelling alone'. (pp68–9)

The 'journey's end' is one of the sweetest love meetings in literature. She cannot write about it, just a few words:

Then two hours across snow fields towards black and white mountains at the foot of which was Chuguchak. Then into muddy streets, and Kitaiski scouting about to discover if Owen was there, while I waited perched on the loaded sleigh, and Owen coming round the corner – and there was Chuguchak. (p70)

He writes:

Thus it was on the seventeenth day without news, when I was at the house of the French-German-speaking couple, disguising my dejection somewhat, but unable not to reckon over to myself the things that might have happened to her on that road, among those people, in that snow, that a strange Chinese in many furs burst in. He had tried me several times in Russian and Turki before I tried him in Chinese, then he tugged me into the street, boasting in a rush of words his prowess and chivalry in bringing my wife to me. She stood, almost unrecognizable to me in her furs, beside a small heaped sleigh in the wintry street. She had brought off the incredible, and we were together, and in Central Asia. (p90)

Eleanor can journey like that, alone, and then she has to write the usual woman's introduction to her letters home;

> I could not have made the journey at all without my husband. If I had not believed him to be at the end of the rainbow I could never have travelled alone those seventeen days by sledge across the snow-covered Steppes of the Great Horde in the dead of winter. And later, if I had not been with him I could not have camped with the nomad Kazaks of the Heavenly Mountains, nor kept house in Turkistan deserts and oases, nor finally crossed the five great mountain passes, all over 16,000 feet high, which form the mountain barrier between Turkistan and India. But men go everywhere, and write about it, whereas, as a woman in a land where white women have seldom and in many places never, been seen, my interests, experiences and sensations were in many ways unique. I am, therefore, venturing to suppose that there are those who will be interested in my side of our 'sentimental journey.' (pp18–19)

What would Isabella Bird, who went up the Yangtze Valley alone in 1896, have made of that, and Ella Maillart who follows Eleanor as a travelling companion in this book but travelled solo through Soviet Central Asia in 1932?

From now on, Eleanor and Owen's journey was together and she writes, 'We are jogging blissfully along on the road from Chuguchak to Urumchi, and travelling with a husband is a lot more fun than travelling alone' (p73). Their companionship is attractive and many of their attitudes are twentieth-century; Percy Sykes and his imperialism are left in the previous century. Eleanor writes:

> We want to travel like vagabonds, wandering through the province as simply and inconspicuously as possible, living as much as possible 'off the country' and as the natives do, both because it is cheaper and more carefree and because we can learn more of the people and the country by doing it that way. But we have to compromise to a certain extent between our idea of the kind of people we are and the Chinese idea of the kind of people we ought to be. This is all because the Chinese officials have their own notions as to how bona fide Western travellers ought to travel, and anyone trying to act like a gypsy is likely to be harried as a Russian refugee and suspected as a spy …
>
> … a white man is no longer treated as a Lord of Creation just because he is white, and it seems that now, to be treated with any sort of respect and consideration one must make it obvious that one is not a Russian. Most Chinese are completely unable to understand anyone enjoying travel for its own sake. They look upon it as a necessary hardship and usually do it very badly. They wear the same clothes and carry the same flowered quilts and white embroidered pillow covers when they travel that they use at home. And if we wear corduroy breeches and khaki shirts and carry army blankets it is because we are poor and have no manners and are therefore not worthy of respect or consideration. And without the respect and consideration of

Chinese officials and innkeepers we wouldn't be able to travel at all. So we are trying to atone for our khaki shirts and our lack of embroidered pillow covers by displaying all the guns, cameras, field glasses, barometer, thermos bottles, and other grandeur that we have, and otherwise traveling like the most respectable of Chinese officials. This involves my riding like a perfect Chinese lady in a springless cart discreetly curtained in blue and white. (pp80–1)

The question of appearance and face had earlier occurred to Owen in a different guise:

Then cropped up the difficulty of clothes. 'Central Asia,' I had thought in my innocence, 'will be grand. I shall wear all kinds of play-acting clothes, and no one will know the difference.' Didn't they! I could not wear the yellow elkhide Mongol-style boots I had bought with rapture in Ku Ch'eng-tze, because I might have been taken for a Russian fallen from the pride of Imperial days. Then, all through Mongolia I had girt myself with a sash of purple cotton, thinking it good enough for the desert, and saved my sash of scarlet silk for Urumchi, where it ought to have been appreciated, but was not. Were I to have worn a red sash, I should have looked too much in sympathy with the Soviets. (p28)

In Mongolia Owen had had to prove that he was not an émigré Russian and discovered the individualistic English traveller:

I told him I was not an Oross, but an Amerikanski, – thinking that in a Russianized version I might come nearer his mark, – but it was a clean miss. 'Well then, an Inglis,' I ventured. At this he glowed with joy, going by an estimate which I afterward found common among the races – except the more sophisticated Chinese – of this part of Central Asia, that the Oross are brute-mad and child-foolish, while the Inglis are devil-mad, and as for their foolishness, who knows? – it is of a piece with their madness. (p17)

A related facet of English individualism is British imperialism; Eleanor observes, as they leave Kashgar and head towards India:

We had left behind all those enchanted places which I was the first white woman to see. In Kashgar there had been the consul's wife and several Swedish missionaries, ... Englishmen come over from India to shoot in the Pamirs. This year one of them even brought his wife. We met them in a garden in Posgam. They had bathtubs and thirteen servants. Our Moses said he was going to strike for thirteen salaries. From Kashgar we became Sahib and Mem Sahib, and were treated no longer as curiosities but as members of the Ruling Race which was fun but needed living up to. (p261)

Owen notes and analyses imperialism (Chinese as well as British) on more than one occasion for, as he says, 'I touch on these things partly because it is the business of a traveler to appreciate, if he can, everything that comes to his notice' (p301). It is not their style, whether imperialism in rule or its concomitant in travel, and Owen mocks it as they leave Chugachak together:

> From now on we were, by ample modern precedent, no longer travelers, but an expedition. We could lounge and stare together as expeditions do, along roads not perfectly understood, perhaps, but at least known, with no more noble duty than the invention of counter-spellings to set up against the spellings on the maps of others, hopefully confounding, in the cause of knowledge, things already well and earnestly confused.
>
> This matter of becoming an expedition had unfortunately slipped our attention in Peking, so that we had not provided ourselves with the distinctive expeditionary insignia of stamped letterheads and personal titles. My wife had even submitted, in filling out her consular papers, to the description of 'housewife.' I had fallen into a loose way of regarding myself as a person interested in people, rather than as a person interesting to people, as a true expeditionary should be. (p91)

Now that they are together we also see their division of interests and can pursue their differences in style. It is worth, too, looking to see if Eleanor's perception is changed now that she is no longer alone. Interestingly enough, she does not maintain a particular interest in women; one wonders why there are no details when she notes:

> Soon after we arrived Owen went to call on the officials, and he hadn't been gone a minute before the postmaster's wife, mother and two babies came in to see me. I showed them all our belongings and they stayed all the time he was gone, but the minute they heard him come in the gate they were off like rabbits. And it has been the same way ever since. They won't come in the room as long as Owen is here, but pop in the minute he leaves. (p235)

What did they talk about? They were Chinese and she spoke their language. And, of the same stay with the postmaster in Aqsu, Owen writes, 'My wife talked with the women, while I talked for hours with the men.' And he does elaborate on their conversations (p298).

On another occasion the omission is more marked. Eleanor describes visiting an old mosque in the middle of nowhere and of being the guests of 'two delightful old *mullahs*' (p122). It is only from Owen that we learn there were women there – women for Eleanor:

> The sheikh of the mosque, an old man with the dignity of much white beard, graciously showed us into his room, which was cool and dark, and served us tea and women. The women were for the benefit of the foreign woman, not of the foreign man. Granted even the cordiality toward strangers, and the

frank, interested manners of the Turki, a sheikh in charge of an important mosque would hardly have allowed his womenfolk to appear before a *parang* (*farang*; Frank) had not the Frank been accompanied by his own woman. Yet the fluttering, delighted women, though they subdued their chatter, were not timid in the presence of strangers; they did not even veil their faces, but showed in their behavior the tolerant way in which the easy-going Turki folk let slide the strict Mussulman standards in regard to women. (p177)

Eleanor half-answers the mystery of her lack of interest in women, in a delightful passage. They have arrived at a small Chinese fort at the foot of the Muzart pass; the colonel is a Tientsin man, Ma Ta-jen – Big Man Ma:

Owen asked the Big Man if he had brought his family with him to live at the fort. 'Well, I have one family here,' he answered. 'I suppose that you, too, have left the mother of your children in a more civilized place.'

He assumed what all the other Chinese officials we have met have assumed, that I am merely a 'travelling' wife and that of course Owen has a more respectable one at home. The Chinese would never expect a respectable married woman to take so rough a journey, and almost any Chinese who has to travel or live temporarily in the interior takes along a temporary travelling wife if he can afford it. They all think it very swell of Owen to have a travelling wife. 'What a fine fellow,' they say, 'travelling with a Tientsin servant and a woman brought all the way from the coast!' But the Chinese officials who are settled in cities where they can have their own regular families have never introduced me to their respectable wives. They have entertained me cordially with the men but the women never appear. (p225)

Owen almost outdoes her. They are taken for an interview with a governor:

One of the most pleasant 'official' interviews I have ever had, and a most unorthodox one, too, seeing that I was accompanied by my wife.

My wife, however, had a most exceptional measure of respect throughout her travels. It was true that conservative people might think her only a 'traveling wife,' since no respectable woman would abandon the dignity of her position as head of a household. On the other hand, the better-informed people admired her spirit and appreciated her interest in her travels. The common people were immensely impressed with the information, which Moses was never tired of putting about, that she had a university degree. I used frequently to overhear lively discussions at inns or by the wayside, something like this: 'These people are Americans; they are of a country new, but very rich. They are not like the English, who are unbending, nor like the Russians, whose affairs no one can make out. The woman? *Ai-ya!* But a very special woman. She has a degree! Yes, a degree. What talent! Undoubtedly her people are officials (that is, because of belonging to the literary class). Her husband has no degree; all his life he has never been more than a merchant. The truth of it is, that all decision is with her; he is only the executor.' (p211)

There is, of course, a language problem for Eleanor with Turki or Kazak women; and it is true that in her letter of 21 July from Kashgar she writes at length of the women of Aksu (Aqsu), and how they dealt with a young woman who had run away from her husband with another man – background details of which Moses found out for her. Then, just before reaching Kashgar, a young woman who had hitched a ride with them got upset and, once again, Moses provides the explanation – man trouble. But there is no sign of empathy with any of the women she describes in that letter, in the way that there was from Lucy Atkinson, Maggie Paton, Anna Forbes or Ella Sykes. It is almost as if she had a clear idea in her mind of her readership, even though her letters are to her family. When she attends a Russian émigré marriage she observes:

> The bridegroom was old enough to be the bride's father and had children as old as she. Urumchi Russians seem to be noted for strange marriages, and as they are all far from home and with little to do but get into mischief they do seem to get most amazingly entangled with each other's husbands and wives. There has been a lot of talk about marriage in Soviet Russia, but somebody should write a book about marriage among Russian emigrants. It would make far more scandalous reading, from tales I've heard of them in other places than Urumchi. Another recent Urumchi wedding was between a man of over seventy and a girl of twenty-one who had had two husbands before him. I have never in a few weeks heard so much gossip of domestic scandals. (p138)

Nearly every time she mentions women it concerns scandals to do with love or marriage. She gives us a clue about her readership, and many about herself, when she writes:

> I am afraid I am too domestic to make a really good exploress, for I simply adore a day in camp all by myself and I always seem to spend it puttering around doing odd bits of mending and washing instead of writing letters or an article on the home life of the Kazaks or something equally profitable. I feel very futile trying to write about this journey. Letters from several editors and a 'literary agent' have expressed interest in my experiences as the 'first white woman to travel overland from Peking to India' or the 'first American woman in Turkistan,' or some such, and implying that the public wants thrills and that any account of my experiences exaggerated to the limit of credibility would be acceptable. Even if I wanted to exaggerate my adventures I'm sure I wouldn't know how. They all seem perfectly thrilling to me, but probably not the kind of thrills the public wants. We have neither been captured by bandits nor attacked by wild animals, but every day seems full of adventures and how can I tell anyone about them! (p206)

Eleanor is sympathetic again through her vulnerability, but no feminist. This problem of twentieth-century travel, when all is much less arduous, is one of which she is very conscious:

> We had looked forward to the crossing of the Muzart as one of the most difficult of all the feats of our travels. I have really been almost disappointed that we haven't had more hardships on this trip. I don't mean just cold and heat, which one can have almost everywhere, but interesting and adventurous hardships which give one a sense of being able to endure and conquer. (p229)

It is a shame if their relative unadventurousness nagged at her, for their approach to their journey has its own twentieth-century validity and their accounts inspired later travellers such as Ella Maillart and Peter Fleming. Eleanor has no chance to let us know whether or not she is a screamer, as Florence Baker did, but she makes no fuss, as several incidents illustrate. Of one she writes:

> I had a new and nasty experience to-day. The cart got stuck in a marsh and we walked on to a Chinese village. The sun was hot so I waited in the shade in front of a little tea shop while Owen went to look for a duck. As soon as he was out of sight all the village children appeared, shouting 'Russian ____' (I didn't understand the second word!), and started throwing mud and stones at me. At first I tried to laugh it off, but when I saw that there were several grown-ups watching them and interfering not at all I was furious, and not having enough of the local Chinese to tell them what I thought of them in any but a laughable manner, I stalked back to the cart as haughtily as I could with bits of mud and pebbles hitting me in the back. The cart was a quarter of a mile away and I wanted terribly to run, but I knew that would only make them worse, so I walked with as much dignity as I could muster, but I've never felt more foolish. (pp97–8)

Owen writes of his part in the matter on his return from hunting in the more consciously explanatory style that we are beginning to expect from men:

> I was angry, and reproached the two men who had been with me concerning the manners of their village. They were abject in apology, but protested that 'it was only child's play.' Bad manners in Chinese children are no bad manners, children, especially boys, are given a license that by our standards is monstrous. Indeed, there is hardly a crime graver than to make a small child cry, or to thwart it in any way. There is even a proverb, *ch'u men pu je san tze*: when traveling, do not annoy the three *tze*; these three *tze* being bearded men (old men), children (boys), and the blind. 'Bearded men' does not in the least refer to foreigners, for the hairiness of foreigners is matter of reproach; but the scantiest beard of a mature Chinese (formerly a man was not even allowed to maintain a beard until he was past forty) is a

mark of reverend dignity. Of the heinousness of annoying children I have already spoken; as for the blind, they are everywhere in China entitled to courtesy, and are commonly addressed as *hsien-sheng*; a term which, as it is ordinarily used for one's teacher, is even more respectful than our 'sir.' Thus, for an affair of children, however unmannerly, too much stir could not well be made. Nevertheless, the villagers were publicly shamed when I reproved them; it was not at all because the children had thrown mud, but because I had mentioned it. An insult in China is not an insult unless you take it up. (pp133–4)

We can see from the extracts that have gone before that Eleanor writes straightforwardly. Sometimes there is an immediacy that has the power of, say, Lucy Atkinson. Owen strives – and succeeds – for scholarship and effect. He also writes more powerfully of conversations because, as we have seen, he glories in languages and in his facility for picking them up and speaking them. As his mother said, 'Owen just learns languages because he can't bear not to know what other people are saying.' Owen also has the knack of getting on with people that is striking. He makes real friends wherever he goes, partly because of his linguistic facility. Ma Ta-jen told him that,

All foreign big-game shooters on their way from India and Kashgar to the Qaraghi Tash to hunt pass by this post, so that in the experience of a number of years he had a lively knowledge of them; but I was the first foreigner he had ever met who could talk with him in his own language; for which reason his interest abounded, and we yarned for hours, explaining things to each other. (p270)

Where narrative style is concerned, Owen is also effective. The contrast between their styles shows strongly in the following passages. Eleanor writes from Kulja on 28 May 1927:

We set out from Urumchi when the moon was pale and young and slender and when we reached Kulja she was very old and tired, but never has a moon made desert sands more magic than this May moon in Chinese Turkistan.
    The reason I know so much about the moon is that we travelled at night because of the heat, and deserts that in the daytime would have been long blistering scorching stretches of sand or gravel were eerie beautiful. Moonlight makes any desert glamorous.
    I keep wanting to shout about how happy we are and to rave about the loveliness of Turkistan and the perfect joy of our days instead of making a sane attempt to describe them intelligently. (p143)

And his version:

Then the moon rose and showed, like a vision, beyond the flickering fires, a pale golden wilderness of glimmering sand and black tamarisks, all enclosed by the sinuous ridges of the dunes, marked with a deceptive sharpness against the faint stars. At the other fires we could see the black shapes of men and hear their deep-toned speech, and at our own the light wavered on dark, bearded faces, and the fox-skin helmets of the Qazaqs and the round sheepskin caps of the Turkis, edged with black lamb's wool. The full magic of the road overwhelmed us. At last we began to hear the strepitant blather of the approaching host of sheep and goats, and dark scuttling waves of them flowed in around us over the dunes. In a few moments we heard also the hortatory bellowing of carters, the cruel crack of whips, and at last the desperate, roaring breath of the ponies as they lugged at the sand-encumbered wheels. (p187)

I expressed the opinion that your arm would get very tired if you wrote like that in a letter home; and the postage would be exorbitant. When their son, David Lattimore, read that, he wrote to me in June 2011 of Owen's writing of his earlier book, about his journey before Eleanor joined him:

Incidentally, you mention the tendency of women travelers to write as they went along. But that is also how my father wrote *The Desert Road to Turkestan* – as dispatches to the *Peking* and *Tientsin Times*. These he composed longhand, on tablets of paper with interleaved carbons. The paper copies he sent to Peking with returning camel caravans that he passed en route. The carbon copies I have seen. They are essentially identical with the published book. So that was before my mother's editing began.

Both Owen and his son make much of the need for Eleanor to edit his work. In Owen's introduction to the 1975 reprint of *Desert Road to Turkestan* he calls it 'too bookish a book'. In the introduction to the reprint of *High Tartary* he writes of the 'cockiness' of the earlier book and adds disarmingly, 'I was a young man who was in fact not too sure of himself, who had not long been married and who was trying to impress his wife.'

I thought that Eleanor herself did not want to write, but according to her son, she certainly had an earlier ambition to do so, and I agree with him that she had 'a style and a voice'. Owen certainly revelled in writing and, however much she pulled his work into shape, he shines through.

Afterwards they were to write together *Silks, Spices and Empire* (1973), an anthology of Silk Road travellers in whose footsteps they had followed. They also collaborated on *The Making of Modern China* (1944) and *China: A Short History* (1947). He went on to become a leading expert on Mongolia, attached to Harvard and other universities, such as Leeds in England, which would have impressed his friends in Chinese Turkestan.

Eleanor died in 1970; Owen did not do so until 1989 though, after her death, as his entry in the *Oxford Dictionary of National Biography* suggests, he was 'deprived of the support and domestic discipline that had made his earlier writings possible. From 1970 to 1985 he wandered ceaselessly.' David Lattimore puts it more personally and pithily:

My father's tragedy was that he survived my mother by 19 years. He kept looking for a replacement, but none met his requirement of a professionally qualified wife who would exchange her career for the role of maintaining him. That model had been discontinued.

In spite of those sad years, Owen's scholarly reputation, and that of adviser to governments, was secure, though in the 1950s he had been a victim of the McCarthy witch-hunt – with Eleanor working on his defence.

In the 1920s, Owen was travelling as a historian in the making; he was interested in people, then and later. Beginning to sum up their journey, he wrote of:

> The progress, now lordly and now comical, in the saddle and by cart, about and across the province, meeting rogues and vagabonds, tatterdemalion soldiers, gracious officials, open-handed merchants, Chinese, Turki, Mongol, Qazaq, and Qirghiz. I wondered if I had dealt honestly by them all. At least I had gone as much as was humanly possible by the custom of the country. As for my own customs, at least I had never called a Chinese a Chinaman or a Celestial; nor, as far as that goes, a camel a ship of the desert, nor a horse a steed. Nor had I written out in detail the menu of a Chinese dinner. Nor had I, in print, got nearer to Nature. Never, in striking camp, had I folded my tent like an Arab. I had not gone behind the back of Mongol or Qazaq to call him a child of Nature, nor insulted the sanctity of any temple by speaking of idols. And I had left poor old Marco Polo and his much misrepresented Trail alone, as much as I decently could ... (p316)

It was the travelling that counted for Eleanor – her 'sentimental journey' or her 'marriage journey'. 'I have never seen,' she wrote,

> so many wild flowers as grow on these rocky hills. We're always wishing we were botanists and geologists or archaeologists or anthropologists or something, but after all it is rather nice being purposeless and we fit much better into the landscape. (p213)

And from Turfan in April, 'I wonder if ever again in our lives we will live so perfectly or be so free and happy' (p112). And from Urumchi:

> We are torn between loving Urumchi and wanting to be off again. This vagabond life is so beautifully simple. Instead of jobs, offices, newspapers, railways, clothes, calls, dinner parties, there are only ponies and the long road, Moses and his frying pan, paper taels to pay for bread and meat and onions, and all the world to wander in till all the tattered taels are gone. (p140)

7 – A Born Traveller

Ella Maillart, *Forbidden Journey* (**1937**; 1983; 2003)
Peter Fleming, *News From Tartary* (**1936**; 1980; 1990; 2001; 2010)

7.1   The Professional (Ella Maillart)
in Chinese Turkestan (from Fleming,
News from Tartary)

7.2   The Amateur (Peter Fleming)
in Chinese Turkestan (from Fleming,
News from Tartary)

Ella Maillart and Peter Fleming only came together – against the better judgement of both lone travellers – because their proposed journey was to be so fraught with obstacles. They needed to pool resources and, having bumped into each other on assignment in Manchuria, they admired each other's talents sufficiently to risk a joint venture.

Maillart held the trump card of having found a Russian couple, the Smigunovs, who knew an obscure way through and, desperate to return to their home in the Tsaidam on the southern rim of Chinese Turkestan, were prepared to act as guides. Maillart sets the scene of her cooperation with Fleming:

> … Hearing me speak of the Tsaidam and the Smigunovs, he had said coldly: 'As a matter of fact, I'm going back to Europe by that route. You can come with me if you like …'
> 'I beg your pardon,' I had answered. 'It's my route and it's I who'll take you, if I can think of some way in which you might be useful to me.' (p18)

Ella Maillart (1903–1997) is the best known of all the women travellers under observation. Indeed, she may well be the only one heard of before by some readers. That is because when she set out with Peter Fleming (1907–1971)

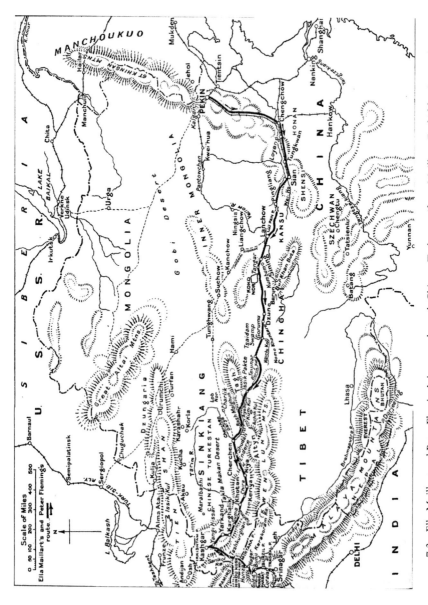

7.3 Ella Maillart and Peter Fleming's journey through Chinese Turkestan (from Maillart, *Forbidden Journey*)

from Peking in 1935 she had already established three reputations: as a traveller, with her book *Turkestan Solo* (1934), the account of a hazardous and determined journey she made alone in Soviet Central Asia in 1932; as an Olympic yachtswoman (1924); and as a world-class skier for Switzerland (1931–34).

Ella Maillart – called 'Kini' in Fleming's book – is different from other travelling companions in an important respect: she was not married to Fleming, nor related to him in any other way. Thus a strong, independent, professional woman of 31 was joining forces as an equal with a 27-year-old man already admired for his *Brazilian Adventure* (1933) and *One's Company* (1934) (describing a search for Communist rebels in Southern China). His *Times* obituary remarks that, 'as a stylist he was in the top flight; as a traveller he was *sui generis*, for his journeys and his manner of recounting them belonged to a school of his own devising'.

Eight years after Eleanor and Owen Lattimore had made the relatively easy journey from Peking to India across Chinese Turkestan the political situation there had changed radically. This meant that, first, the two reporters, Maillart for a French newspaper, Fleming for the London *Times*, felt they should bring back an account to the outside world of what was going on and, second, they would be unable to obtain permission to do the journey at all. Thus they came to do it covertly, a fact which gives a distinct edge to both accounts.

And yet, such a woman could write a few months later, when, through an enforced delay, Fleming had gone off hunting,

> Ever since we had reached the flat solitude of the Tsaidam [the] mountains [to the south] had been beckoning to me, but there was no persuading Peter to sacrifice a week to go exploring, and I had given up the hope of getting to know them. Now, with my rucksack on my back I could spend three days in going, at any rate, some little distance up the valley. It was a way of becoming my own master again, of ceasing to be a mere fragment of a caravan. Of course Peter was chivalrous and pretended that I was very useful, but he could not realize how much I longed to shake off the inertia that had taken hold of me since I began travelling with him. I no longer took the lead, no longer shouldered any responsibility. I was one of a group, and my capacity for decision was blunted.
>
> But it was no use, Peter returned from his hunting, happy at having had a good day while I minded the house … Peter said he wanted to get on. (p122)

How had that happened? The paradoxical key seems to be in their relationship. A paradox because they did not have one in the way most of the other couples did: they had no legal or formal emotional tie, nor did they have a romantic one. They were comrades in arms. Their relationship was, therefore, in theory, unimportant to their journey. And yet it is crucial. Maillart half-realises that in one or two of her asides, but she is ultimately left baffled and frustrated.

The following passages by Maillart are essential to an understanding of their journey and of Fleming's ability to travel as he wanted to, rather than as she wanted:

> Every night Peter would repeat his refrain: 'Sixty lis nearer to London.' He did it to annoy me, and I would tell him to shut up, for I wanted to forget that we had, inevitably, to return home. I even lost the desire to return home. I should have liked the journey to continue for the rest of my life. There was nothing to attract me back to the west. I knew I should feel isolated amongst my contemporaries, for their ways had ceased to be my ways. In London I had thought that Peter was in revolt against town life. Now I saw him impatient to get back to it and I wondered whether he had only been indulging in a well-bred affectation. Yet how was I to know whether he was being sincere now or merely paradoxical, or trying to mystify me? Only his own compatriots, I thought, would be able to resolve these riddles. What is certain, however, is that Peter seemed to be less afraid of finishing up in the depths of an Urumchi prison than of getting home too late to shoot grouse in Scotland. We were about to cross one of the most magnificent hunting grounds in the world. Yet the fact that Tibetan yaks and wild asses, ibexes and markhors of the Hindu Kush were within range would not change his mood. A surprising companion! Or was it only that he wanted to accomplish the unique exploit of shooting, in the same year, 'tur' in the Caucasus, duck in Shanghai, antelopes in the Koko Nor and deer in Scotland? (p89)

On 15 August 1935, Maillart writes:

> We had been six months travelling that day and we opened a bottle of brandy to celebrate the occasion. Peter, a dilettante, like all good Etonians, remarked that it was the first time in his life he had stuck to anything for more than six months. (p270)

Maillart was right about his dilettantism – Fleming will confirm that in a passage praising Maillart; what was perhaps not so obvious was that it was both true and untrue. He was a professional dilettante. His kind of Englishman had been trained – firmly but unobtrusively – for generations to be both a dilettante and to lead, to rule and to win.

Percy Sykes, educated at Rugby, was in a similar tradition; but Fleming, as an Old Etonian, was expected to and would expect himself to perfect the art. Maillart notices little signals:

> I listened ... to Peter, noting that an unwritten law has decreed that it shall be considered a sign of good breeding for an Old Etonian never to speak of 'Eton' unnecessarily but always of 'School,' without saying what school. (p165)

We have seen how Percy Sykes had a nose for understanding local custom and manipulating it to his own advantage when he persuaded a Persian administrator that his reputation in Europe for hospitality would suffer unless he allowed Sykes to have his own way. There are numerous examples of Fleming doing the same and this links up with Fussell's description of the mode of English male travelling, already quoted in my introduction, as 'a powerful strain of lawless eccentricity and flagrant individuality' and a 'commendable distrust of authority' (p78).

Fleming's biographer – Duff Hart-Davis – also Fleming's godson and son of his close friend Rupert Hart-Davis, understands those matters; he writes, introducing an illustrative text:

> By that stage of the journey Peter had developed to a high degree the art of manipulating 'face' and using its subtle but very real pressures to secure food, animals, free passage, or whatever the expedition needed at the moment. As they entered Khotan, for instance, they needed fodder for the animals. The mayor was out, and the shrewd 'old-fashioned Chinese in charge of his yamen was very properly alienated by my vagabond appearance – dirty shorts and Red Indian face and knees and arms. But I took his rebuffs coolly and, after referring to my friendship with several men of consequence in Khotan, I not too ostentatiously wrote down his name and rank; then I made as if to leave him, my demeanour expressing well-bred regret at such churlish treatment of a foreign traveller. This mild and oblique intimidation shook his nerve, and before long we got the fodder'. (Hart-Davis p180; Fleming p294)

Maillart is conscious of Fleming's background; it would be difficult not to notice it superficially for, as she writes, 'Peter warned me that his affected manner and languid Oxford accent had driven his last travelling companion nearly crazy' (p9). She makes frequent references, too, to the 'Old Etonian', one of them following an incident similar to that noted by Hart-Davis. Fleming sets the scene:

> Towards dusk we came to Chira, a fairly considerable bazaar. I dragged myself along, too hot and tired to care that I was losing face by travelling on foot. Just outside the bazaar there was a parade-ground, equipped ... with a hundred-foot-high wooden tower ... From the summit of this tower an officer with a megaphone was drilling two or three hundred cavalry ...
> ... When I moved on along the edge of the parade-ground I was spotted from on high. There were shouts from the tower which I knew were meant for me, but I ignored them and it was not until two panting orderlies were on my heels that I turned and registered polite surprise. They led me back. ... When we reached the foot of the tower the officer shouted (but not to me) an order; and a man who looked like a sergeant left the ranks and addressed me in Russian. I judged it prudent to conceal my knowledge of this language and said facetiously to the bystanders 'What kind of aboriginal

speech is this?' The feeble sally got a laugh, and in China once you have got a laugh the battle is half over.

The officer on the tower asked me, in loud and peremptory Chinese, if I was a Russian. Mimicking as best I could his over-bearing tones, I replied that I was an Englishman. Had I a passport? Yes, of course; 'passport have not, this remote place what manner arrive?' (The audience was with me, now). The officer said he wanted to examine the passport. I replied that when I had reached my inn, and washed, and drunk tea, I would be glad to show my passport to anyone; at present I was hot and tired and dirty and in no mood for affairs of this kind. In the end, after further exchanges on these lines, I was allowed to go. I felt – though one can never be sure – that I had not lost face ... (pp291–2)

Maillart, who had arrived earlier in the town, was only told about this charade when he joined her. Giving only spare details of it, she sums up:

The situation might easily have taken a nasty turn, but the Old Etonian succeeded in extricating himself with flying colours. He got the laughs on his side by addressing the officer on his high perch, not inappropriately, as 'Do Ta jen' ('very great man'). (p203)

Maillart may well not have realised then the full significance – how Fleming, from his background, manipulated her too – a manipulation which he describes bare-facedly and self-deprecatingly, as only his kind could:

Perhaps one of the main reasons for our getting on so well was that Kini always had a certain friendly contempt for me and I always had sneaking respect for her; both sentiments arose from the fact that she was a professional and I was eternally the amateur. The contrast showed all the time. Kini believed that the best way to get a thing done was to do it yourself; I believed that the best way to get a thing done was to induce somebody else to do it. It was I who shot the hares; but it was Kini who, noticing that if Li or a Mongol skinned them the liver and kidneys were always thrown away, taught herself to do the job. If anything wanted mending or making fast, if a box needed repacking, if one of the saddles was coming to bits, it was always I who said, 'Oh, that'll be all right', always Kini who expertly ensured that it would be. On my side it was partly laziness and partly incompetence; on Kini's it was the knowledge, acquired from experience, of how important the little things can be. In so far as you can audit a division of labour, ours would have worked out something like this:

I did: all the shooting; most of the heavy manual labour; all the negotiating; all the unnecessary acceleration of progress; all the talking in Chinese and (later) Turki.

Kini did: all the cooking; all the laundering; all the medical and veterinary work; most of the fraternizing; most of the talking in Russian.

I suppose I was the leader, because I made decisions more quickly, guessed more quickly, knew more quickly what I wanted than Kini did. But she did all the work that required skill or application, and almost all the work that was distasteful or annoying rather than merely arduous, the work that gets left undone if there are only second-rate people to do it; we both knew that she was, so to speak, the better man, and this knowledge evened things out between us, robbed my automatically dominating position of its power to strain our relations. We had complete confidence in each other. (pp167–9)

All that flattery was real, and yet it was not real. A little later he says that he could not talk fluently, except nonsense, but he prided himself on his writing, on telling a good story and that was a very good, very English, very male, very Old Etonian good story. While on the journey he was turning over in his mind what he would write about Maillart in his book, he also knew what he had written home to his friend Hart-Davis about Maillart and his fiancée, the actress Celia Johnson (whom he calls 'the Crackwit'):

> ... The fourth member is a dashing Swiss girl, who (this is important) may take some explaining to the Crackwit if she hears about her. Her name is Maillart ... I met her in London in the summer, said 'See you in China,' and forgot about her. But at the time I ragged the Crackwit about her, pretending to have been greatly struck, and that is why I have said nothing to her (the Crackwit) about this woman ...
>
> ... We remain on speaking terms without difficulty, but as far as the Affections go she will never mean more to me than a yak. All the same I feel guilty towards the Crackwit and worry a lot about not having told her about the Other Woman, though I'm sure it was better not to. So if, Peking being what it is, the news comes through and the Crackwit asks with a forced laugh 'What about Peter's Swiss?', will you explain? It's, a silly situation and would never have arisen if I hadn't cracked jokes about the girl last summer. On re-reading this, I seem to have been unduly derogatory about the Swiss. She is very enterprising and what you might call a good trouper. It's just that she isn't my cup of tea. (p158)

And in a later letter to Hart-Davis (the biographer does not give dates for these letters, and Fleming may well have chosen to write differently later):

> The Swiss is bearing up well, and we remain on speaking though not always in my case on listening terms; she is an honest soul and quite useful. I do hope Celia is all right. (p164)

Perhaps Fleming thought that Celia might read that letter or surely he would not have been so patronising; it certainly contradicts his published panegyrics.

It is obvious that Fleming admired Maillart – he could not fail to; but he would make no concessions to her way of travelling. She could dominate on some matters, such as health; when she persuaded him in Peking to be inoculated against typhus she writes:

> Peter maintained that no louse would dare attack his 'iron' skin, and I had great difficulty persuading him to go. But I pointed out that if he were taken ill it was on me it would fall to nurse him and that he must therefore obey orders. (p12)

But on the central issue she had no effective weapon. She realised that she had made a mistake – even though, when she made the decision to travel with him there seemed little choice. She wrote early on in her account, even before they had left 'civilisation':

> Though I liked the companionship and it had considerably ameliorated the anxiety of our wait at Lanchow, it nevertheless deprived me of the greatest thrill the sense of discovering had given me on previous journeys. I had lost the intense joy, the intoxication, of blazing my own trail and the proud sense of being able to get through alone, to which I had become accustomed. Above all, a piece of Europe inevitably accompanied us through the mere fact of our association. That isolated us. I was no longer thousands of miles from my own world. I was not submerged by, or integrated into, Asia. Travelling in company, one does not learn the language so quickly. The natives do not make their own of you. You penetrate less deeply into the life about you. (p46)

Fifteen years later she wrote this into her 'philosophy of travel' when she contributed a chapter with that title to *Traveller's Quest* edited by M.A. Michael, and she elaborated further, still drawing on that Chinese Turkestan experience:

> Detachment was slowly becoming part of me. It was normal to belong nowhere, or everywhere; to feel one is an eternal traveller ... I discovered I was richly contented, away from my people and my friends – without a roof, without a wood fire, without bread even. In winter at twelve thousand feet of altitude with two cups of barley flour a day; at ease in a reality which was a void. (pp121–2)

That word 'reality' is essential to an understanding of Maillart's travel. Her friends realized that when, to honour her on her 80th birthday, they compiled a book and called it *Voyage Vers le Reél* (Voyage Towards Reality) (1983) 'Was I typical of our age when I wanted to learn how to grasp reality?', Maillart had written, and continued:

> What goes under the name of spiritual problems of the modern man became a fact for me when I saw that having had all I wanted, I was nevertheless miserable. Material security, welfare, humaneness – they were not sufficient

ideals to me. Now at last I know with absolute certainty that we travel to find ourselves. By placing ourselves in all possible circumstances which like projectors, will illumine our different facets, we come to grasp all of a sudden, which one of our facets is full, uniquely, ourselves. Through it, go beyond it, having then exhausted our particularism. (p123)

So, in the end it did not matter so much that she travelled with Fleming and he wanted to travel differently and get different things out of the journey; for she discovered her own truth through her own perceptions:

When I crossed Asia with my friend Peter Fleming, we spoke with no one but each other during many months, and we covered exactly the same ground. Nevertheless my journey differed completely from his. One's mind colours the journey as if one wore individually tinted spectacles. It is our mind we project outside and ultimately decipher when we think we meet the 'objective' world. (118)

And what was Fleming thinking; what did he get out of it? He explains:

Of certain stages of a journey in Brazil I once wrote, 'continuous hunger is in many ways a very satisfactory basis for existence'; and in Tartary it proved its worth again.

But there were days, or parts of days, when no such material stimulus to thought and conversation, no such gross foundation for peace of mind, were needed: days when we rode or walked for hours, singly or together, filled with contentment at our lot. The sun shone, the mountains were alluring on our left, and we remembered the virtues of desolation and felt keenly the compensations of a nomad's life. Each march, each camp, differed very slightly from the one before; but they did differ, and we appreciated the slight but ever present freshness of our experience as much as we appreciated the tiny changes in the flavour of our food.

We took, besides, a certain pride in the very slowness and the primitive manner of our progress. We were travelling Asia at Asia's pace. In Macaulay's *History of England* ... he speaks with smug Victorian condescension of 'the extreme difficulty which our ancestors found in passing from place to place'; and there was a certain fascination in rediscovering a layer of experience whose very existence the contemporary world has forgotten. We had left the twentieth century behind with the lorries at Lanchow, and now we were up against the immemorial obstacles, the things which had bothered Alexander and worried the men who rode with Chinghis Khan – lack of beasts, lack of water, lack of grazing. We were doing the same stages every day that Marco Polo would have done if he had branched south from the Silk Road into the mountains. (pp166–7)

The 'slowness' described in his narrative does not tally with the journey as it really was, at least as it appeared to Maillart, bridling against his constant urging onwards.

As for the 'objective' world which Maillart mentions, for all their differences, they had one thing in common, as Fleming explains:

> ... that was our attitude to our profession (or vocation, or whatever you like to call it). We were united by an abhorrence of the false values placed – whether by its exponents or by the world at large – on what can most conveniently be referred to by its trade-name of Adventure. From an aesthetic rather than from an ethical point of view, we were repelled by the modern tendency to exaggerate, romanticize, and at last cheapen out of recognition the ends of the earth and the deeds done in their vicinity. It was about the only thing we ever agreed about. (p27)

Maillart confirmed:

> I appreciated Peter's brilliant intelligence, his faculty of being able to eat anything and sleep anywhere, and also his sure grasp of the kernel of any situation, of the essential point in any argument. I appreciated still more his horror of any distortion of facts and the native objectivity with which he recounted them. (p9)

In spite of their shared passion for the truth, Maillart and Fleming did see things differently, even objectively. He writes of a meeting with a provincial governor:

> General Shao, an elderly but vivacious little man with stubbly grey hair and beautiful manners, welcomed us in the innermost of many courtyards with cakes and fruit and tea. With him was his young and attractive wife, formerly a Moscow-trained Communist, whom marriage (it is said) saved at the eleventh hour from execution. (p48)

And Maillart writes:

> Shao Li-tze proved to be an affable little man, dressed in Chinese clothes. He had made a stay of several days in Paris in 1916 and could recall a few French words. We were received in a room furnished with Spartan simplicity. Shao Li-tze's wife was young and lively. Having made a prolonged stay in Moscow, she spoke excellent Russian and it was in that language we exchanged the usual polite greetings ...
> ... As the governor talked, I was studying his young wife. With her slim fingers she was peeling pears for us. I wondered whether she had not come back from Russia holding Communist beliefs and whether she did not secretly wish to see Shensi in the hands of the Reds. (pp24–5)

For Fleming, Mme Shao Li-tze was a 'Moscow-trained Communist'; for Maillart she had been in Russia and it was interesting to speculate about whether or not she held Communist beliefs and sympathies. So much for objectivity!

Other differences in their accounts are more obviously subjective. Fleming did not travel fast and furiously easily; he suffered, and sometimes Maillart won. Fleming writes of their first and last bus ride, which was much delayed, 'Occasionally one of the other passengers reappeared, announced that we were starting at once, and disappeared. I began to get angry' (p50). She responds:

> Peter was furious. I was enchanted. The delay gave us an opportunity of lunching at the Chinese inn where the Smigs [Smigunovs] had stayed, and making the acquaintance of our friend Norin's old cook who had arrived from the north ... (p28)

Very soon Fleming had earned the name of 'galloper'. And yet there was a different, controlled, side to the galloper; the one that could outwardly show English sang-froid, if he chose:

> Peter suffered more than I from our compulsory inaction. He could, however, remain outwardly impassive and smiling. That was our greatest asset in dealing with the inn-keeper, with the inquisitive police, with the scratchers at our paper windows. Never did a gesture of Peter's betray the hastiness that often characterizes Occidentals. (p56)

Fleming was as able to manipulate himself as he was others to achieve an objective. But behind the scenes the reality was very different, as he writes of the same occasion:

> So for a time I played endless games of patience on the k'ang while Kini read or sewed or wrote up her diary. But gradually, as the glow of breakfast faded in our bellies, we became restless.
> 'Let's go up to Lu's.'
> 'Wait till I've finished this chapter.'
> 'How much more have you got?'
> 'Ten pages.'
> 'Hell, that's too much. Come on. I'm going now.'
> 'Oh, all right ...'
> So off we went, giving our by now celebrated performance of caged tigers down the long main street. (p78)

Once again, it seems they are doing what Fleming wants, but it would be a mistake to think they had no fun together, far from it. They laughed a lot and had the sort of joking relationship which in traditional societies may exist between, for example, a mother-in-law and son-in-law – those who have a relationship which requires them to be friendly, even though there are, by the nature of things, opportunities for tension. There are many incidents that illustrate their 'joking relationship'. At Tangar they stayed with a missionary couple called Urech; he was Swiss, she was Scots. Maillart writes:

> Visitors were so rare at Tangar that young Malcolm, aged three, had never seen any. He called us 'the Mongols,' the term being synonymous with 'foreigners.' He also had a great success when he called Peter 'the old Maillart.' Only Peter was not flattered. Mrs Urech was quite proud when she found that Fleming, the brilliant author by whom she had just read an article in *The Reader's Digest,* and the young man whose coming she had been warned of, turned out to be one and the same person.
>
> 'Malcolm!' she said. 'Take a good look at the famous man we have the honour to entertain in our house.'
>
> 'Then he isn't a Mongol?' asked the puzzled little boy.
>
> 'No,' I said. 'He is what is called in Europe a "special correspondent." He writes in the newspapers about what he has seen. Only he has a curious way of doing things. For instance, he says my linen takes up too much room, though actually it consists of three sweaters and three pairs of woollen pants. And all the time it is he who has my cases bursting with his enormous boxes of tobacco ...'
>
> Then Peter: 'If you don't stop grouching I'll wire to *La Vie Parisienne* to recall you!'
>
> And I: 'Mrs Urech, I've told him a hundred times that *Le Petit Parisien* and *La Vie Parisienne* are two entirely different periodicals. And, just imagine, he thinks I ought to be satisfied with a camel crossing Asia! Of course that won't stop me from having a horse. I don't see why he should be the only one to play the lord.
>
> 'Well,' he protested, 'you'd be a lot better off on a camel, since you are accustomed to it from your other journeys.'
>
> 'No,' Mrs Urech intervened, 'she ought to be able to get on ahead and prepare supper for the lord.'
>
> 'I know,' I said, 'I am to be cook to my interpreter ... Peter, I've been given dried apricots, onions ...'
>
> 'Been given!' You've been robbing Mrs Urech, that's what you've been doing. I know the old sea-dog, Mrs Urech. Give her back those apricots, you! We don't want them.'
>
> 'Listen to him, Mrs Urech! He who wants to cross Tibet and doesn't even know what scurvy is ...'
>
> Just then I noticed something the Chinese servant had brought in and involuntarily I cried:
>
> 'Oh, two kinds of jam to-day.'
>
> Peter was scandalized. 'Really, Maillart,' he protested. 'You are a disgrace to the expedition.' (pp70–1)

One of Fleming's accounts of their 'joking relationship' reads:

> Occasionally we discussed without relish the books we should one day have to write about this journey. The prospect of sitting down and committing

our memories to paper was welcome to neither of us; but at least I knew that I could get the horrid job done quickly, whereas Kini was sure that she could not. Travel books in French (at least the ones that I have read) are commonly more vivid and exclamatory than travel books in English; and I used to tease Kini by concocting apocryphal quotations from her forthcoming work: '*Great scott!*' 'S'écria Pierre, dont le sangfroid d'ancien élève d'Eton ne se froissait guère que quand ses projets sportifs s'écroulaient,' 'Voila mon vinchester qui ne marche plus!' (p170)

And it would be a mistake to think that Maillart came away from their journey resentful or regretful. It is I who have teased out the moments of frustration and, in conjunction with Fleming's background, made out a case. Maillart experienced times of great pleasure with Fleming and she understood the differences in their temperament well enough for them not to be a constant bone of contention.

The following passage, which fits chronologically into her account in much the same place as his long analysis of their relationship fits into his, shows, nevertheless, that Maillart's greatest moments of joy tend to occur when she is taking an initiative.

... a tent-pole had been lost *en route*. There was no timber in the region, so it could not be replaced, and I went off to look for it. Walking along at an even pace I felt in great form, filled with such joy as I used to experience setting out on my skis on very dry winter mornings. There on the high table-lands of Asia I was singing, *I'm sitting on top of the world.*

I even laughed at the wide heavens. It was an odd situation Peter and I were in together at the centre of the continent. Indeed, it was like a situation in a novel, and if I were writing a best seller, it should be that very day or never that the hero and heroine fell into each other's arms in mutual love and gratitude ... Well, novel-readers would have to go without.

Peter was the best of comrades and I had found that I could be absolutely frank with him. It is true that our enterprise bound us to each other to such a degree that, living as we did, like two castaways on a desert island, our conversation at supper, evening after evening, revealed the fact that the same thoughts had struck us simultaneously in the course of the day. But it was only our egotisms that worked together, each helping the other. I could see clearly where we parted company. We both liked to spend our leisure in the open air, he shooting, I ski-ing ... But then? Peter thought me too serious and I did not understand British humour (as serious in the eyes of an Englishman as it is for a Chinaman to 'lose face'). I had the bad taste to lay down the law about the art of living. Peter was bored by my craving to understand the thousands of diverse lives that make up humanity and bored, too, by my need to relate my own life to life in general. How could anybody be so crazy as to want to find out whether men's efforts brought about an improvement in human nature? Peter was troubled by none of these things. In his imperturbable wisdom he looked on human beings as characters in a comedy. As to his deeper self, his timidity usually made him hide it beneath a facetious dignity. Except at rare intervals, he seemed persuaded that his concerns were of no interest to anybody ...

I found the tent-pole. That was what mattered then. And success made me sing as I returned to Peter, who stood waiting for me to appear in the plain he dominated. (p148)

Maillart and Fleming discuss their relationship in some detail in their books – partly, perhaps, to tantalise a prurient 1930s readership. From the similarities in some of the passages, it is fair to assume that they also discussed it together. Fleming, for example, in the long passage about her superior qualities already quoted from, makes a remark that has distinct echoes of that just quoted from Maillart:

By all the conventions of desert island fiction we should have fallen madly in love with each other; by all the laws of human nature we should have driven each other crazy with irritation. As it was, we missed these almost equally embarrassing alternatives by a wide margin. (pp167–8)

It is reasonable to suggest that, in the 24 hours previous to the tent-pole incident, Maillart had broached her general unhappiness and that they had attempted to thrash it out. The passage of frustration at the beginning of this chapter is only 20-odd pages earlier. They came to some sort of accommodation. One of the problems was that Eton, for all it had prepared Fleming to sail through life – bravely and with style – had not prepared him for Maillart. He might be comfortable enough with a respectable English wife of his own kind, and, perhaps, with a 'travelling wife' but no matter how hard he tries to show otherwise – and he writes as a well-travelled, intelligent, sophisticated man – he found it difficult to think of women as equals or to come to terms with women who were. In yet another endeavour to give Maillart her due, he wrote:

I had no previous experience of a woman traveller, but Kini was the antithesis of the popular conception of that alarming species. She had, it is true, and in a marked degree, the qualities which distinguish these creatures in the books they write about themselves. She had courage and enterprise and resource; in endurance she excelled most men. (p26)

What Fleming means by these remarks concerning other travelling women is not clear; the very ambiguity underlines his attitude. Then we see him distorting his account of a particularly difficult day. It had started with one of the horses, Cynara, evading capture for some hours; Fleming writes:

Every man, provided that he does not raise blisters or other impediments on his feet, can walk in a day at least half as far again as he imagines. The muscles responsible for placing the left foot in front of the right foot, and the right foot in front of the left foot, do not tire quickly; it is the feet that count. My own feet are almost as little sensitive as hooves, and as the hours of march dragged into their early 'teens I had nothing to complain of save tedium, anxiety, and the staleness of sustained exertion. But water would have been welcome – doubly so when a keen north wind bore down our line of march ... When night fell we were past talking, past hoping, past thinking. We moved numbly, each bounded in a nutshell of discontent. At half-past seven we gave it up and halted, pitching the tent on a slope of stony desert. We had been marching, at a good pace for camels, for fourteen hours without food and with only two or three halts, none longer than five minutes; Kini had done the first seven hours – the most strenuous, because of catching Cynara – on foot. (p218)

She writes:

At six o'clock we were still on the march. Lashed by an icy wind, I held on to the slight shelter provided by the camel's load ... We were going along a water course, but a dried-up water-course ... Peter had just torn the entire sole off one of his shoes and come up in great distress. What was the good of wearing out man and beast by marching vainly for fourteen hours on end? I put my foot down, and insisted that, water or no water, we pitch the tent before nightfall. (pp168–9)

Fleming finishes his account of that day with another of his tributes to his companion:

I got, during our seven months together, so used to regarding Kini as an equal in most things and a superior in some that perhaps I have paid over-few tributes to her powers of endurance ... I should like to place it on record that, at the end of fourteen hours' march in the middle of a hard journey (rising almost always before dawn, eating almost always a little less than enough), Kini went supperless to bed without, even by implication, turning a hair. The best that I can do in the way of eulogy is to say that I thought nothing of it at the time. (p218)

Fleming meant it as the highest praise; he would not know what you were talking about if you pointed out that Maillart did not feel the need to say the same sort of thing about him, particularly since her account suggests that his endurance on that occasion was slightly less than hers, contradicting his account in a kindly but convincing way. And it was a tribute indeed for, in addition to his opinion of women travellers in particular, an occasion described first by Maillart is his more usual opinion of women in general:

A decided-looking and heavily-laden young mother joined our caravan a little way out from Bash Malghun. Her baby was given to crying at night and to vomiting; in short, 'did all that the dear little things do.' Thus the somewhat peeved Peter. He went so far as to predict all sorts of difficulties. He did not like women. 'You have to be always helping them,' he said. 'The moment they appear, complications begin.' And he was afraid that this one might turn the men against us. However, as he looked at the child, tied on the donkey and getting shaken, Peter finished by observing: 'Poor little chap! He hasn't much of a life.' My compassion, on the other hand, went out rather to the mother. (p173)

Fleming's version:

Shortly before noon we were joined by a lady with two donkeys, on one of which she rode; the other carried a light load of household goods, on top of which was more than firmly lashed a yearling child. This infant relished very little the delights of travel and lodged almost continuous protests; but its mother – a domineering person with a harsh, masculine voice – abused the donkeys so roundly that most of her offspring's cries were drowned. (p226)

For all that Maillart travelled as Fleming wanted, rather than as she preferred, and that she did the washing, sewing and cooking, she was not steered towards women and womanly affairs in the way that Ella Sykes and Eleanor Lattimore were and, as will emerge, Doreen Ingrams was. This meant fewer opportunities for gleaning women's lore. Nor, anyway, could she speak the language of the Chinese or Turki women. When she could communicate, as with Mrs Urech, there were sisterly relations.

Often Maillart's accounts of women are visual ones and usually it is of the beauty of those she is observing. There was one glaring exception; on one aspect of women in China she had the same views as Ella Sykes and she could not avoid noticing it wherever she went and being horrified anew each time. She writes of footbinding on more than one occasion; of Tungkuan she wrote:

The women had beautiful, regular faces, and round their heads, like a narrow turban, wore a black veil. They were all going in the same direction and I followed them. Their mutilated feet, looking like pointed stumps and hitting the ground with a dull clatter, made my heart sick. When they walk their knees seem to be devoid of flexibility. The effect was of a caricature of a ballerina dancing on her toes. (p21)

In Chingchow she noted in the main street that 'the ground was so slippery that the women, because of their stunted feet, had to carry long sticks to support themselves' (p32).

That evening, Maillart and Fleming spent the night with a missionary and his wife; the latter confessed to Maillart that because of lack of security in the area, 'in four years she had never rested properly at night. But amongst the compensations for all the uneasiness there was one that I found touching.

She had helped to abolish the torturing of the women's feet out of shape' (p32). And again:

> Life in Kansu is really wretched. Squatting in front of their mud hovels the women were stitching at thick cloth slippers for their husbands. With vacant faces and dressed in dusty jackets and trousers, they seemed to have no sense of feminine coquetry except in the matter of their stunted feet. These they shod with embroidered materials attached to little curved wooden heels. Many times I saw mothers on the side of the road tying up the feet of tiny girls – poor resigned little things! – with dirty bandages. (p44)

And what did Fleming make of bound feet? 'The streets of Lanchow are romantic. The women hobble round the puddles on bound feet, their sleek heads shining like the shards of beetles ...' (p63).

As for their own appearance, there is a charming vignette concerning their arrival in Kashgar which epitomises their relationship, their characters, and their journey. I am saving it for the Conclusion.

Following her experience with Fleming, not surprisingly, in spite of their comradeship and achievement, Maillart either travelled alone or with other women. In 1939 she went through Persia and Afghanistan with someone she calls only Christina (Annemarie Schwarzenbach), and in 1945 she took a short walk in Southern Tibet with a woman she calls B – Beryl Smeeton. In her introduction to Smeeton's 1961 autobiography Maillart wrote a few simple but telling lines:

> Once more I am convinced that it is really people who matter most. A landscape or an idea may be of great importance, but in the end it all depends on who sees the Yangtze River, for instance, or who talks about freedom. (pxiii)

And she wrote of Smeeton a line that applied equally to herself, still travelling in her 84th year: 'It is a rare joy to meet a born traveller.'

Postscript

On reading this chapter Ella Maillart was unconcerned with any analysis of her relationship with Fleming. She wrote back,

> Here I am without *Forbidden Journey* ... but try to find the page on the way to the Pamir, I climb alone a steep mountain, try to see Mustagh Ata ... when descending ... am *very* afraid to slip ... & I say something *important*: that I cannot die before I have found why we live ... or the purpose of living ... I think you might use it in your book. (2 December 1987)

In her book she wrote:

> ... what mattered was myself, I, who was living at the centre of the world – that 'I' who did not want to disappear without accomplishing something

worthwhile. Something that would carry me on, that would save me from nothingness, and satisfy – however humbly – the craving that existed in me. (pp268–9)

The physical travelling – let alone the travelling companion – was, therefore, unimportant. It was the spiritual travel, or quest, that mattered. And so the past was irrelevant because the quest was not yet ended.

Their relationship, and the contrast between Fleming's account and her own, may have been unimportant to Maillart at 84, but for the biographer to be able to stand Maillart against the other half of a double mirror, is to produce reflections that may be illuminating.

Following our correspondence, I had the chance to meet Ella Maillart. For her, a private woman, and one who had that day fallen and grazed her face, the meeting in London was probably only an irritation. For me, despite the passage of time, despite her air of distraction, she was the physical manifestation of the Maillart of her books.

And yet, in my writing, I have drawn out a dimension of her that she does not recognise. I was conscious from the start of avoiding a spiritual side of Ella, brought out more in some of her other books, that was essential to her. She recognised it clearly for she wrote to me after our meeting, 'Congratulations for the thoroughness you put in the way you work. Am glad we met: we "function" on different wavelengths' (17 March 1988). I thank her for the colon which suggests she was glad we met because we were different, not that she was simply identifying a gap between us.

Of course, we see ourselves differently from how others see us but, in the end, I may have been as far distant from Ella as I saw her from Peter Fleming, from whom I tried to protect her. The question then must be, how much validity is there to my view of her? That is the dichotomy of biography. Without corresponding with and meeting Ella Maillart, I might not have had to acknowledge it to myself so clearly.

8 – Liberia, Wherever it Was

Barbara Greene, *Too Late to Turn Back* (**1981**; 1991; originally published as *Land Benighted*, 1938)
Graham Greene, *Journey Without Maps* (1935; **1971**; 2010)

8.1   Barbara Greene and Graham Greene as they set out
(courtesy of Rupert Strachwitz)

Few female travelling companions can have entered the fray less prepared than 27-year-old Barbara Greene. In the 1981 introduction to the reprint of her account of the journey with her cousin, she writes, capturing the air of insouciance that had existed 46 years before:

> Graham's and my adventure together began when we met at the wedding reception of his brother Hugh, where we were all merrily drinking champagne – I think that was in 1935 [it was October 1934]. Graham had already made his plans for going to Liberia. Travel books to out-of-the-way places were popular at the time, Graham had a family to provide for, and his publisher had advanced him the money for a new book. From childhood on he had enjoyed adventure stories and unknown Liberia sounded hopeful, but he did not like the idea of going alone. He was trying to persuade

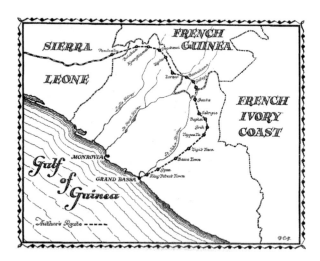

8.2   Barbara Greene and Graham Greene's Liberian journey
(from Greene, *Too Late to Turn Back*)

8.3   Barbara Greene and porters in Liberia
(courtesy of Rupert Strachwitz)

someone, anyone, to go with him, and only after everyone else had refused did he ask me and I promptly agreed to accompany him, though I had no clear idea of exactly where he was going to. (pxii)

The champagne wore off and 30-year-old Graham realised the enormity of what he had let himself in for, but Barbara was undismayed:

Whatever qualms Graham may have suffered, I think that my own reaction was chiefly one of excitement. Everything sailed along so quickly and perhaps I was also a little flattered by the attentions I was receiving. It was unusual then for young girls to adventure off into the wilds ... Apart from getting my visa and some injections, I really had nothing else to do. I am ashamed now to admit that I had no idea how much work was needed when preparing for such an expedition, how the question of medical supplies (among a hundred other things) had to be gone into with great care ... Graham saw to everything and I felt sure that he knew what he was doing though I now wonder whether I really thought about it at all. (ppxiii–xiv)

Graham, writing 45 years after their undertaking in *Ways of Escape* (1980), suggests that he was only a little more prepared than his cousin:

I had never been out of Europe; I had not very often been outside England, and to choose Liberia and to involve my cousin Barbara ... in the adventure was, to say the least, rash. My invitation to her can only be excused because I had drunk too much champagne at my brother Hugh's wedding, and I never expected her to accept. I did my best afterwards to discourage her. (pp37–8)

Barbara writes of their relationship on that journey:

Graham and I were both rather shy people; ... we were really only acquaintances when we set out together and – strange though this may seem – we were still not more than friendly acquaintances when the long journey came to an end after three months. Even under the worst conditions we were invariably polite and courteous to one another; we never argued. If we disagreed on any subject we dropped it immediately, partly because the heat and sheer exhaustion drained all surplus energy. That was probably a good thing, for although it led to long silences the silences never became bitter or resentful. Graham took all the decisions and made all the plans. I merely followed. Looking back now I realize also that I was never, at any time, in the least bit helpful, but on the other hand I never, never complained. (pxiv)

And Graham responds:

Luckily for me my cousin appeared unmoved by the reading material I sent her, for she proved as good a companion as the circumstances allowed, and

I shudder to think of the quarrels I would have had with a companion of the same sex after exhaustion set in, all the arguments, the indecision ... I made the wrong one, and because of the difference of sex we were both forced to control our irritated nerves. Towards the end we would lapse into long silences, but they were infinitely preferable to raised voices. Only in one thing did she disappoint me – she wrote a book ... I hadn't even realized that she was making notes, I was so busy on my own. (p38)

And, of how the book came to be written and published, Barbara explains:

The account I wrote of the journey was never meant for publication. Graham had already published his *Journey Without Maps*, which was not a straightforward travel book but became a more abstract account of a journey into the interior of life itself, far deeper and more complicated than anything I was capable of doing.

Throughout the trip I had kept a diary in which, however weary I felt, I recorded the events of the day in some detail. When, a few years after our return to England, my father became seriously ill, I rewrote the notes I had recorded (keeping strictly to the truth) and made them into something I could read to him every morning to amuse him and keep his mind off his troubles. It was by chance that the manuscript fell into the hands of a publisher, who insisted on bringing it out exactly as I had written it. No facts were ever verified, nor were the local customs that I had so blithely and ignorantly recorded. (ppxv–xvi)

It is probably true to say that Barbara Greene (1907–1991) and Graham Greene (1904–1991) are the only travelling companions in this study that might conform to an imagined stereotype. Just as Ella Maillart and Peter Fleming were unique in their travelling relationship, so, at the other end of a spectrum, were Barbara and Graham Greene. Paul Theroux writes in his sympathetic, if male-oriented, introduction, to Barbara Greene's 1981 reprint:

What might have seemed trivial or unimportant about *Too Late to Turn Back* in the Thirties now – over forty years later – is like treasure. What if Waugh had had such a companion in Abyssinia, or Peter Fleming's cousin had accompanied him to Manchuria? What if Kinglake, or Doughty, or Waterton had had a reliable witness to their miseries and splendours? We would not have thought less of these men, but we would have known much more of them. (pxxvi)

Leaving aside Ella Maillart's overlooked illumination of Fleming, I would like to change the questions: what can Barbara tell us about what made an apparently empty-headed young woman from a comfortable 1930s background tick? How did she cope with the journey? What did she contribute to it? And what in the end did she get out of it?

'Liberia, wherever it was,' Barbara writes at the beginning of her book, 'had a jaunty sound about it' (p1). She did not go to Liberia at the beginning of 1935 because she loved Graham Greene, nor because she wanted to travel, nor to see the Dark Continent, nor because she wanted to discover herself. She went in a champagne bubble, as if someone had suggested meeting for lunch at Fortnums the following day, or a drive up to Oxford for a ball.

Barbara had so little aim in her life beyond enjoying herself before the journey that she claimed, even in her 1981 introduction, to be only 23 years old on the journey. Her son has suggested that this was because what might pass as acceptable for a young woman would not for a 27-year-old. She had an added reason for this subterfuge, writing that any Liberian reader 'should be kind and generous and pass over all inaccuracies and shortcomings, remembering that it was written by a very young girl' (pxvi). I only wish that when we corresponded I had realized the discrepancy in her stated and actual ages; I would have quizzed her and I know she would have given me a gem to add here. (Graham, too, got his age wrong – he was 30, not 31.)

Graham has already illustrated how little conscious he was of his tall, taciturn cousin in unflattering shorts by his admission that he did not even realize she was making notes; while she says that she wrote a detailed diary every day, and of one occasion she writes of the villagers, 'They watched us with interest as we sat writing in our diaries' (p140). One wonders really why he thought he needed a companion if her presence was of so little note to him.

Barbara also tells how everything was done for her in preparation for the journey. She had only to secure a visa. That was not especially difficult once she had found the Liberian consulate; but that in itself required a little ingenuity. And yet, each knowing of this slight difficulty, they did not think to advise the other. Perhaps more than any other moment in their journey, the two accounts of that task illustrate their relationship and the differences between them, particularly of all kinds of style. She writes:

As I could not find where the consulate was from the telephone book, I approached Thos. Cook. The numbers in what must surely be the most deserted street in London had apparently all been changed, for the number I was looking for was now a church. It was all very difficult, but I said to myself: 'Don't give up. Things will be more difficult than this in the jungle.' And so, with new life in me, I eventually managed to track down the Consul in his lair. It was a strange office, small, dirty, and very untidy. A meal was obviously just over, for dirty plates were lying everywhere about the room. The waste-paper basket was full of them. I had brought a friend with me, a Dutchman, and I began to feel glad that I was not alone, for I was not welcomed very warmly. Perhaps I had disturbed their afternoon sleep, or perhaps they were not used to visitors, for they did not seem to know what to do with me. There were two dark young men, and they spoke with a strong accent. 'Liberians,' I thought. 'Pale kinds of half-castes.' And if I had not been getting a little tired of sitting there doing nothing I would have got excited at the thought. They could not understand what I wanted, or that one should want to go to Liberia at all. I explained again. I waited. Then one of the young men spoke to the other in another language. To my great astonishment my companion joined in the conversation. They were all Dutchmen. After that we suddenly found ourselves the best of friends. I paid my guinea, and I got my visa, a large red seal stuck into my passport. (pp2–3)

In his account of following in the Greenes' footsteps – *Chasing the Devil* (2010) – war correspondent Tim Butcher provides evidence that Graham travelled to Liberia on behalf of the Anti-Slavery Society to look into the trade there. Other Greene biographers suggest a British Foreign Office connection, for which there is also some evidence (and he was certainly in intelligence in West Africa during the Second World War). Graham gives no hint of this, except for references to dodging government controls; for him it was a personal African adventure from which, as a writer, he hoped to make money. Indeed, he starts his book as the established novelist he was:

The tall black door in the narrow city street remained closed. I rang and knocked and rang again. I could not hear the bell ringing; to ring it again and again was simply an act of faith or despair, and later sitting before a hut in French Guinea, where I never meant to find myself, I remembered this first going astray, the buses passing at the corner and the pale autumn sun.

An errand boy came to my help, asking me whether I wanted the Consul, and when I said yes, that was what I wanted, the boy led me straight to the entrance of St Dunstan's Church and up the steps and into the vestry. It wasn't the sort of beginning I'd expected when I was accumulating the tent I never used, the hypodermic syringe I left behind, the automatic pistol which remained hidden underneath boots and shoes and bags of silver in the money-box. They were preparing for the harvest festival; the vestry was crowded with large dressy yellow blooms and litters of vegetable marrow; I couldn't see the Consul anywhere. The errand boy peered among the flowers in the dim light and at last pointed to a little intent woman bent above the blooms. 'There she is,' he said, 'that's her. She'll tell you.'

I felt very self-conscious, picking my way among the vegetables in St Dunstan's, asking: 'Could you by any chance tell me? Is the Liberian Consul –?' But she knew and I left that street for another.

It was three o'clock and lunch at the Consulate was just over. Three men, I could not distinguish their nationality, overcrowded the tiny room which was deeply buried in the huge new glittering office block. The window-sill was lined with old telephone directories, school textbooks of chemistry. One man was washing up lunch into a basin stuck in the top of a waste-paper basket. Unidentifiable yellow threads like bast floated in the greasy water. The man poured a kettle of boiling water from a gas jet over a plate which he held above the basket; then he wiped the plate with a cloth. (pp15–16)

That compartmentalisation between Barbara and Graham continued throughout the journey. He was wont to march on ahead each morning and it led on one occasion to their being separated almost irretrievably. Barbara describes what happened with an intricacy and vibrancy worthy of a novelist; part of her description reads:

Finally the path simply died on us, and we were left facing a thick, impenetrable wall of jungle. It stood deep and solid in front of us. We stood there, huddled together on the jagged thread of path, while I thought – this is a moment to think quickly. I could, of course, do nothing of the kind. Like ton weights one thought after another dropped heavily into my mind. Obviously we had lost Graham, and obviously it was going to be extremely difficult to find him again ...

However hard I racked my brain I could not remember the name of the village we were aiming at, and the men had forgotten it too. It began with B, but that was not enough to be of any use. The name of the village we had come from, of course, I had never known, but probably the men would be able to find their way back there. Would Graham turn back when he realised that we were lost, or would he go on and wait for us? ...

Strangely enough I was not in the least worried. I had grown so stolid of late, so phlegmatic, and I simply decided that it would be a waste of precious energy to fuss till I was quite sure that my cousin had disappeared for ever ...

The men were getting restless and gave me nasty looks. 'We go back,' I said firmly.

Actually there was nothing else we could do, with that wall of African bush staring us in the face. If only I could remember the name of the village. I could remember Jbaiay, the name of the village we did not go to, but the other – a far simpler name – had completely slipped my memory. I was determined not to let the men see that I was puzzled. If I found as we were walking that I still could not remember it, we could go back to the last place.

'Missis say go back,' said Laminah to Mark, and Mark shouted out something in a native dialect.

The men growled, and the headman slowly made his way towards me, pushed on by the others. He made some sort of a speech, which was heartily encouraged by the carriers, but of which I understood nothing except the words I had been expecting, 'Too far.'

The man with the money-box was standing beside me and seemed to be on my side, which gave me infinite confidence. Actually I was feeling amused at the whole situation – such a ludicrous huddle of humanity, such a chattering, in so many different dialects, like the tower of Babel – and my brain was incapable of taking in the seriousness of the situation.

I smiled sweetly at the headman. 'I go on,' I said. 'And now for heaven's sake, shut up.' He did not understand, but he smiled back his vague, pleasant smile, and shook his rattles rhythmically in his hand. The men were sitting along the path in a row on their cases, grumbling.

I turned on my heel and walked down the narrow path with the boys and some of the men. I did not look back, but presently I heard the rattles of the headman following me, and I decided the other carriers had made up their minds to come too. After all, they would be very foolish to go on sitting in the middle of the forest ...

Suddenly out of the blue and in the nick of time a ragged old man appeared on the path. In his hand he carried a clump of bananas, and as I saw them the name of the village flashed through my mind. Bamakama! ... It was certainly a strange way that the old man took us. With a sure instinct of direction, or else a real knowledge, of the paths of the forest, he ran ahead, the green and yellow bananas in his arms, on his bare, flat feet. Down little, tortuous ways, crossing larger paths, over streams, like a bloodhound with his nose on the scent, never hesitating, never stopping.

As I followed I realised the chief reason why I felt so little upset at the situation I now found myself in. I was revelling in the relief from the boredom of walking without excitement. Trekking to-day had been an adventure. Circumstances were providing me with plenty to think about. The shouting every few moments was something new, and consequently interesting out of all proportion ...

I was just beginning to long for food when we came to a big broad river. We gave another shout, thinking that this time it would be carried along the water, when it was answered immediately.

There, on the other side of the river, sat my cousin and his men, waving their arms excitedly. (pp89–94)

And Graham, what did he make of that near fatal adventure?

After half an hour I was anxious but ... There was nothing we could do if they had lost their way, and my cousin's lot really would have been happier than mine. My cousin had Laminah and the cook and Vande, the beds and mosquito-nets, and most of the food and more than half the carriers. I tried to make up my mind what I should do; it would be no use chasing each other all over French Guinea. I decided to go on, just as my cousin, I learnt later, had decided to go back. But at last when I was on the point of giving the order to march, for fear we should be caught in darkness in the bush, an answer did come, from between the big trees, from across the water, and presently a tired angry band rejoined us. Among the many paths which had to be closed with sprays, one had been left open and they had taken it. The path had narrowed into nearly nothing at all, but they went on, Laminah cutting a way for them with the sword he wore, until they reached a closed wall of greenery and knew they were lost. In such densely overgrown country it was easy enough to be lost completely within a mile of a village and for all they knew they might be ten miles from any other human beings. If it had not been for the river I should have gone straight on to Bamakama without knowing that they were lost, and if Laminah had not found a man who guided them to the St Paul, a piece of luck they couldn't have expected when once they had strayed off the main path, we should have been permanently separated, for my cousin had no idea of the route I intended to follow the other side of the St Paul. (pp151–2)

In spite of the difference between Ella Maillart and Barbara Greene, that incident shows a similarity: how a travelling companion, either deprived of initiative or not previously familiar with the attractions of taking it, rejoices in having to do so. Graham leaves out Barbara's positive part, and it is noticeable that at a time when he is in a position of waiting rather than acting – often the female role – his flair deserts him, in his writing, too.

The compartmentalisation of Barbara and Graham is shown in a different way during that same shortcut through French Guinea from one part of Liberia to another. There the atmosphere is decidedly French and, enjoying the hospitality of a French-influenced village chief, each sees the sexuality of the situation directed towards themselves, almost as if the other were not there. Graham writes:

The daughters were the prettiest women I had seen in Africa. They lay round and over him like kittens ... there was a distinct atmosphere of sex and relaxation about the scene ... The chief sat grimly on the floor among his girls, with only the faintest suspicion of enjoyment about his mouth, and poured the warm sweet delicious wine into the enamel cup. He drank and passed it to me; I drank and passed it to my cousin. Back it went to the chief and was refilled ...

The favourite daughter could speak a few words of English; her thigh under the tight cloth about her waist was like the soft furry rump of a kitten; she had lovely breasts: she was quite clean, much cleaner than we were. The chief wanted us to stay the night and I began to wonder how far his hospitality might go. (pp161–2)

Barbara writes:

... He gave some [of the wine] to a few of his wives, who drank and passed the mug to the little daughter. She loved it, lapped it up with enjoyment, and laughed more than ever. Then we all drank, taking a sip in turn and passing on the old tin mug, laughing and wiping the sweat off our faces. The chief said something to his daughter.

'My fadder says you very fine woman,' said the daughter to me, and we all laughed.

The wives were leaning back on one another, laughing with the chief and giggling at Graham. The chief gaped at me, watched me with staring eyes. The moment had come, I could not help thinking, when he should burst into romantic song. One could hardly carry on with this scene without music.

'My fadder says you very fine woman,' said the girl again and again, in the same voice, like a broken gramophone record.

The hut was hot and stuffy, filled with the scent of black bodies, and almost overpowering in its atmosphere of sex and drunkenness. The chief was wearing some magnificent rings and bracelets. Without much hope I rather wished he would give me a few.

'My fadder says you very fine woman.'

'I wish she'd stop saying that,' I thought ... (pp104–6)

Barbara, a well-brought-up young Englishwoman, takes the sting out of the sexuality of the experience through humour and a suggestion of farce. Since much of Graham's book has an undertow of sexuality, particularly in what one might term the flashbacks, perhaps Barbara's presence there was intrusive; or perhaps he wished to protect her in print. But the blotting out of part of her continues into his illness, already referred to in my introduction.

Until the climax of his unidentified but debilitating sickness, Barbara admits that she had little to do but put one foot after another on daily marches – the novelty and pleasure of which gradually wore off. It was Graham who carried the expedition, usually competently, in spite of his inexperience. Of one occasion Barbara writes:

I sat down somewhere and took off my shoes. My feet were bleeding. But for Graham the real work of the day began. By means of interpreters who could not understand one another, he had to find huts and food for the men. This was a long and irritating business, and the only thing on our trip that caused me continual astonishment every day to the end was the way my cousin managed to do this always with unfailing patience. (p45)

In an earlier draft of this chapter I wrote, 'It is hard to see where Barbara could fit in, particularly in male-dominated societies where negotiation with her would not be taken seriously.' Since then, I have read Lady Dorothy Mills' *Through Liberia* (1926), an account of her solo journey a decade earlier during which she had to negotiate relays of porters and fresh supplies in each village, with only a minimal consistent and reliable entourage. Nevertheless, Barbara's role as a non-housekeeper is marked when compared with the women companions in the preceding chapters. But, on the night when Graham was at his most perilously ill, according to Barbara's version she took charge:

Graham was tottering as we got to Zigi's town; he was staggering as though he was a little drunk. He could get no rest from the carriers while he was up, for they came to him as usual with all their troubles, but I managed to persuade him to go to bed. I took his temperature and it was very high. I gave him plenty of whisky and Epsom salts, and covered him with blankets, hoping that I was doing the right thing. (pp173–4)

It is worth noting here, although Barbara does not, that she had trained as a nurse, even if she had not practised. Later she went to bed 'but did not dare to sleep very much in case my cousin should call out' (p176). He rather ungraciously records:

> I remember nothing of the trek to Zigi's Town and very little of the succeeding days. I was so exhausted that I couldn't write more than a few lines in my diary; I hope never to be so tired again ... I remember trying to sit down, but immediately having to deal with the town chief over food for the carriers, trying to sit down again and rising to look for threepenny-bits the cook needed for buying a chicken, trying to sit down and being forced up again to dress a carrier's sores. I couldn't stand any more of it; I swallowed two table-spoonfuls of Epsom in a cup of strong tea (we had finished our tinned milk long ago) and left my cousin to deal with anything else that turned up. My temperature was high. I swallowed twenty grains of Quinine with a glass of whisky, took off my clothes, wrapped myself in blankets under the mosquito-net and tried to sleep. (pp212–13)

Of course, Graham was ill; he probably remembered little; his diary notes were of the sketchiest and he made assumptions from past performance. But, in the same way, he seems to seek to minimise her ability to march endlessly day after day by suggesting that, expensive as it was, he hired four hammock carriers for her; later it emerges there was also a hammock (and expensive carriers) for him but,

> My cousin used a hammock and needed four carriers, but I reduced my hammock-men to three: I hadn't used the hammock yet and unless I went sick I saw no reason why I should ever need to use it. (p145)

We know two things from her account: one is that occasionally for a few minutes she used the hammock; second, she did her full share of walking and in other ways she was by no means a burden physically. She writes, for example:

> I was feeling most extraordinarily well. My feet had nearly healed and were getting beautifully hard. The long walks seemed to suit me, and although the heat was almost too much of a good thing, it now seemed to tire my mind only and not my body. (pp83–4)

From the two accounts, I felt it was fair to assume that Barbara's version is more correct, and that Graham was exaggerating her use of the hammock and minimising his own.

Tim Butcher, travelling 74 years later, had a happy meeting in Zigida. An old man, who would have been 15 when the Greenes passed through, remembered how 'they arrived in hammocks. It's a difficult journey, you know, through those hills.' Butcher notes how Barbara used the hammock from time to time and adds, 'In contrast, Graham Greene only admits to using his towards the end of the trip when the fever got so bad he was barely conscious.' It was in

Zigida that Barbara says her cousin's illness began. The old man's memory and, indeed, Graham's account, suggests that he was already feeling under the weather as they approached the village.

Graham's need to tell a good, different, unique story has already been touched on in my introduction. Barbara explains how differently she sees her account. She writes, for example, 'I was far too stolid in my nature to be able to imagine beauties and excitements where my eye did not see them' (p124). And, when they met a missionary anthropologist who wanted to tell them many of the secrets of the local inhabitants, Barbara admits:

> With all honesty I confess I was incapable of understanding nearly everything that Dr Harley said to us. Sleepiness, so overpowering that it became an agony, crowded into my brain. I could listen to all he said, but two minutes later it was all forgotten ... So do Life's most interesting moments pass us by. With deep shame I confess this. It would, perhaps, have been better if I had read up this subject before attempting to write this book, so that I would have something to offer to those who are yearning for knowledge, but I had decided to write a book of truth. And that is the bitter, humiliating truth. I had failed utterly and completely to profit by the teaching of this great man. (pp120–2)

In case the reader should judge Barbara's intellect too harshly by that admission, Graham has to write a similar one: 'I am not an anthropologist and I cannot pretend to remember very much of what Dr Harley told me: a pity, for no white man is closer to that particular "heart of darkness", ...' (p173).

Barbara comes over as a simple, straightforward, unaffected woman. In spite of her inexperience, she does not flinch from a convincing appraisal of her cousin's rather more complex character:

> I got out my diary and wrote down what I thought of him. His brain frightened me. It was sharp and clear and cruel. I admired him for being unsentimental, but 'always remember to rely on yourself,' I noted. 'If you are in a sticky place he will be so interested in noting your reactions that he will probably forget to rescue you.' For some reason he had a permanently shaky hand, so I hoped that we would not meet any wild beasts on our trip. I had never shot anything in my life, and my cousin would undoubtedly miss anything he aimed at. Physically he did not look strong. He seemed somewhat vague and impractical, and later I was continually astonished at his efficiency and the care he devoted to every little detail. Apart from three or four people he was really fond of, I felt that the rest of humanity was to him like a heap of insects that he liked to examine, as a scientist might examine his specimens, coldly, and clearly. He was always polite. He had a remarkable sense of humour and held few things too sacred to be laughed at. I suppose at that time I had a very conventional little mind, for I remember he was continually tearing down ideas I had always believed in, and I was left to build them up anew. It

was stimulating and exciting, and I wrote down that he was the best kind of companion one could have for a trip of this kind. I was learning far more than he realised. (p7)

To read Graham Greene's account of his boyhood – particularly his schooldays at a school where his father was headmaster, *A Sort of a Life* (1971) – is to become more sympathetic towards, and understanding of, the man of 30 with whom Barbara became vaguely acquainted in Liberia. The reputation of *Journey Without Maps* is high within the canon of clever 1930s books by male travellers (including those of Fleming) but it helps to have read both Greene's autobiographical books to appreciate many of the otherwise obscure allusions contained in the account of his interior/exterior journey.

Even if one presumes to understand him better, his attitude towards his cousin is almost more disconcerting than Thomas Atkinson's complete dismissal of Lucy from his written accounts. At least one felt, from her writing, that they were warmly engaged when they travelled. That was not, apparently, what Graham wanted. He lived in a world of his own as he walked ahead, as he jotted in his diary and, particularly, as he wrote his book. The content of the book obviously grew much more in the writing than while he travelled, for he makes it clear that profound thinking was not what trekking through Liberia was all about:

I was usually alone with a carrier or a guide who couldn't speak English, for Mark and Amedoo could not keep my pace, and I had to try in vain to occupy the mind, to think of things to think about. I would calculate: I can think of this place or that person for so many hundred steps, and I would have a sense of triumph when the thought lasted me for a few dozen steps further than I had hoped. But usually it was the other way; ... (p156)

He had an idea of what he was after, however; he gives several clues:

There seemed to be a seediness about the place you couldn't get to the same extent elsewhere, and seediness has a very deep appeal ... there are times of impatience, when one is less content to rest at the urban stage, when one is willing to suffer some discomfort for the chance of finding – there are a thousand names for it, King Solomon's Mines, the 'heart of darkness' if one is romantically inclined, or simply, as Herr Heuser puts it in his African novel, *The Inner Journey*, one's place in time, based on a knowledge not only of one's present but of the past from which one has emerged ...

... It is not, of course, that one wishes to stay for ever at that level, but when one sees to what unhappiness, to what peril of extinction centuries of cerebration have brought us, one sometimes has a curiosity to discover if one can from what we have come, to recall at which point we went astray. (pp19–21)

That was how he saw it as he set out; later he was to write:

> ... suddenly I felt curiously happy and careless and relieved. One couldn't
> I was sure, get lower than Duogobmai. I had been afraid of the primitive,
> had wanted it broken gently, but here it came on us in a breath, as we
> stumbled up through the dung and the cramped and stinking huts to our
> lampless sleeping place among the rats. It was the worst one need fear, and
> it was bearable because it was inescapable. (p126)

He wanted to, and managed to, cut himself off from his companion. She was
there when he needed her. But I had to recognise my own reactions rather than
Barbara's when criticising Graham as it were on her behalf, for she wrote to me
after reading this chapter, among other matters which appear in the Conclusion:
'I was perfectly content to leave all initiative to my cousin and I also absolutely
understood his wish to be as much alone and undisturbed by me as possible'
(2 January 1988). And, in spite of that side of his journey, one should not see
Graham as harsh or unresponsive to those around him. Barbara writes:

> Graham, contrary to all the advice that he had received in Freetown from
> the Europeans, had an excellent method of his own for dealing with the
> men. We had been told that it was useless to expect obedience or honesty
> unless we showed by the most primitive methods what strong masters we
> were. Graham, however, from the beginning treated them exactly as if they
> were white men from our own country. He talked to them quite naturally
> and they liked him. They knew where they were with him, and apart from
> their everlasting cries of 'Too far,' they did everything he wanted them to
> do. (p68)

And he wrote of the inhabitants of the villages they passed through, and of
their carriers:

> Their laughter and their happiness seemed the most courageous things in
> nature. Love, it has been said, was invented in Europe by the troubadours,
> but it existed here without the trappings of civilization. They were tender
> towards their children ... they were tender towards each other in a gentle
> muffled way; they didn't scream or 'rag'; they never revealed the rasped
> nerves of the European poor in shrill speech or sudden blows. One was
> aware the whole time of a standard of courtesy to which it was one's
> responsibility to conform. (p80)

As for Barbara, she was quickly licked into shape by the journey and her
true, warm and responsive nature given free rein. First the superficial things
changed:

> It is strange, and perhaps rather horrible, how quickly we adapt ourselves
> to our surroundings. My life in England had been laid in pleasant places.

All my life I had been used to well-cooked food and beautiful clothes, a lovely house filled with people who smoothed out for me as far as possible the rough patches on my road through life. I was taken care of and spoilt both by my family and my friends, and the little, dull, tiresome everyday household things were automatically done for me. I had liked to find my evening clothes spread out for me ready pressed on my bed, my bath ready for me, and then to come down to dinner lit by candle-light. Beauty, comfort, and a good deal of luxury had been part of my life. I was used to it, and I knew that when I returned to England it would immediately become part of my life again. In Liberia I was surrounded by rats, disease, dirt, and foul smells, and yet in a very few days I had sunk to that level and did not mind at all.

We never had enough boiled water to wash really properly. Our clothes were never clean. The bristles of my hair-brush were eaten away entirely by the rats in this dirty village. It was my own fault, for I had left the brush out of my suit-case, but it meant that there was nothing I could do except throw it away; and so for the next two months – till I reached England – I did not brush my hair again. It got stiff with dust and stood out round my head like a halo ... my face was burnt and brown, and the dust was so rubbed into it that it took me literally weeks when I got to England to get it to look normal again. I kept my nails short, but they got broken round the edges. I was quite certainly not a thing of beauty, a joy for ever. But it did not worry me. It was all part of the existence we were leading and seemed to be perfectly natural. (p49)

Her reaction to the women she met was not superficial: it was deeper than language, particularly when there was no common one spoken; and she was a participant, not an observer:

The village girls crowded into my hut with me and watched with great interest while I changed my shirt and washed. I did not mind their being there. They were charming, and smiled at me so excitedly and shyly. When I washed myself they could not understand what the soap was, but loved the way it made the water fluffy. They dipped the tips of their fingers into it when I had finished, and then gazed at the bubbles as they gradually disappeared. I broke off a small corner of the soap and gave them a piece, and it was passed round eagerly from hand to hand, till one of them tried to eat it. They stroked my arms, not rudely and inquisitively as they had done in the last village, but gently, which I learnt later was a sign of approval. Although we could exchange no word, we laughed together and felt friendly and happy.

The women had their breasts, and sometimes the whole of their bodies down to the waist, cut in strange patterns during their time in bush school. Some of the very young girls in this village were quite lovely; they held their heads high and moved gracefully. But disease soon ravaged their bodies. The older women looked gaunt and withered, and unattractive in their nakedness. But in spite of the sores and the unhealthiness there was a freshness in the village, a cleanliness of spirit, and a charm that came straight from the heart. Their manners were good and dignified. The women realised at once when I no longer wanted to have them near me, and gracefully withdrew and left me alone. Somehow we came very near to understanding one another, and I felt I was among people I liked. (p58)

Graham's perception of these same women was quite different:

Only a few of the women broke the monotonous ugliness of the place. The adults had been beautifully and elaborately cut in bush school; the patterns were like metal plaques spread from the breasts to the navel; and there was one small girl in a turban with slanting, Oriental eyes and small neat breasts who did appeal to a European sexual taste even in her dirt. To their eyes she was probably less attractive than the village beauty who gazed at herself all day in a little scrap of cracked mirror, a girl with swelling buttocks and smeared and whitened breasts which hung in flat pouches to her waist. It was curious how seldom they did appeal: perhaps sexual vitality was lowered by the heat and the marches, but it was partly, I think, their lack of sexual self-consciousness. They weren't, until we came near to the Coast and 'civilization', interested in the sex of their visitors, but only in their colour or their clothes. The nakedness was monotonous; it brought home how few people, and for how short a period of their lives, one can see naked with any pleasure. (p129)

For Barbara there was a sisterhood with the women she met, one she felt in whatever way she could communicate. At three different places they met missionary women who spoke her languages. (Although Barbara's father was English, her mother was German; they had met in Brazil, where Barbara was born.) The husband of the first missionary had been drowned and she had stayed on, unable to go anywhere else, and become strange. Barbara puts her on paper as an experienced writer might – on their first meeting building up to a climax more effectively than her cousin; but as they leave, she writes of 'the lonely – desperately lonely, woman' (p85). Mrs Harley whom they met next was grieving for her dead son. Barbara noted:

I did not understand these things, but I felt that I wanted to take the brittle fingers of the little white woman in mine and comfort her. But I knew I could bring her no comfort. I was only a stranger passing through. It brought no pleasure to her to have the loneliness broken for a day or two. I was only a burden to her that had to be borne, like the many, many other burdens that lay on her shoulders. (p112)

And the third chance encounter just as they are ending their journey:

We had come to another mission and were welcomed by the German missionary and his wife. I cannot remember anything about the man, but the picture of the woman lies enshrined in my heart. She was fat, large and kind, and her straight greyish hair was pulled with great force back from her red face and pinned into a tight little bun behind. She looked exactly the kind of picture that springs to mind when one tries to imagine an old-fashioned, middle-class German *Hausfrau*. She was perfect in every detail. It was almost as if she had dressed the part for a joke to go to a party, and she remembered everything, down to the black woollen stockings. But her heart was as large as her body and she seemed to exude kindness from every pore. She gave us iced fruit drinks and delicious gingerbread, and provided – ever true to her character – little paper serviettes so that we might delicately wipe our rough red fingers. And suddenly she nearly made me weep, for she put her hand softly on my head and said, 'Mein armes Kind,' exactly as my mother used to say to me when as a child I was feeling sad. And I realised that what I wanted more than anything else was to be petted and spoilt a little bit and to be made a fuss of. When I wanted to thank her as we said good-bye I could hardly say a word in case my voice should tremble, for since the day before I could never be sure of my mood from one moment to another. (pp190–1)

If Barbara did not contribute much practically to the journey and if, in many ways, Graham thought of himself as alone – however courteously he speaks of his cousin in retrospect – what did she get out of it? She asked that question herself over 40 years later, by then author of several books and widow of a German count and distinguished diplomat, and answered:

What, I sometimes wonder, did that journey bring me? Did it enlarge my horizons, change my ideas or character? Unconsciously I suppose it must have done, as till then I had floated lightly on the surface of what I now realize was a very privileged existence, and I remember clearly how Graham's wider experience of life and his independent views often amazed and astonished me; but how far they changed me, is hard to judge for I was at the age when every day opens new windows to wider views. That I was forced to stick through all difficulties to the end showed no particular merit on my part, for we soon reached the point of no return ... I was never able to return to Africa again. Nevertheless ever since those days I have kept in my heart a dream of pure beauty and peace, a vision of moonlit villages in the jungle, friendly people dancing to the twang of a native harp and the beat of a drum, simplicity where material values were of no account and where understanding could be reached without words. In dark moments I needed only to remember those evenings and I was immediately filled with gratitude that I had been given the gift of life and the opportunities to experience such rare moments. That, I suppose, is the treasure that I brought back from my journey through Liberia. (ppxiv–xv)

As for Barbara's relationship with Graham, that became warm and close in later life, as Jeremy Lewis illustrates in his history of the extended family, *Shades of Greene* (2010). Graham wrote to her in the lead-up to the re-publication of her book in 1981, 'Please don't have any misgivings about the re-issue of your wonderful book – it will get superb reviews.' And, post-publication, he added, 'I was glad to see a good review by Theroux saying that your book was nearly as good as mine. Perhaps he should have said a better book than mine' (p474).

They corresponded regularly, she living part of the year on the island of Gozo, he in Italy. And when I asked if I could send this chapter to him through her Barbara replied,

I've just had a letter from my cousin Graham who tells me that if I have given my permission to quote from my book, he agrees to your quoting from his. He is far too busy, he says at the moment to read your mss. So please take this as his answer ... Graham by the way, found the idea of your book very amusing! (13 January 1988 and 5 February 1988)

There is something reassuring about his reliance on her judgement all those years later.

9 – Wife of Ingrams

Doreen Ingrams, *A Time in Arabia* (**1970**; reissue planned 2013; Arabic translation 2011)
Harold Ingrams, *Arabia and the Isles* (**1942**; 1966; 1998)

9.1   Doreen Ingrams with cameleer Suleiman at Wadi Gubhudh

(All images courtesy of Leila Ingrams)

9.2   Camp during first detailed survey of Hadhramaut (by Europeans), 1934, Wadi Sei'ar

9.3   Doreen Ingrams in Syrian headdress (out of respect) with Zahra

When is history? My husband, talking as a legal historian to a class of new, women students, reported afterwards, 'They had only studied European history from 1942; how can that be history? I was alive.' Writing about Doreen Ingrams (1906–1997) is a bit like that.

She lived in South Arabia, mostly the Hadhramaut (part of today's Yemen) for ten years from 1934, acceptable enough as 'historical' time; but she wrote up her account from her earlier diaries in 1969/70 with retrospective perceptions that were becoming 'modern' – which shows in refreshing ways. What is more, how do you write historically about a woman you have met and talked to, strangely quickly become friends with, sisters even. It is not possible, therefore, to put her under the same historical microscope that I have presumed to do with earlier women travellers.

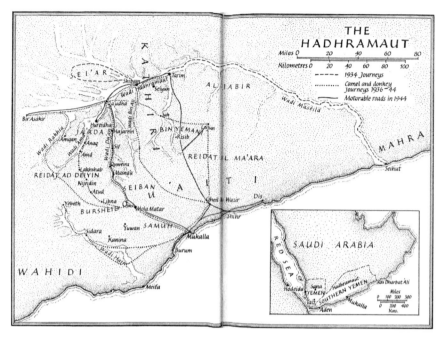

9.4   The journeys of Doreen and Harold Ingrams in the Hadhramaut
(from Ingrams, *A Time in Arabia*)

9.5   Harold Ingrams – at peace ceremony,
Hammumi tribe surrender, 1937

9.6   Harold Ingrams – lunch halt during
Hadhramaut survey

Doreen's later reworking of her stay in Arabia and her travels there shows in
specific ways. One is that, writing long after her husband Harold's well-known
and admired account of his life as a political officer from 1919 in Zanzibar,
Mauritius and Aden, and later British Resident Adviser to the Hadhramaut
States, she wanted to say something different. Linked to that, because she
was writing at the beginning of a resurgence of interest in matters concerning

women, she chose to concentrate, to a large extent, on the women she met and the concerns of the women of the area.

Second, she felt able to discuss issues that were previously omitted from women's travel writing for reasons of convention. Intimate relationships between women living in seclusion in Islamic societies and menstruation are examples that stand out.

The latter may seem trivial. Certainly Diana Shipton (who appears in the next chapter) was dismissive when I raised it with her in conversation; she was not ready, modern as she had become, to discuss such matters; one didn't; all women went through it, put up with it and that was that. But, imagine being a woman traveller in the days before tampons, even modern sanitary towels. How did Lucy Atkinson and Florence Baker cope? We can only speculate. But Doreen Ingrams in an appealing and informative no-nonsense way writes of a journey she made:

> We had three donkeys, one for Hasan, one for me, and one for our goods. In my diary I made a list of the luggage for this trip: 1 camp bed, 3 rugs, 2 Arab pillows (these were long and hard), 1 overcoat, change of clothes, STs, powder, toothbrush, etc., cigarettes, matches, notebooks, pencils, large saucepan, small saucepan, serving spoon, 2 enamel plates, mug, canvas water bottle, kettle, lantern, torch. The disposal of sanitary towels was always a problem on the stony plateaux, and the best I could ever do was to scratch a hole and bury them under a heap of stones. These memorial cairns were to be found all over the deserts of the Hadhramaut. As for other natural functions it was not easy to perform them unseen when there was not a rock nor a tree in sight for miles, so I followed the example of the ostrich and, having walked a good distance from the camp, turned my back on it, satisfied that if I could not see the beduin they could not see me. (p94)

Even she does not discuss the other aspects of inconvenience that may go with menstruation – such as how one's health, stamina, equilibrium, etc., might be affected. When Barbara Greene talks of being on the verge of tears and notes that 'since the day before I could never be sure of my mood from one moment to another' (p190), was she about to menstruate? Would she have seen the missionary woman differently depending on the answer to that question?

Even Marika Hanbury-Tenison, travelling round Indonesia in 1973, mentions only in a list of necessities to be bought in Singapore, 'Those boring female requisites.' Marika is modern in her language, talking naturally of a young woman with 'full, perky breasts' (p46) and retelling anecdotes about women 'having it off' (p172), and another sticking a crocodile's egg 'up her arse' (p202). When she talks of her own 'aches, pains, and swollen legs' (p46), is she telling us what hell menstruating in the jungle is? Or is it some other complaint? It is not a trivial matter for women travellers nor for the women who identify with them.

One of Doreen Ingrams' main advantages is that she spent ten years in Arabia – she and Harold were the first Europeans to make the Hadhramaut their home. She settled down straight away to learn the language and, through it, the people and their customs at more than a superficial level. She can describe them from numerous personal experiences:

> No water was available for ablutions before prayers and this started a discussion as to whether they were really necessary. 'Hanafis', said Seiyid Hamid with disapproval, 'do not mind if they have touched a woman between ablutions and saying their prayers, but we Shafa'is insist that we must wash again.' This made him a butt for jokes as he had touched my arm when emphasising a point and had then said his prayers without washing. I was reminded of an old seiyid who carefully covered his hand with his shawl before shaking mine in case I might be menstruating. Sa'ud, when playing cards with her brother Alawi, youngest of Seiyid Bubakr Al Kaf's three sons, would sometimes tease him when he was about to say his prayers by touching his hand and saying with a giggle, 'Now you've got to wash again as I've got blood.' Men and women after having intercourse must wash thoroughly, including their hair, before saying prayers, and this too was a source of ribaldry in the harem, for when anyone came in with wet hair everyone would call out, 'We know what you've been up to!' (pp33–4)

Doreen was not constantly moving on. She made friends with women living in the harem and records conversations with them. One of the reasons she waited so long to publish her memories is that she wanted to cause as little offence as possible to her women friends. As a wife, she was often shunted into women's affairs, but what a bonus for her general readers and for scholars (as well as for herself in terms of friendship). In a chapter entitled 'Harem Life' she writes, as an introduction:

> Harold at once got down to discussions with the two minor Kathiri Sultans ... While they discussed the future of the country Hasan Shaibi took me sightseeing and I was greeted everywhere by cries of 'Woman, Christian woman!', which brought the Tarim women, usually shy and in the background, edging forward to have a closer look.
>   ... Seiyid Umar invited me to visit his Number One wife, Shfa, who was very quiet and looked worn out with child-bearing; she was then expecting her eleventh, which would be Seiyid Umar's fourteenth child as he had three more by his second wife, a younger woman whom he had married because he wanted her, whereas Shfa was a rich relative chosen for him by his father. The laws of Islam allow a man to have up to four wives providing he can treat each one exactly the same as the other, so that it was usually only rich men who could go in for polygamy. No Al Kaf wife would dream of sharing her home with another wife, as sometimes happened in less wealthy families, and a new house had to be built or rented each time a man married ... The fact that a number of women in the Hadhramaut put up with having co-wives did not for a moment mean that they were any less jealous or were made any less miserable than a Western woman would have been in

such circumstances, but they were more fatalistic about it, saying 'It is our custom and we must bear with it'. (pp19–20)

With the special entrée that she obtained to various households Doreen was able to go much deeper into relationships; she touches too, without using the word, on lesbianism in the harem – a useful addition to the literature. In studies such as *Surpassing the Love of Men: Romantic Friendship and Love between Women from the Renaissance to the Present* (1985) by Lillian Faderman, the subject began to be explored historically as far as European society is concerned but it did not include those in Islamic societies, often visited by women travellers. In Seiyid Bubakr's house Doreen mentions:

Ayesha, who drifted aimlessly about and spent a good deal of her time in the Sultan's harem where she had a special girl friend to compensate for an emigrant husband, and perhaps also to console her for the loss of three children who had died in infancy, a very common occurrence; there was also Raguana who, apart from Fatima, had the most outstanding personality in the harem. She was taller than most Hadhrami women, with a good figure and the striking looks of a film star, which she might well have been had she grown up in another environment for she also had a most compelling, deep voice. As the only one in the harem who could read we often listened entranced while she spoke the words of the Quran. I would watch her at the sewing machine or coiling up her hair, fascinated by her grace and the serenity in her expression, which masked an intelligence and interest in the world around her that might have led her to a more satisfactory and fuller life had she been educated and emancipated. As it was she wasted her undoubted gifts in harem badinage and, like Ayesha, sought consolation for a husband who had gone abroad in the affection of other women. (pp25–6)

Doreen elaborates on the background conditions through her living recollections:

Every now and then Seiyid Bubakr put his head round the door to see how things were going. When he found us laughing hilariously over some silly joke he said to me with the air of a father deprecating his youngsters' antics, 'Arab women have no manners, you should tell them how to behave. They need teaching.'

'It is a pity they cannot read or write', I replied.

'I don't mean that', he said, 'they need to be taught manners. If they are taught to read and write they will start writing to men.'

Whenever Seiyid Bubakr appeared in the harem there was an atmosphere of strain as everyone was a little afraid of him. His voice was gruff and rather forbidding and he was very much 'the Boss'; Fatima could not even go to bed until her lord was ready to do so. Most of the time she bore no resentment at his authority but I did sometimes see her frown with vexation when he refused her some request, or shrug her shoulders with frustrated anger at his open handed generosity which often meant more work for Fatima and more spending of her money as well as his own.

This domination by men had the effect of making women more carefree, for they had few serious problems to solve. Husbands were found for them, they did not have to go out to work or try to compete with men in any way, and though their lives were circumscribed they had a definite pattern and they knew just what they could or could not do without male sanction. None of them had the worried, anxious expressions so often seen on women's faces in more sophisticated societies; instead they were like nuns with that composure and serenity which one associates with convent life. But being shut away from the society of men did lead at times to attachments – even passionate attachments – to other women. (pp28–9)

Doreen's remarks about Seiyid Bubakr's generosity are given added piquancy when set beside Harold's on the same subject, comparing him to sixth-century Hatim al-Tai, of legendary hospitality:

His wife, to whom he has been married for thirty years, is as kind and charming as he is, and although, of course, she is not seen, men say to you confidentially: 'There's only one other person in the Hadhramaut like Seiyid Bubakr, and that's his wife,' because her influence spreads out unseen. He is the simplest and most generous of men, and although his charity is done without a flourish it is so widespread that he is called the Hatim Tai of Hadhramaut. I think everybody who has stayed with him will agree that he is the best of hosts, and while he provides extremely comfortable and well-fitted rooms with all European comforts for his European guests, he himself sleeps on a mattress on the floor. (p263)

And Doreen's conversation with Seiyid Bubakr on education is reminiscent of the one Ella Sykes had in Persia. Where Doreen and Ella differ is that the former lives in more analytical and open times for women, enabling her to pursue the matter further:

On this occasion our conversation was serious but most of the time in the harem we talked trivialities, and I was often struck by the contrast between the conversation of men and women. The men would discuss politics or history or poetry, which would have bored most of the women just as they were not infrequently bored by Sherifa Alawiya [an intellectual woman], yet with their intelligent minds they might so easily, with a little education, have entered more fully into the lives of the men. 'They are no better than sheep,' I have heard men say, but whose fault was that? The men were afraid that if women were taught to read and write they would want more freedom, and with freedom there would be an end to morality. Ideas about immorality were often a reflection of the men's ideas about the behaviour of women in the west who kissed in public, wore indecent clothes, and generally behaved in a manner which no Muslim would like to see his daughter imitate. Rahima Jaffer [from a well-known Aden family] once told me that in Aden many Arabs were convinced all European women were immoral as they could not see how a woman could dance in a low evening dress with a man if she did not also sleep with him. In Hadhramaut the men seemed to think that so long as the women had no opportunity of meeting men they would lead chaste lives, and as far as men were concerned this was largely true, but when young women had their passions roused by early marriage and were then frustrated by divorce or the husband emigrating, it was not surprising that, having no outlet for even a mild flirtation with a man, they turned to their own sex. (pp62–3)

As an example of what she means by the passions of early marriage and of the uninhibitedness of harem conversation, Doreen writes:

I was told that once alone with the bridegroom a bride must not utter a word as he takes off her ornaments one by one, not even if he fumbles trying to undo the numerous clasps of her necklaces. Seiyid Bubakr, according to Fatima, was so bored with all this that on their wedding night he took a pair of scissors and cut the necklaces off her. (p68)

Doreen's life was far from confined to the harem; indeed, often and increasingly over the years, she travelled on Harold's behalf when he was trying to spread the concept of peaceful coexistence among previously warring Arab tribes. It was not unusual for her to be introduced on these tours as 'Wife of Ingrams the Friend of the Hadhramaut' (p51). Of a particular occasion she writes:

… it was appreciated that Harold had achieved something no one else had been able to achieve and he was greeted by everyone as, 'Friend of the Hadhramaut'. I was made strikingly aware of this changed attitude when some children, who always reflected adult opinion, called after me, as they often did, 'Christian, Christian', but immediately a small boy cried out, 'she is not a Christian, she is the female Ingrams,' I knew we had been accepted. (p65)

Travelling without Harold did breed other epithets too, linking Doreen in a broad geographic and cultural swathe with Eleanor Lattimore:

After supper that evening my bedroom was crowded with women from neighbouring houses, dressed in bright colours but with red predominating as it was the fashionable colour for the evening. Jemila served tea and I was soon being asked the usual questions, which by now had become very tedious. They stroked my hair, touched my clothes, and tried to reason out why I behaved so oddly, roaming the countryside without my husband. One woman had the answer, of course my husband had another wife to look after the home and I was his 'travelling wife'. (pp49–50)

Harold writes of Doreen's obviously invaluable work; in a chapter called 'The Signing of the Truce' he refers to the settlement of a difference in which she was involved:

> Perhaps one of the greatest surrenders of those days was that of the royal wives at Seiyun. Sultan 'Ali was completely under their thumbs and it was extraordinarily difficult to get them to consent to send their sons to Aden to the Chiefs' college. D. conducted a campaign in the background as she could carry it well into the enemy's trenches. Finally they gave in and Hussein, the eldest son, and Majid were selected to be educated. It was not easy to get Hussein as he had already been booked for a girl aged fourteen or fifteen by an anxious mother who thought it was high time she was married. (p306)

Doreen writes of the matter so that we appreciate the mechanics of it, see from the inside out:

> ... I was assigned to getting the consent of the Kathiri Sultan's family for two of his sons, Hussein and Majid, to go to the college. This was one reason why I frequently called on the women of the royal household who lived on the top floor of the high palace set in the heart of Seiyun. There the wives of the Sultan and his brother, their daughters, mothers and grandmothers, shared a string of rooms and were waited on by some twenty female servants. All joined in argument with me; not one of them liked the idea of the precious boys going out of their sight: it was not customary, it was not necessary. Hussein was to be married to his cousin, a girl already sixteen which was verging on old age for a bride, and Majid was delicate, needing special food and attention. I spent hours drinking tea, chewing melon seeds, and arguing, breaking off only when they rose to say their prayers, covering themselves from head to foot in orange cloaks, standing in line murmuring, bowing to the ground, kneeling and rising, like a row of brilliantly coloured flowers swaying in the wind. I am glad to say that they finally gave in, whether because they got tired of my pestering them or because the Sultan used his authority I do not know ... (pp46–7)

When one reads about the lives of the Hadhramaut women, it is remarkable how Doreen was accepted the way she was, doing, as it were, man's work. Harold writes, for example of particular leaders,

> [who] were anxious that I should go up to the Wadi 'Amd and sign on the Ja'da, but there was still much to do in Wadi Hadhramaut and I promised to go later on. In the meantime they took D. off with them and she and 'Alawi were to go up the wadi and see what the situation was.
>   From Hureidha they visited every village up the wadi to 'Amd, the capital. 'Alawi and his Javanese servant rode one camel and D. and Jamila, the Al' Attas maid and a woman of character, rode the other. Jamila taught D. beduin war songs and when she had learnt them they proceeded up the

wadi singing duets. D. took down details of thirty-two major feuds in the wadi. Almost everywhere the villages were divided against themselves and everywhere the cry was the same: 'Give us peace.' One gentleman discussed the matter from a second-storey window. He apologized for not coming down but explained he was busy carrying on a war single-handed against all his neighbours. (p298)

It seems clear that Doreen had discussions with both men and their women about the need for peace and, even, that the women urged her to put pressure on their men.

Doreen's travelling life was not without its discomforts and dangers, as one might imagine in an undeveloped and unsettled area. There were nights spent insecurely in the open because a vehicle did not turn up, and there was the extortion of protection money as they passed through the areas of different tribal factions. After the Ingrams' peace began to bite, Doreen wrote of a journey, 'Neither beduin carried a gun, the first time I had ever travelled with unarmed beduin' (p79).

She did not have occasion to prove herself as some nineteenth-century wives did but she needed to have strong nerves, nevertheless, for one never quite knew how people might react. Her confidence is expressed through a typical early experience:

While Harold went in for a long discussion with the Sheikh of the Awamir I had a look round and was immediately the centre of attention. 'Come to my house' whispered a dark complexioned woman seizing my hand, 'Come to mine' said another. 'No mine' shouted a third. By now both my arms were being held and I was being pulled in all directions. The strongest woman won and, followed by a screaming crowd, we jostled each other along the narrow lanes until we reached a small door. 'Not here, not here' shouted several women and I was dragged away in spite of protests by the lady of the house. Another even more determined woman pulled me towards her front door, where, with the help of a friend, she pushed me inside banging the door shut behind us. The friend hastily ran along the passage to lock another door that led to the street and I was then taken upstairs, but we had not even reached the guest room when the crowd was upon us, though how they got in I do not know. A hefty man thrust his way through the women, caught hold of my hand and said in English, 'Come on, come on, not good here. I know, come on.' I was annoyed at his officiousness as I had not been in the least apprehensive among the clutching women, but as he continued pulling at me until he got me through the protesting women and out into the street I began to wonder what he thought was going to happen. I shall never really know but I suspect he was afraid they were over-excited at their first sight of a European woman and might unintentionally harm me: there were times later on when I was nearly stripped in the excitement of seeing if I were the same colour all over. (pp21–2)

Later, when she went on tour without Harold, Doreen took pains, in spite of her acceptance, to conform to certain customs. She writes of one of her Arab companions:

> There were many more villages and at each one we dismounted to talk to the Muqaddam (headman). I always make sure Seiyid Hasan rides ahead as I know it would greatly offend his dignity if a woman were to ride in front of him when we come to a village. (pp97–8)

And of appearance and appearances she notes:

> For some time Harold and I had been wearing Arab clothes when we were outside our own home, a custom that began when Seiyid Bubakr gave Harold his first *futa* [loincloth] and Fatima asked me if I would wear a sarong, saying it would be much more comfortable than a short dress when sitting on the floor. The sarong, however, was not worn as an outdoor garment and I felt unbearably conspicuous walking through the streets in a short skirt, so I adopted what at that time was the outdoor dress of women in Syria, a long black skirt and a cape that covered head and shoulders. This was no protection against the sun but it hid my hair and the low neck line of my Western cotton dress. Wearing Arab clothes can be described as 'dressing-up', but it has to be remembered that we were the only Europeans in a country where traditional customs were held very dear and where there was much suspicion of Christians. To be the only woman in a country showing her legs, or her hair, does not help to make you feel at home, whereas I found that conforming as far as one could to local customs made one not only more acceptable but more at ease. (pp71–2)

Harold writes of the same conversion, showing not only his male concern with appearance and how it relates to appearances, or 'face', but also with an immediacy of style which this chapter so far hardly allows him:

> These days, too, marked my initiation into the constant wearing of Arab clothes. Hitherto when on the road I had worn a turban for practical reasons. It was infinitely more comfortable than a topee and served a variety of purposes – shade by day, warmth by night, sieve for water, a bag for goods, and, being brimless, it enabled me to take bearings without having constantly to push my hat up. This time I had worn it since leaving Mukalla, even in the towns.
>   As it was Ramadhan, our friends could only ask us to meals after dark. They knew we did not like to eat in splendid isolation and dinner was tiresome for them when they had a meal at sunset. In a day or two I was asked to the sunset breakfast by Seiyid 'Abdur Rahman.
>   'Would you mind eating on the floor – Arab food?' he asked doubtfully. I explained that I very much preferred it and that I was used to such meals

in Zanzibar days. Next day it was at Seiyid 'Umar's. I saw the brothers and others in whispered consultation, plainly about me.

'Alawai, the architect, came over and asked me to come out of the room with him. He produced a fine new sarong.

'We should be very pleased if you will wear it.' Having adjusted it to his satisfaction, we returned to the room to be greeted with pleased smiles and exclamations of 'Wallahi! 'Arabi. You are no longer an Englishman, you are a Hadhrami,' Seiyid 'Abdur Rahman said: 'We have always treated you and Duri [Doreen] as of the family, now we feel that you really are.'

I did not at first wear the garb by day, but every house I went to provided me with a new sarong, so that soon I never wore anything else. Indeed, from the point of view of comfort, I should be sorry to return to trousers again ... (pp258–9)

They were not like other 'colonials' in several respects; Doreen writes of the term 'memsahib' used when she first arrived in Aden in 1934:

... a name which even in those far off days conjured up to me the worst type of British woman abroad. The fact that I had a rather unconventional approach to life in a colony may have been partly the result of having been on ... the stage in the days when touring showed you a world of 'digs', slum life and mixing with anybody and everybody, all far removed from the protective shell of my parents' home. But I had also married a man with an independent mind who refused to conform to the mystique of the British in the colonies, the social round that excluded 'natives', the formalities of calling, dress, and way of talking to the 'lesser breeds', all of which were supposedly keeping up British prestige, or so I was assured on the occasions when I questioned British behaviour. (pp4–5)

Doreen's comfortable home had been that of the Rt Hon. Edward Shortt KC, Liberal Home Secretary between 1919 and 1922, and Isabella (née Scott). The baby of a family of four siblings (two much older), she had been briefly educated at a private school and then, with a sister, by a governess before the two were sent to a Swiss finishing school, for which Doreen was a bit young. In spite of her incomplete education, she later taught herself through avid reading. Her piano teacher felt that, if she practised, she could become a concert pianist; instead, in 1924, aged 18, she went on the stage. She married Harold Ingrams (1897–1973) in 1930 when she was 24 and he was nine years older. He was the son of a parson and teacher at Shrewsbury, where Harold himself was educated, and an army officer during the First World War. By the time they went to South Arabia, she had already accompanied him to Mauritius where he was Assistant Colonial Secretary. But they eschewed the colonial life there and Doreen began to learn basic Arabic and to translate from French to English an eighteenth-century history of Mauritius. Their attitudes were unconventional for their time and background; Doreen adds:

It always seemed strange to me that so many British women could live for years in Aden without ever speaking to an Arab other than their servants or the shopkeepers. They had no interest in the 'natives', did not attempt to speak a word of Arabic, and were astonished if a compatriot did not conform to their way of life – bridge, tea parties, the exclusive British club. This was not true of missionaries, nor of wives of political officers who were often as immersed in local Arab life as their husbands, but it was true of many Service wives and a good many mercantile families, not only British but French, Italian or Greek, and certainly there was only a handful of foreign women who ever went into an Arab home. Yet in Aden the Arab women were often more educated than those in the Hadhramaut. (pp125–6)

Even when some well-meaning attempts were made, they could come unstuck through 'colonial attitudes', as almost happened when the British Council opened a club for women in Aden; Doreen writes:

The strictly purdah bandage-making parties ... were successful in attracting a number of the more secluded women especially as they were thought to be working in a good cause ... When we had filled the first half dozen cases with bandages I asked the president of the Red Cross to accept them. Not for the first time I was amazed at the tactless and patronising way in which a European spoke to Arab women. She looked at the first case and said, 'The bandages all look very neat on top, perhaps I'd better look underneath to see if they're all like that.' It may have been intended as a joke but Arab women are as aware as anyone else when they are being treated like children and naturally resent it. Kibre ingliz, 'English pride', was an expression often used by Arabs and frequently deserved. (pp126–7)

Harold confirms her description of his views and endorses hers:

I get most of my fun out of learning other people's languages and living among them and sharing their life. If you know and understand people you rarely want to fight with them. I think the greatest compliment I was ever paid was in Mauritius, where I was described as international. To be aggressively English always seems to me the most unpleasant form of 'patriotism'. (p270)

And he concludes his book, writing of South Arabia:

It is an Arab country and Arab it must remain. It should never be necessary for any large number of aliens to be in it either for administrative or other reasons. Those of us who are there respect the customs and life of the people. We do not set ourselves up as rulers of the country but merely try to pass on to them any experience or knowledge we have which may be of value. If the weekend-visitor of the future goes away having seen Arabs dressed as Arabs and living in houses of Arab architecture and does not find endless outward and visible signs of European occupation our labours will not have been in vain, and we who know it will hope that inwardly and spiritually the character of the Arab has not suffered by our presence. (p354)

Doreen later had occasion to test his hopes of 1942:

When I returned to the Hadhramaut in 1963 the number of British living in or around Mukalla filled me with misgiving. Inevitably with the increase in their numbers they had become isolated from contact with the natives. I was even told that it was not safe for a European woman to walk down the main street. I proved this to be the complete rubbish that I knew it to be, but it only showed how out of touch the British had become that such a thing could even be suggested. (p152)

One of the bonuses of Doreen's book is the possibility of looking ahead from the place and the woman of 1934–44; she is not quite sure which woman she is:

It is only too easy to be wise after events and I have to think hard to remember what I felt about colonialism in the 1930s knowing how I feel about it now. I think I probably accepted it as an institution but rebelled against the division between rulers and ruled; in any case I was brought up to believe it was the right of people to rule themselves, one of my earliest recollections as a child was some official function in Newcastle when, dressed as a colleen, I curtsied to the wife of the guest of honour and handed over a bouquet with the words 'From a little Home Ruler'. Certainly by the 1940s I doubted if colonialism was there to stay ... The genuine affection and respect of most colonial officials for the people of the country in which they served and their wish to promote their welfare are not to be denied, but paternalism by its very nature denies the right of free expression to children. (pp152–3)

In spite of Harold's 'progressiveness' and, in spite of the freedom Doreen had, and that she exercised, there are signs that, in the end, what her own society then expected of a woman in her position chafed. Her work was certainly respected by her own society. Bernard Reilly, the British Resident in Aden when Ingrams arrived as an officer in 1934, ends his 1942 introduction to Harold's book:

In all his work Ingrams has been encouraged and supported by the indefatigable collaboration and help of his wife. The name of Doreen Ingrams is as widely known as that of her husband, and in this story of life and work in Mauritius, Zanzibar and southern Arabia will be found a vivid description of efforts in which they have shared in the toil and in the success. (px)

But Doreen was, after all, seen as only a wife, so that when she writes the following we know what it means:

> Our first visit to the Hadhramaut in 1934–35 lasted nine weeks, during which time we covered a great deal of ground, literally as well as figuratively ... We found out as much as we could about the tribal organisation, the economy of the country, and the social conditions, and we mapped a good deal of hitherto unmapped territory, all of which was published in Harold's official Colonial Report No 123 and then later in his book *Arabia and the Isles.* (p9)

That 'we' becomes a throwaway but infinitely revealing line in Harold's account : 'We made an early start in the morning of December 11th, but after lunch most of us slept, except D. who wrote up some of the journal ...' (p221).

Of course, it should be said that Doreen's diary only contributed to the Arabian part of Harold's book. Of the relationship between her own book and her diary, she opens her foreword:

> During the years that I lived in the Hadhramaut I kept a diary. It was the first time that Europeans had ever made a home in that country and at first each day's entries took up many pages, but gradually there were only unusual events to record for what had seemed strange at first had become commonplace. It is these diaries that are the basis of this book.

Written at the end of the 1960s, that shows a refreshing lack of the self-deprecation which has become familiar. But in the 1930s and 1940s her self-image was not so clear-cut. There was the perennial wifely task described first by Harold: 'These proposals were submitted on the 21st January, 1935: months followed in which detailed reports on the country were prepared (D. typed over 900 foolscap pages in all) ...' (p245).

In 1939 Doreen supplements that when, arriving in Singapore in 1939, on an official tour to visit Hadhrami migrants, she observes, 'Here Harold could start writing his report and I could do the typing' (p90). (When Doreen read my first draft of this chapter, she asked me to take out any of my conclusions that seemed to claim she had done something; but her daughter tells me that she 'also advised Harold on many things to do with his writing'.) And when they visited Yemen:

> During the six weeks we were in Sana Harold was having discussions with the Imam or his Foreign Minister about the frontier problems and matters connected with the tribes on either side of the frontier, and I was often kept busy coding and decoding telegrams to and from Aden. (p121)

Harold writes, obviously sincerely, in his introduction:

> I have dedicated this book to my wife, not because (though it is quite true) 'without her help it would never have been written,' but because without

that help there would have been little to write about. I hope I may be forgiven for saying that she, like many others, is an exception to Freya Stark's dictum that 'The British appear to be popular wherever they go until they come to settle with their wives.' Nevertheless, as we all know, there is a lot in that statement and if I may add one word more to those contemplating a Colonial service career, it is, choose a wife who will not only share your life but that of the people amongst whom she and you will live. (pxiii)

And presumably one that can settle down to office work.

We can see from both Ingrams' accounts a team that was fulfilled in its work, however ambiguous the status of one of the team members. They received joint medals; one for bringing peace to the Hadhramaut (1939), the other for their contribution to geographical science (1940).

On her visit to the Hadhramaut in 1963, Doreen found that the first school for Beduin girls that she and her friend Rahima had set up nearly 20 years earlier in Mukalla, and in which they had done some teaching, was still going strong. Sa'ad, the Beduin mother, who had taken charge, was still there; hundreds of girls had since passed through her hands, and some had gone on to be teachers and nurses. Doreen had also been responsible for the setting up of a school for blind children and the organisation of relief and emergency medical centres during the famine of 1943–44.

By the time she published her book, 26 years after leaving Arabia, Doreen had established a career in the British Broadcasting Corporation Arabic Service where she was able to focus attention on Arab women, as she travelled round all the Arab world. Even when I met her, as she robustly and gracefully faced her eighties, she was working with her younger daughter, Leila, on a 16-volume work, *Records of Yemen 1798–1960*. Leila continues to research and write on that part of the world to which her parents contributed so much and is preparing for publication the autobiographical manuscript left by her mother. Leila has been approached by descendants telling her that 'Duree [Doreen] will never be forgotten for all she did – we thank Allah!'

At our meeting, Doreen radiated the sort of energy and fresh mentality that, as I was fortunate enough to experience them, too, in Barbara Greene Strachwitz, Ella Maillart and Diana Shipton Drummond, make me wonder if there isn't something in this travelling business.

10 – Not the First Englishwoman

Diana Shipton, *The Antique Land* (**1950**; 1987)
Eric Shipton, *Mountains of Tartary* (1951)

10.1   Diana and Eric Shipton picnicking near Kashgar
(from Steele, *Eric Shipton*)

'Spirit of Place' has been a term used in discussing male travel writing. D.H.
Lawrence's people, Paul Fussell (1980) suggests, 'discover their identities
through their response to place' (p143). It may well be that, in conclusion, I
shall claim that our travelling women are most interested in the interactions
between people in foreign places, so it is worth pausing to look at 'spirit of
place' from a different angle.

A reviewer of Edward Hoagland's travel book about the Sudan, *African
Calliope* (1979), adds an element that may be relevant to women's travel
writing when he approves and laments:

There is less 'destination' writing – scenic descriptions clogged with
adjectives – than there would be in a book by an English writer with a
similar brief ... part of Hoagland's methods is to use recorded conversation
rather than over-heated words of his own to evoke atmosphere or chart the
high temperatures. It is always a puzzle to me why English travel writers
make so little use of conversation. All eyes and no ears, I suppose, besides
natural shyness at being linguists.

10.2 The British Consulate, Kashgar and (right) 10.3 Front entrance to the British Consulate
(both from Shipton, *The Antique Land*)

And Diana Shipton, writing of her time in Chinese Turkestan in the 1940s, adds to the literature:

Describing scenery is liable to the restrictions of photographs of scenery. Carefully selected words may make beautiful sentences, as a carefully arranged, well lighted photograph may make a beautiful picture. But neither wholly catches the atmosphere, the feeling of space, air, colour and the fullness of the composer's own emotions. I am tempted to avoid describing scenery altogether. Accurate, geographical description is not my sphere, nor can I attempt poetic flourish. But the whole beauty of country, of different kinds and in different moods, is what makes travel worth the doing and so must be some part of a book of travels. (p165)

Perhaps Mildred Cable, the missionary who travelled round Chinese Turkestan with her companions Evangeline and Francesca French between 1923 and 1938, caught the real point when she wrote in *The Gobi Desert* (1942) about the Caves of a Thousand Buddhas at Tunhwang:

It must have been the unbroken quiet of this place, the remoteness of the oasis and its great solitude, which produced an eerie sense that the caves were guarded by the presence of those who once worked here so busily. Generation after generation, century after century, they had lived the absorbed life of creative artists, handing on, when their own time came to die, that great tradition of a production in which no individual artist is glorified, but in which an unnumbered crowd of craftsmen make their humble contribution toward the whole. (p50)

Perhaps it is not, as Lawrence suggested, that people take their identities from places, but that places take their aura from the people who live in them over time.

Diana Shipton (1917–1996) was following in the footsteps of several of our travelling companions when in 1946 she arrived in Kashgar with her husband Eric Shipton (1907–1977), the new Consul General. Ella Sykes, Eleanor Lattimore and Ella Maillart had passed through and recorded their impressions but they were transient. Catherine Macartney (1877–1949) lived there for 20 years. Her husband, later Sir George Macartney, was Britain's first Consul General but he did not write a publishable account of his 28-year stay to place side by side with *An English Lady in Chinese Turkestan* (1931; 1985). The bachelor establishment he had set up was rather different from the gracious family home created by his wife that was to greet later travellers and into which Diana Shipton settled. Diana was conscious of the ghosts and her inheritance:

The dream-like atmosphere of our arrival did not fade for a long time. In fact, I wanted it never to fade. I did not want to 'get used' to Kashgar, or to forget the extraordinary fact that I was in Central Asia. This feeling was not as pretentious as it may sound. There was no particular merit in my being in Kashgar. I did not aim to instruct anyone about it, nor to be 'the first Englishwoman' to do something or other. I only wanted to keep alive to the significance and interest of the country and the people all round me. In the large comfortable Consulate it was all too easy to slip into an unimaginative, domestic slumber; to nod gently over one's own small affairs. Yet a chance to see this part of the world would most probably never come again and I did not want mentally to sleep.

In 1946 air travel to Kashgar was still restricted to the use of a few Chinese officials. From whichever direction the ordinary traveller approached it, the journey was rough and the comforts few. Arriving at the British Consulate the sudden transition from the harsh desert to a well-appointed English home, seemed literally fantastic – as if by a turn of some magic ring, the whole place would disappear. This sounds over-lyrical, and by some Western standards the house left plenty to be desired. But for me the first impression of luxury and comfort, after the hard journey, was never quite dulled. The present house was finished in 1913, and whatever its faults in design, (for instance many of the rooms were dark and sunless, two guest-rooms were at the end of a rough, stone corridor, beyond the kitchen regions), it was a solid, well-built house, very superior to the modest, native-style mud house which Lady Macartney describes as her first home in Kashgar. Such things as glass in the windows, which I took for granted, were a luxury to her; her furniture was mostly home-made and comical. I walked in to a completely furnished, ready-made home. It was strange to think of the

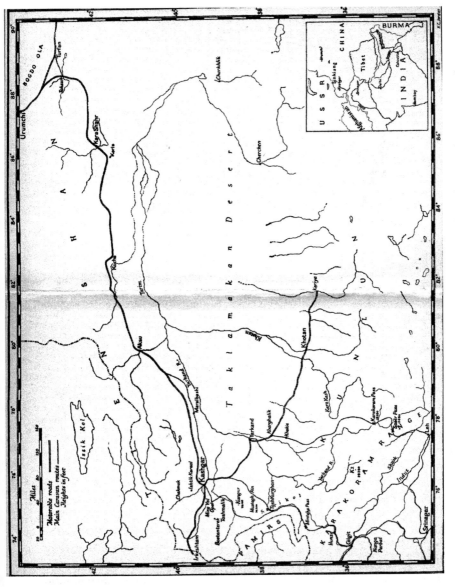

10.4   Chinese Turkestan and Kashgar, location of the British Consulate (from Shipton, *The Antique Land*)

many ideas and tastes which had built up this whole. Now I was free to
add my own individual touch. (pp40–1)

Diana met Eric Shipton in 1939 in Kashmir where her father, F.F.R. Channer,
was in the Indian Forestry Service. The following year Eric took up his post
as Consul General, for the first time, in Kashgar. There he stayed, much
circumscribed by political events and attitudes, until October 1942. Arriving
back in England at the end of the year, he married Diana ten days later. He was
35; she was ten years younger. He was known then as a mountaineer – several
times before the Second World War he had been a member of Everest teams
and he was to write several books about his mountaineering experiences;
indeed, the spirit of mountains imbues *The Mountains of Tartary*.

Between 1942 and 1946 the couple saw little of each other. He was sent to
Persia and then to Hungary. He was in Vienna when the cable came asking
him to take up, again, his post in Kashgar. Diana, whose first son had been
born six months before, was scarcely less excited at the prospect of spending
time in Central Asia. After a lot of heart-searching, she decided that young
Nicky would be better left in England.

How different was Diana from her predecessors, not only those who had
gone before in Kashgar, and how different were her travelling experiences? At
first sight one might have expected the travel to be very different. There were
aeroplanes and cars. But, because of the political and security situation in the
area, it turned out that Diana's travel from India to Kashgar was no different
from how it might have been a hundred years before – over the towering,
forbidding and hazardous mountains on the back of an animal. And in other
things little had changed. Catherine Macartney approached Kashgar in 1898
from the north (through Russia) instead of the south-west through British
India but, at that moment when the Macartneys left Osh, after a long train
journey followed by days in a *tarantass*, and found themselves at the foot of
the Tien Shan (Celestial Mountains), Diana and Catherine Macartney had
much in common. Catherine wrote:

Off we started, making an imposing procession, the yak leading, followed
by eight or nine baggage horses, while we and the servants brought up the
rear on horseback.

I had never ridden before, and had no idea what I must suffer to become
a horsewoman. ...

Finally I was mounted, and off we started, I innocently thinking how
comfortable it was to travel on horseback. After the first hour I began to feel
stiff, then I got stiffer, until I was simply in agony, and felt as though every
joint in my body was dislocated. Each movement and jolt was excruciating,
but I dare not stop and dismount, for I was sure that in my present condition
I should never be able to swing my leg over the bundle again.

So we went for six hours, and when at last we got to the Russian rest
house where we were to put up for the night, I had to be almost carried in,
and laid down gently on some bedding, feeling the most miserable home

sick creature in existence. How was I to live through sixteen awful days of such travelling? I was quite sure I should not survive it, and I must confess that I pulled the blanket over my head and wept bitterly. (pp18–19)

And nearly 50 years later Diana writes:

It is curious how quickly one forgets the dismal parts of an experience. In retrospect I see this journey to Leh as a sun-lit path winding among green oases or forbidding mountains; two weeks of exciting new adventure, of beauty and delight. The aching tiredness, the Rest House always round the *next* bend, the small irritations, seem to have faded from my mind. The only trouble which has not faded is my deep-rooted dislike of riding – a deep-rooted fear, really. This was the subject of continual argument between Eric and me. 'If you come to Asia you must ride,' Eric said. I have gradually learnt that he is right. Along mountain paths, narrow and twisting, walking is pleasant; when endless miles of dull desert stretch round you, it is a wretched business. A good, sturdy pony will cover the distance comfortably and fast. But I never learnt to enjoy riding. (pp19–20)

That was Diana's plight in theory; she shows us what it meant in practice as they approached Leh:

When still six miles from Leh we could see the green, welcoming oasis across a stony stretch of desert. Near us the Indus flowed placid and green. In the distance snow mountains gleamed and lower hills were lightly etched in shades of blue. I had given my horse to Amir Ali and felt completely at peace as I trudged along. My contentment was soon shattered. Coming towards us over the desert, in a dusty, noisy cavalcade was an alarming number of horsemen. This proved to be a deputation of Indian traders come out to escort us into Leh. My heart sank at the prospect of a spirited ride in the middle of this cavalry. It was out of the question to walk. A compromise was reached by Eric galloping on ahead with the main party, while a handsome young Sikh, who spoke English, very gallantly offered to accompany me. He never quite understood what all the fuss was about and I hope never realized what remarkable unhappiness that six miles caused me.

Eventually we reached the main gate into Leh and everyone dismounted. Feeling dishevelled and dusty, my legs still shaking from the ride, but trying to look dignified, I accompanied Eric in a 'triumphal' walk through the bazaar. (p23)

Eric would hardly be expected to have the same memories or perceptions of that occasion:

Near Leh, the Indus Valley widens out. The southern flank, freed for once from overshadowing precipice, lifts gently to the distant snow-peaks of the Zaskar Range. For once there is natural verdure along the banks of the great river, which flows with unwonted placidity between green meadows and willow thickets. Here, on 15th September, we found a large deputation of traders who had come out to meet us. We were provided with spirited ponies and escorted swiftly over six miles of sloping desert to Leh, where we found, somewhat to our embarrassment, that a pompous reception had been arranged for us. Our arrival apparently was welcomed as a sure sign that the profitable trade-route to Yarkand and Kashgar was at last to be reopened. A heavy burden of responsibility seemed to have descended upon our incompetent shoulders. (pp66–7)

It would be difficult to suggest a more English, male, account. Eric would not think to mention Diana's difficulties; if he noticed them, it is not what would be of interest to his readers, nor should it be. Not once does he mention Diana's trials as she struggled to keep up with a riding and mountaineering husband in a land of horses and mountains. He writes in his more autobiographical book *That Untravelled World* (1969) of Diana, '... she had spent much of her childhood in jungle camps, and among the many things we had in common, she shared my love of wild country ...' (p137). Diana would undoubtedly agree with that but she never quite imagined what that love might entail.

Diana's dislike of riding and her admission of it is the first break with the past. The women in the previous chapters nearly all rode, and did so for hours on end without complaint. Even Catherine Macartney, a complete novice, soon knuckled under. Diana, however, was prepared to write, as they crossed the desert towards Kashgar:

We listened eagerly for the sound of a motor but heard only the interminable jingle of the ponies' bells. My lofty desires to abandon 'modern' travel; my longing to try the simple life had evaporated a little. Two days in a despised machine now seemed infinitely preferable to ten more on a horse or my own feet. (p37)

Diana was a child of a new age. She is prepared to grouse, too, about other discomforts that would not have been noticed by Florence Baker as she fielded the spears:

It was arranged that while everyone else rode, Lhapka [a servant] and I should go by 'mappa' – a small horse-drawn vehicle with two high wheels, no springs and a wooden platform covered by a coloured, rounded hood.

On Sunday morning I began one of the most painful experiences of my life. It was just punishment for my cowardly fear of riding. All the bumps, ditches, holes and ridges of which I complained on our lorry drives, were intensified. While the driver perched on the shafts – leaping off most skilfully to lead his pony over the more difficult places – I tried every corner of the mappa in a search for relief. I sat far inside the cab in dark obscurity; I crouched, I knelt, I lay with my feet outstretched; finally I decided that the extreme edge of the platform, with my legs dangling out, was the most comfortable position. I have read of Europeans travelling hundreds of miles in a mappa, before the advent of motor cars to Sinkiang. I feel that I must be spoilt and degenerate, lacking stamina because of easy mechanical transport. By the end of a mere forty miles I felt shattered and spent. (p65)

Diana does not feel the imperative, felt by her predecessors, male and female, to keep up appearances not only in front of the 'natives' but in print; the image of the stiff upper lip is bent into a human shape more easily identified with by today's reader. She can write without blinking, 'We followed along the bottom of the ravine and were only occasionally checked by a hard wall of sandstone, where I and our dog had to be pushed and pulled to the top' (p72).

In the next passage Diana explains her difficulties with climbing but that is, in some ways, only incidental, for she also suggests a clash between logic and intuition – two forces traditionally said to represent respectively male and female. The third character, the Sherpa Gyalgen, had been with Eric Shipton on his Everest expedition and his 1939 Karakoram one. Diana writes:

Although Eric has climbed mountains since the age of fifteen, I have never done more than walk among them. The feel of mountain country and the beauty of hills I have always known. But steep places frighten me and I had never before attempted anything that I could, strictly speaking, dignify by the name of a 'climb'. Difficulty, of course, is relative to the climber's skill. I do not want to give the impression that I now tackled something difficult, as the term is accepted among climbers. It was certainly a sheer rock face and a fall would have hurled one into a deep gorge, of which the bottom was invisible. But the rock was firm, the foot and hand-holds were good and in climbing terms it was 'easy'. This was scant consolation to me; my fears had little to do with reason. It was Gyalgen's gentle, soothing encouragement and not Eric's logical assurances, that got me to the top. We were often to have arguments about 'difficult' climbs during our expeditions. Fear of heights in some degree must be familiar to everyone who has been among mountains.

Presumably the real climber gains confidence as he learns the technique – learns to control his feet, his hands and the rope. He must learn mental control, too. Although Eric never asked me to tackle anything that he considered severe, he did, quite rightly, ask me to try small climbs which he knew were easy and absolutely safe. He was convinced that with practice I should learn how to move and also to control my unreasonable fears. It was like our arguments about riding and I found it hard to follow his advice or to believe his assurances. But in this case the rewards seemed to me so much greater that I tried harder to conquer my fears. I only introduce the sorry story of my personal cowardice to explain that 'difficult' climbs relate to my own low standard. (p83)

Gyalgen was a man and understood that it was not logic that was needed. So is it only western-educated men who believe that logic is superior? Certainly, with the Sherpa's approach Diana was able in the end to enjoy something special:

> The reward of my first 'climb' was very great. To the north and south snow peaks stood high and sparkling against a bright sky. The soft misty-blue folds of the lower mountains merged imperceptibly into the deep red-browns of the smaller hills. On either side flat deserts and wide river valleys rolled up towards our range. The hills immediately round us were a complicated pattern of shapes. They rose in sharp and delicate spires, in heavy blocks, in pyramids like those of Egypt; all were divided by the huge canyons. From our narrow ledge we peered down into one of these terrifying ravines. It took nine seconds for a stone we dropped to hit the bottom.
>
> My enjoyment of the huge scene was a little spoilt by the prospect of having to go down again, always the disadvantage of climbing up. This time I chose the slanting shelf. With the rope to prevent me from slipping and two men to guide me from in front, I crept carefully down on my seat. It was an easy descent and I regretted my silly apprehension. (pp83–4)

Eric's account of that same climb reads:

> The next morning, before starting back to Kashgar, we followed another gorge, and again, although with considerably more difficulty, succeeded in reaching the watershed at a minor peak, some 10,500 feet high. The storm had passed, and though the wind was still strong, the air was very clear. The same terrific rockscape lay to the south at our feet, again enclosed by an outer line of towers. Beyond stood the great peaks of the Pamirs looking incredibly high and sharp. Northward, across a wide expanse of desert hills, red and gold, the western ranges of the Tien Shan were arranged in a vast arc, mauve below, dazzling white above in their mantle of freshly fallen snow. (p101)

That was not the only occasion when Gyalgen's Oriental sensitivity suited Diana's temperament better:

> Our last day was particularly strenuous as Eric and Gyalgen were led ever higher and higher in their excitement, while I panted in the rear ...
>
> In places snow lay deep and when I floundered up to my waist Gyalgen came a long way down again to rescue me. Whatever his faults in the house, on these mountain trips I loved him dearly. He never seemed to tire; he treated all my outbursts of despair and cowardice with calm and encouragement; he stoutly maintained that I was almost capable of tackling Everest; he would usually wait to see if I could manage some narrow ledge or airy corner. (p112)

On another occasion the consulate tailor joined the party and Diana had a comrade:

> The hill-side was steep and crumbling; both the tailor and I were put on the rope with Gyalgen, to give us moral support. I was glad to have someone with me, if possible, more nervous than I.
> ... Down the dripping rock wall, through the dark passages, along the unwholesome by-pass to the series of big scrambles we went. The tailor, Sola [the dog] and I again had to be helped. I felt sorry for the tailor because whereas I was expected to need help, he was heavily chaffed and mocked by the others. (pp86–7)

In spite of his apparent carelessness about Diana's needs when climbing, it is important to note how Eric felt about her and mountains, for of the Kungar peak, which he had known before, he wrote, 'I had the exquisite excitement of introducing it to my wife ...' (p106).

The days of exploration of the kind that had allowed Samuel Baker to prove himself a man were in the past; new forms of machismo were perpetually being sought. It was not always Eric and mountains; Diana noted of the society in which she moved in Kashgar:

> Prussian officers, I have read, used to be trained to drink. With typical efficiency, they made what should be a pleasure into a solemn duty. Judging from my small experience amongst the Russians in Sinkiang, they seem to have a similar idea, but omit the efficient training. Drinking became a duty. There was no escape from the ceremony of endless 'toasts'. At my first few dinner parties in our Consulate I made the uneducated mistake of sipping my wine as I felt inclined, and imagining that my guests would do the same. The only toasts I was accustomed to were standard ones at the end of the meal. I discovered that neither the Russians nor the Chinese drank except when invited. They must have considered me very inhospitable. An invitation meant draining the glass to the bottom and any reluctance was regarded as an insult. Men who preferred wines to vodka or brandy were labelled 'women' by the Russians. Our non-drinking Mussulman staff never escaped this epithet and monotonous mockery. The whole question of alcohol began increasingly to exasperate me. Eventually I abandoned all efforts to please, I drank exactly as much as I chose to drink and no more. (p103)

A picture is forming not so much of a woman putting herself down in the traditional way, but of one down-to-earth in a new, post-war, second-half-of-the-twentieth-century way:

> The surrounding hills were low and lacked grandeur, there was nothing to relieve the monotony and only one thing occupied my mind – a cup of tea. It was one of those patches, which one is inclined to forget when thinking or talking, so glibly, of the joys of mountain treks. There were

inevitably moments when one was too tired, cold or hot, hungry or merely irritable, to enjoy the general experience. Living a simple life the simple things loomed large and important. On many occasions the scenery had to be very impressive indeed, to take precedence, in my mind, over a passionate longing for a drink of water or an end to the day's march. Again it was a question of mental control, and I certainly did not have a sufficient share of it. I often wondered whether men like Gyalgen, Kapak, or any of the Kirghiz who accompanied us, had more self-control than I had, or whether they were more tough, or perhaps, more insensitive. They appeared to react much less quickly to changing temperatures and while I would put jerseys on and take them off a dozen times in the day, they would wear the same padded suit in the cold dawn and the heat of the sun. Such details as a limping horse, swarming flies or a smoke-filled tent, appeared to leave them unmoved. Perhaps this insensitivity results in mental dullness in other directions; but I often envied it, and I suspect could copy it without much damage to my fancied intelligence. (p140)

What seems more likely – and Diana has already suggested it – is that the comforts of civilisation are beginning to create a softness in the traveller. Eric fought against it with his mountains but Diana no longer had the cultural incentive to struggle. She faces the ultimate question squarely, in a way that the hardier Lucy Atkinson of an earlier age did not have to:

Because one likes simple things oneself; because one finds native ways interesting; because it is 'picturesque' to see slow ploughing with an ox and a donkey yoked together, the dignified camels, the women sitting on their doorsteps spinning, two men making a false breeze over a satisfying pile of wheat, while a third tosses it high to free the chaff; because one sees a people apparently unhurried, unharassed by 'modern' progress, one tends to laud a primitive way of life. It is like looking back and thinking how delightful it would have been to have lived in the eighteenth century. But like the hero in the play, *Berkeley Square*, one would inevitably find all sorts of unattractive manners and habits, many discomforts to which one is no longer accustomed, if one attempted to live that primitive life oneself. The simple people of Sinkiang may have advantages over us, but forced to live their life one would, no doubt, lose a good deal of one's rosy romanticism about the subject. Eric once asked me if I would rather lead the life of a Kirghiz woman or that of a restricted English housewife. Personally, I regard the latter with considerable horror; I tend to idealize the former. But to be honest, I do not know if I could discard all the ordinary comforts, advantages and entertainments of an English life, for the narrow, though free and open-air existence of a nomad. (p132)

Certainly it was not a Kirghiz need to climb mountains: as Diana remarks when they are being sheltered by some nomads, 'Why we came there to struggle up ice mountains and weary ourselves among the hills, for no apparent gain, must have been a question the Kirghiz never answered' (p165). As for the watcher watched, Diana acquired a refreshingly inverted view about that:

> Becoming part of a moving circus, takes a little getting used to. At first I felt annoyed by this constant curiosity and the complete lack of privacy. But it was as much a part of Asian travel as the desert or the dust – something one must accept. I became so accustomed to the interested crowds that I was quite offended if, by chance, people did not gather round to stare; as if our travelling show had had a poor reception. Only at Kuntigmes I lost my temper with one woman. Her curiosity knew no limits and having examined everything I possessed, she began gently poking me; presumably to find out if English women were formed in the same way as Kirghiz women. (p174)

Little had changed over the years in that respect and the same applied to other aspects of female society. Diana's first account of experience with Islamic women (apart from any she met as a girl in India) comes during the crossing of the Karakorams from India to Turkestan:

> The next day we had a long, slow, gasping climb up to the 17,500 ft Khardung Pass. There was a narrow, well defined path, but as we crawled up I began to feel the unpleasant effects of altitude, and each step was an effort. I was too nervous to ride. The way down was even worse and oddly enough my headache and sickness increased. All pretence of a path failed, and there was a sharp descent over rock and ice. The ponies, slipping and falling, were ruthlessly kicked and lashed; boxes and baggage rolled down the slope. We began to realize that Mohammed Kurban had provided too few men for the number of ponies. The caravan was quite out of control. Through all this pandemonium struggled the dispenser's wife, a young Mohammedan girl in the cumbersome purdah garment which covered her like a tent, and only allowed her a small mesh to see through. The entire journey she sat on her pony, thus heavily draped, clutching her baby, sick and cold, without any interest in the country or any knowledge of how long her agony would last, a gallant and incongruous figure. She rode over places which I found far too alarming. Once she and her baby were thrown to the ground when their pony tripped and fell. I longed to help her but she spoke only Pushtu; and she seemed numbed into a pathetic resignation. (p28)

It was a slightly different situation in Kashgar:

> In all the celebrations of Christmas Day the women could take no part, shut away by their Mussulman rule of purdah. So I decided to give them a 'purdah party' on Boxing Day. I had no idea of the number of women hidden away in the rabbit warren of the Consulate. I simply laid out as many cakes as remained from Christmas Day and opened a tin of cigarettes 'in case anyone smoked'. The servants were forbidden to come near the

drawing room, and one or two more unorthodox of the women offered to bring in the tea.

Before the first purdah party I gave, Mrs Chu and I waited until, very late, the guests began to trickle in, shedding their long white coats and little veils, in the hall. Everybody had made an effort to put on their best clothes ...

Soon all the seats were taken, the tea and cakes were rapidly disappearing, and I found that everyone smoked! Cakes and cigarettes were often secreted inside the coat, for future use. The trickle had grown to a flood; more and more women poured in; I and my helpers worked frantically; searching the house for chairs; impatiently ordering more tea from the men in the kitchen; opening new tins of cigarettes; and finally snatching a secret store of cakes, which had been kept by the servants, and hurling them into the fray.

There was no stiff silence and restraint. The room bulged with women; those who had had no chair sat on the floor; everyone talked at once and screamed across to friends opposite; helpers picked their way about with trays of cakes and tea, falling over crawling babies or bumping into each other, so that tea poured on the carpet and cakes were trampled underfoot. The babies were being fed by their mothers, or were howling, others chewed any available cake, ash tray and cigarette, or made a quiet pool to add to the general fun.

Gradually the storm died down, the food was finished, the cigarette tins were empty, and the exhausted helpers sipped their tea.

Then someone suggested dancing. A woman fetched her long two-stringed 'guitar', and one or two reluctant guests were persuaded to perform. The two elaborately dressed and elderly wives of the Jemadar opened the show with a slow shuffling dance; a plain but self-possessed girl sang one of the harsh Turki songs; and finally two pregnant women took the floor and shuffled, too. But the interest was half-hearted and the performers embarrassed. Mrs Chu spoke Turki and I asked her to announce the party was over, how delighted I had been to see them all and so goodbye. Everyone thanked me profusely and streamed into the hall where veils were carefully put on again before going out.

Lhakpa and Gyalgen were disgusted with the chaos left in the drawing room and railed against the greed, dirtiness and even dishonesty of all Turki women ...

Although I counted ash trays to see if any were missing, I enjoyed the unaffected hearty atmosphere of my purdah parties far more than the stiff, embarrassed parties of men. (pp91–3)

There are advantages and disadvantages to meeting a 'historical' character. So enchanting and sympathetic a view of her purdah parties had Diana presented that one of my first questions to her had to be, 'Did you make a particular point of interesting yourself in women and their concerns during your time in Kashgar?'

'No, not really,' she replied disarmingly.

She was 30 years old when she left Kashgar after 18 months there; she was approaching her seventies when I met her, exactly 40 years later, and a lot had changed. She had done some living since then, learnt some harsh lessons about men and women and their relations, and her reactions had become more woman-aware than they were when she published her book in 1950. By then she had joined Eric at Kun Ming in Yunnan Province where he had become Consul General just before the Chinese Revolution of 1949. She left precipitately in January 1951, three-month-old John in her arms, five-year-old Nicky clutching her skirts. Eric stayed behind to maintain a British presence. In 1955 Diana and Eric divorced.

Eric's description in his autobiography of the breakup of their marriage and how he realigned his life is of a frankness it is impossible to imagine from, say, Percy Sykes. Eric died in 1977. More details about Eric and the women in his life, including Diana, are contained in Peter Steele's biography, *Eric Shipton: Everest and Beyond* (1998).

Meeting Diana, by then Diana Drummond and living alone, and talking about everything under the sun, particularly men, put Eric at a disadvantage – not that she was malicious; they remained friendly until his death – but because, learning of their split, enjoying the warmth of her personality, discussing women's issues, I could not resist looking for hints of things to come in their books. They are like a trail.

Without having met one of the characters, would this chapter have been different – probably. Recreating history and biography are also a question of perception.

Diana closed her book – in the process of being reissued by Oxford University Press when we met:

This book, begun in a place where time was unrestricted, has had to be finished in the harassing domestic routine of a child and a house. It is difficult to think of two existences more different. How I long to see Rosa Beg's cheerful face and to hear Gyalgen explaining with elaborate reason why he has used up the week's butter ration.

But one must go forward to new experiences, only looking back in deep appreciation of the interest, the fun, the beauty, the novelty and the hazard one has had in a past experience. (p219)

Having lived, as it were, with so many women in Kashgar, I had to go there myself in 1992. I thoroughly enjoyed the Sunday Market which all visitors then went for but, as emerges from the chapter 'Spirit of Place' in *Chinese Footprints: Exploring Women's History in China, Hong Kong and Macau* (1997), Chinibagh lives more kindly in my mind through the accounts of my predecessors than it does in my memory. And as I end that chapter,

How then does one define 'spirit of place'? To describe a place as 'steeped in history' is not only a cliché, it is also misleading. 'Spirit of place' comes not from a place being dunked in history for a while to stew; it comes instead from the people who have been steeped in that place over time, as if they were peppercorns or lemon rind. Their aura, or essence, pervades it then, and now. That may be obvious in a place like the Forbidden City in Beijing, where every marble alleyway reeks of what has happened there over centuries. In Chinibagh today, 'spirit of place' may have to be absorbed through the mind's eye – something in addition to imagination – of the beholder. Training the muscles of the mind's eye is one of the pleasurable exercises of the historian. (p152)

11 – Conclusion

… that the world shou'd see to how much better purpose the Ladys Travel than their Lords, and that whilst it is surfeited with Male Travels, all the same Tone and stuft with the same Trifles, a *Lady* has the skill to strike out a New Path and to embellish a worn-out Subject with a variety of fresh and elegant Entertainment.

Mary Astell, draft preface, 1724, to Lady Mary
Wortley Montagu, *Turkish Embassy Letters* (Halsband 1956 p467)

… who does not know the difference between their books – especially their books of travels – the gentleman's either dull and matter-of-fact, or off-hand and superficial, with a heavy disquisition where we look for a light touch, or a foolish pun where we expect a reverential sentiment, either requiring too much trouble of the reader, or too much carelessness in the writer – and the lady's all ease, animation, vivacity, with the tact to dwell upon what you most want to know, and the sense to pass over what she does not know herself … Ladies have been known to write the dullest and emptiest books – a fact for which there is no accounting – and gentlemen the most delightful, but here, probably, if the truth were told, their wives or daughters helped them.

Lady Eastlake, 'Lady Travellers', *Quarterly Review*,
vol. 76 (June), pp98–137, (London, John Murray, 1845)

An Unpretending Narrative

In the Introduction I raised several questions concerning style, content, perception, perspective and focus. Taking 'An Unpretending Narrative' as a theme, and using the writing of two couples who have not so far had a voice of their own as a starting point, it is time to suggest some conclusions. The familiar travelling couples will supply their own echo.

In 1917, two American journalists, wife and husband, Louise Bryant (1885–1936) and John Reed (1887–1920), each working for a different newspaper syndicate, arrived in Russia just before the Bolshevik Revolution and watched it take place. His account – *Ten Days that Shook the World* (1919; **1977**; 2006) – is an often-reprinted classic; hers – *Six Red Months in Russia* (1918; **1982**; 2002) – is reprinted but is little noted in the annals of the Revolution, in spite of its unique interviews with revolutionary women. Louise and John go to Moscow for a mass burial of revolutionaries against the Kremlin wall, though neither suggests that the other is with them. He writes of a moment in the ceremony:

Slowly the marchers came with their coffins to the entrance of the grave, and the bearers clambered with their burdens and went down into the pit. Many of them were women – squat, strong proletarian women. Behind the dead came other women – women young and broken, or old, wrinkled

11.1   John Reed and Louise Bryant, 1918
(courtesy of Houghton Library, Harvard
University (MS AM1091 (1401))

women making noises like hurt animals, who tried to follow their sons and husbands into the Brotherhood Grave, and shrieked when compassionate hands restrained them. The poor love each other so! (pp229–30)

And she sees it her way:

> Women all around began to sob and one quite near me tried to hurl herself after a coffin as it was being lowered. Her thin coating of civilisation dropped from her in a moment. She forgot the revolution, forgot the future of mankind, remembered only her lost one.
>
> With all her frenzied strength she fought against the friends who tried to restrain her. Crying out the name of the man in the coffin, she screamed, bit, scratched like a wounded wild thing until she was finally carried away moaning and half unconscious. Tears rolled down the faces of the big soldiers. (pp190–1)

Marika and Robin Hanbury-Tenison travelled round Indonesia in 1973, to many of the places visited by Anna and Henry Forbes nearly a century earlier. He was researching the plight of minority people in his capacity as Chairman of Survival International; Marika, who died of cancer in 1982, aged only 44, accompanied him, as she had done to Brazil a couple of years before, purely out of interest, though she was a professional woman – the cookery editor of a national newspaper. He writes in *A Pattern of Peoples* (1975):

> In the evening we reached a Chinese trader's house where we stopped and fed on mouse deer and rice. Most of the Chinese have been forced to move from the rivers of Western Kalimantan to settlements around Pontianak where life is not easy for them and they are said to be cheated and abused, their possessions confiscated and their liberty threatened. We, ourselves, had seen a frail old Chinese lady surrounded by a crowd of shouting youths, who had jostled and teased her while she defended herself with her umbrella. All this had come about since the coup of 1965 when many Chinese were massacred as suspected communists. Guerrilla activity in the north, as well as jealousy for their financial domination continues to make their life difficult. (p85)

11.2   Marika and Robin Hanbury-Tenison (courtesy of Robin Hanbury-Tenison)

And her version in *A Slice of Spice* (1975):

> Coming back, we saw a scene which brought home to us how much the Chinese were hated throughout the country, and although we had felt the tensions already, this was the first time we saw open hostility between Indonesians and Chinese.
>
> A bunch of students crowded onto the ferry, carrying bundles of school books, their clothes meticulously clean, although many of them looked as though they were about to fall to pieces through endless washing.
>
> An old Chinese lady stood in the centre; her small feet were planted widely apart to bear the weight of a heavy body which sagged onto swollen ankles above minute embroidered slippers. She wore the baggy pants and

high-necked shirt, criss-crossed frogging, of her country. Her hair was so tightly scraped back into a dull grey bun that it accentuated the naked look of lashless, narrow eyes in a wrinkled, jaundice-coloured skin.

I did not see what started it off; we were just aware of a sudden scuffling and some of the older Indonesian students began to bait the old lady, shouting insults at her in the now familiar, high-pitched tone of the Indonesian language. The others quickly joined in, screaming and yelling, surrounding her in a circle, like the savages they despised in their jungles. The other passengers watched impassively and we did not dare to intervene, although we were both itching to, as the Chinese lady stood her ground, ignoring their obvious taunts, staring in silent stoicism at her miniature feet.

When the ferry landed, the boys had worked themselves up into a state of mob mania and, as she crossed the planks onto the shore, were brave enough to start touching her clothes, and jostle her along the heat-steaming tarmac. Her temper snapped and she began screeching back at them in Chinese, flourishing her umbrella like a female Errol Flynn and beating around her in a really fearsome way. By the time she reached the end of the street, the crowd had dispersed and I had the feeling that the prices in Chin's, or Chee's or whatever shop it was that her family monopolized, would be rising within the next twenty-four hours and credit would be cut to a minimum. (pp62–3)

Those four extracts follow a pattern of contrast already established in earlier chapters: the woman and the man in each pair have written about the same incident but they have seen it in a rather different way. The women write, as it were, from the inside, tightly focused; they experience what they write about or they identify with what they are seeing. They write in detail, intimately, with immediacy. The men write as observers, with a larger canvas, and from a wider angle.

In a finely-crafted email giving me permission to use their extracts, Robin Hanbury-Tenison writes that 'they demonstrate clearly what I have always said: that [Marika] was a much better writer than me' (24 August 2011).

Work continues by linguists, literary critics and feminists on the comparison between how women and men express themselves and what, if any, significance any difference has. In the early stages of such studies, they looked mainly at the spoken word and fiction. Although I am by no means the first to publish an exploration of travel writing, much in this Conclusion was drafted ahead of later studies. In preparing now for publication, I do not ignore later work, such as the marriage of gender and imperial history, exemplified by Susan Morgan's analysis of Anna Forbes' travel account, with its 'feminine imperial rhetoric' (p71), nor the feminist theory that it is difficult to make generalisations about the nature and behaviour of women, but I do stick to the courage of what my own reading originally suggested.

Sara Mills, writing of 1850–1930 in *Discourses of Difference: An Analysis of Women's Travel Writing and Colonialism* (1991), posits an explanation for several passages I quote throughout my exploration:

Because of their oppressive socialisation and marginal position in relation to imperialism, despite their generally privileged class position, women writers tended to concentrate on descriptions of people as individuals, rather than on statements about race as a whole. (p3)

It is a tempting theory, but I'm not sure that I have provided evidence for it. I think women wrote about individuals, rather than the general, for other reasons. And my primary concern is not with the theoretical and analytical. I have lived too long and intimately with these travellers for that. I have accepted them, the women at least, on their own terms. What I feel they usefully provide us with are insights for each reader to pick up and react to.

And there are many ways of interpreting. Billie Melman writes of what she calls co-writing in the chapter 'An Orientalist Couple: Anne Blunt, Wilfrid Scawen Blunt and the pilgrimage to Najd' (1995): 'Blunt himself is presented in the preface [of *Bedouin Tribes of the Euphrates* (1879)] and throughout the book as the analytical traveller, capable of abstract thought (juxtaposed with Lady Anne's passion for details)' (p281). For her, that is Wilfrid Blunt's way of making clear his superior position within their relationship.

H.V.F. Winstone's (2005) biography of Anne Blunt suggests what her passion for details signifies when he writes of that earlier book, 'In six months she produced the first part of a two volume work of surprising authority on a part of the world they had as yet explored only cursorily' (p145). There, Anne is the scholar. Her husband's less than laudable part in the book's production is elaborated on later in this sub-heading.

So far I have compared the accounts of women and men who travelled together to the same place and, except those co-writers in the Introduction (and including the Blunts), wrote separately. The women are in a clearly defined situation with the perspective and perceptions that it brings. But, in exploring the travels and travel writing of women and men, there is an element so far missing. Doreen Ingrams wrote in response to a copy of the draft Introduction and Conclusion:

There seems to me to be such a great difference between a woman who travels alone and a woman who follows her husband that a comparison between two such women writing about the same period would be interesting. (29 October 1987)

Perhaps we can think of the woman travelling without a man as someone against whom to measure both the travelling companion and the man.

Paul Fussell in *Abroad*, travel analysis almost entirely of men travellers, looks at Evelyn Waugh as a travel writer. He suggests that the way Waugh made the day-to-day routine of travel fascinating was through 'sheer style' or, as Waugh himself put it, 'Letting phrase engender phrase.' Fussell continues:

Someone is sure to ask why I've not dealt with the travel books of Freya Stark, and I will have to answer that to write a distinguished travel book you have to be equally interested in (1) the travel and (2) the writing. In Stark's works, admirable as the travel has been, the dimension of delight in language and disposition, in all the literary contrivances, isn't there. Her reward is due not from criticism but from the Royal Geographical Society, which has properly conferred upon her medals and grants. She could never say, as Waugh does, 'I regard writing ... as an exercise in language, and with this I am obsessed.' She could never say, as Waugh does, 'Style alone can keep [the writer] from being bored with his own work.' (p197)

And of D.H. Lawrence, Fussell proclaims that, 'Like all literary travel writers worth reading, he played a spume of imagination upon empirical phenomena, generating subtle emotional forms and structures to contain them' (p155). But Doreen continues in her letter:

Incidentally, I disagree entirely with Fussell! Freya was obsessed by language and style – hence, as she told me, she wrote her first book, *The Valleys of the Assassins*, nine times – & I feel sure she will want to be remembered as a good writer rather than as a traveller who wrote.

11.3 Freya Stark on her desert travels, 1930s
(from Moorehead, *Freya Stark*)

In 'Travel Writing and Gender' (2002), Susan Bassnett confirms that Freya succeeded, describing 'an ability to write beautiful, often lyrical descriptive prose'.

Freya Stark (1893–1993), a professional traveller and writer who usually travelled alone (and notably in high heels), is an obvious candidate for comparison; she reinforces her suitability when she writes in *A Winter In Arabia* (1940) of Doreen Ingrams, to whom, with Harold, she dedicated the book:

(She) would come in from the office where she combined the functions of Treasurer, Private, Political and Oriental Secretary, and Chief Typist; she would give a passing look to her adopted daughter sitting over its mug of milk in the morning sunshine. (p61)

Doreen is a product of her situation; Freya of hers.

It happens that for the first part of that book Freya has two travelling companions, an archaeologist and a geologist, but they are both women. Freya has been to the area before and is known by the people; the presence of the others does not change her status.

To prevent the possibility of one woman alone giving a false impression, I have chosen another in similar circumstances. Several of our travellers were, in previous chapters, in Chinese Turkestan at much the same time as Mildred Cable (1878–1952) who was there between 1923 and 1938. She travelled as a professional – a missionary in her own right who had studied science at London University – in the company of two other missionaries, Evangeline and Francesca French.

They were typical of a transition that gathered pace as the nineteenth century progressed from missionary wives such as Maggie Paton, seen only as appendages however hard they worked beside their husband, to paid single missionary women in full charge. Martha Vicinus has graphically described the process of middle-class women escaping 'the confining domestic world of married women' as 'out of the garden, out of idleness, out of ignorance, and into adventure' (Haggis 1995 p51). Mildred Cable wrote a string of books about these 'adventures', the best known and loved of which is *The Gobi Desert* (1942).

With the introduction of Freya and Mildred, it is possible to compare the writing of unattached women and that of our travelling companions and their men, to see how different it might be.

Freya Stark writes about the hospitality of Sayyid Abu Bekr's house in Seiyun which Doreen and Harold Ingrams have already described (they call him Seiyid Bubakr):

... the splendours of Sayyid Abu Bekr's new house, which I had seen beginning, had blossomed into what their owner must feel sadly now and then is almost a hotel. All travelling Europeans, including every member of the Air Force, stay there, except Harold [Ingrams] who prefers, when he can, to live with the sayyid in his old and less sophisticated home. Here we too spent some days enjoying ash-trays and velvet chairs, mosquito-netted beds, and the hours of Big Ben on the wireless, with electric light splashed round us in a regardless way – till nine o'clock, when it went out. A row of little bulbs runs round the court, each one supported on a pseudo-Greek column, as it were Atlas with a pingpong ball upon his shoulder. Gone is the Eastern charm of Seiyun and its pleasant conversations with Leisure all around. Only the bath, an Eastern institution by birth, has retained its oriental delights; ... (p21)

It is not fanciful to see there an edge, not so obvious in the other two accounts, which comes from a travel writer who has trained herself not only to notice every detail but to describe in a style that bites, one not about gender but another level of perspective and perception. The perspective has something to do with past experience, and that includes formal and informal education.

Freya Stark was born in Paris where both her parents were studying art; she spoke three languages by the time she was five. Later she lived in Devon and still later her mother ran a silk factory in Italy, where Freya worked. During the First World War she was a nurse on the Italian front. In Italy she also learnt Arabic from a monk and subsequently took a degree in Arabic at London University. In 1928 she started travelling alone in the East – wandering ever further east, Lebanon, Syria, Iraq and Iran – and writing about her travels. She had already visited and written about the Hadhramaut when, aged 44, she returned in 1937 – a mature and experienced woman, traveller and writer. Her short-lived marriage was still to come. Her independence of mind and movement were unchallenged (though bouts of ill-health meant that she had to be rescued when far from medical help, once by the Royal Air Force).

The education of travelling couples, and their professional backgrounds, is revealing. Lady Fanshawe (1625–1680), wife of Charles II's ambassador to Spain in 1664, wrote in her autobiography that she learnt sewing, French, singing, lute, virginals, dancing. She talks of 'my mother's education of me which was with all the advantages that time afforded' (p32). But her mother died when Ann was 15. Sir Richard Fanshawe (1608–1666) went to the famous school kept by Thomas Farnaby in Cripplegate; from there he went to Jesus College, Cambridge, in 1623, and so to the Inner Temple. But, law proving distasteful, he went abroad to learn foreign languages and thus entered the diplomatic world.

Rose de Freycinet (1794–1832) was educated at an institution for demoiselles of which her mother was the head. In 1817, Louis de Freycinet (1779–1842) was captain of a French ship with the responsibility of bringing back to France not only *la gloire* at that time of intensive naval exploration (from the 1760s) but also an amplification of the world's knowledge of physical geography, and all that meant. He had already worked in the Ministry of Marine on editing and publishing the reports and atlas of a previous French expedition.

Lady Londonderry (1800–1865), who accompanied her husband to Russia in 1836 on a semi-diplomatic mission, had a succession of unsatisfactory, often cruel governesses. The Marquis of Londonderry (1778–1854) was educated at Eton and was then commissioned into the army, later becoming a Member of Parliament, as well as an ambassador.

Two of the women, Ella Sykes and Eleanor Lattimore, had been to university; the former's Oxford education was limited to what was available to women there towards the end of the nineteenth century. Lucy Atkinson, daughter of a school teacher, was a governess. Maggie Paton was the daughter of a church minister who wrote and published, so she had presumably received some education. Anna Forbes spoke French and German before she went to Indonesia, but did not know Latin as Henry did. Fanny Stevenson married for the first time at 17; her editor does not mention education before then, though she did become an art student at the age of 35. Ella Maillart spoke Russian, picked up on her travels, and wrote in English as well as French, her mother-tongue (though *Forbidden Journey* is a translation). Doreen Ingrams ended up, too young, at a Swiss finishing school, and was thereafter self-educated. Diana Shipton went to several schools from which 'I emerged totally uneducated; I would love to have gone to university.'

All the men were formally educated – Atkinson and Paton by their own efforts after an educationally-deprived childhood. While Eleanor Holgate Lattimore had been to Northwestern University of Illinois, Owen's university life was to post-date his first travels; but he did go to an English public school.

Barbara Greene makes a usefully revealing remark concerning informal education, or socialisation, in a letter she wrote to me about her understanding and falling in with Graham Greene's wishes:

> It had nothing to do with my education as a girl. After all I had three brothers and I was educated for six years in a co-educational boarding school. Intellectual opportunities were always alike for both sexes during my childhood and we girls never for one moment thought of ourselves as different from the boys. Later on of course the boys had to put their minds more on to their future careers whilst we girls rarely bothered about careers and were able to continue to float along and live a pretty superficial life up to the time of marriage. (2 January 1988)

All the men were professional: they earned their living or depended for their reputation upon their reason for travelling. Few of the women were. Lucy Atkinson gave up being a governess on marriage and Doreen Ingrams an acting career. Eleanor Lattimore subsumed her ambition into that of her husband. Louise Bryant continued as a journalist after marriage. Ella Maillart, journalist, traveller and writer, did not marry.

An easily overlooked aspect of perception (linked with experience) is age difference. It is interesting to note that between the married couples who travelled together there tended to be a gap which might be relevant. Sir Richard Fanshawe and Louis de Freycinet were 16 years older than their wives. Between the Londonderrys there were 22 years; the Atkinsons, 18; Patons, 17; Bakers, 21; Ingrams, nine; Shiptons, ten. Fanny Stevenson was ten years older than her husband, Eleanor Lattimore six years older than hers, and Ella Sykes and Ella Maillart four years older than their companions. Barbara Greene deliberately lowered her age to excuse any defects in her published account.

Lack of education or experience does not, of itself, suggest less effective style, nor less interesting content. It may, however, suggest a difference – one that tends to veer away from erudition. The issue has been raised, particularly in the Sykes chapter and the one on Ella Maillart and Peter Fleming, of how much a man's educational background affected his relations with his female companion and how far it allowed him to manipulate the local culture for his own ends when he travelled. That background can also affect his perception or, at least, the reproduction of it on paper.

Annie and Thomas Brassey, during their 1876/77 journey round the world in their yacht *Sunbeam*, stop in Hawaii. As they wait to see the famous high divers, on almost the only occasion that Thomas (Rugby, Oxford – law and modern history – and the House of Commons) describes people, he writes (contained in Eardley-Wilmot):

A number of the more youthful inhabitants of Hilo, of both sexes, entertained us with a display of the art of swimming and diving. One active girl leaped repeatedly from a height of twenty feet into the river. In the intervals between their performances, these amphibious people climbed up the rocks that overhung the river, where they gathered themselves into the most picturesque groups of bronze-coloured yet shapely humanity.

> Fronte sub adversa scopulis pendentibus antrum;
> Intus aquae dulces, vivoque sedilia saxo,
> Nympharum domus.

There were few garments to mar the symmetry of their forms, but there was not the slightest taint of immodesty in the scene. A sculptor, looking on with the cultivated eye of a trained artist, would have revelled in the graceful movement of the forms displayed before him; while a painter would have appreciated not less the harmonious colours of the picture, in which the olive flesh-tints formed such an admirable contrast to the dark lava rocks on which the swimmers reclined. Many a laborious student of the Academy has racked his brain in the vain effort to produce a composition, on canvas or in marble, with not one-half the beauty or the truth to nature of these fortuitous assemblages of graceful figures. (p171)

While Annie, whose *Oxford Dictionary of National Biography* does not mention education, is at her most uncontrived, or 'unpretending' in *Voyage in the Sunbeam* (1899; 1984):

We found a large party assembled, watching half the population of Hilo disporting themselves in, upon, and beneath the water. They climbed the

11.4   Lord Brassey at the wheel
(from Brassey *The 'Sunbeam' RYS*)

almost perpendicular rocks on the opposite side of the stream, took headers, and footers, and siders from any height under five-and-twenty feet, dived, swam in every conceivable attitude, and without any apparent exertion, deep under the water, or upon its surface. (p271)

In the Introduction, Thomas Brassey's description of how Annie wrote raised the question of the conditions and circumstances of writing as a possible influence on the style produced. The accounts of many of the women were written at the time, as diaries or letters, and published soon thereafter or long after by others (in the case of Rose de Freycinet, Lady Londonderry, Effie Ruskin, Florence Baker and Fanny Stevenson) with little change. Anna Forbes' account was, three years after their return, 'pieced together from letters written home, from my journal, and from recollections' (pviii). Ann Fanshawe, Ella Sykes, Louise Bryant, Ella Maillart, Doreen Ingrams and Marika Hanbury-Tenison wrote later narrative accounts based on their contemporaneous record. Diana Shipton wrote a narrative account in Kashgar from her diary. With the exception of Robert Louis Stevenson's *Vailima Letters* (1972), Owen Lattimore's earlier *The Desert Road to Turkestan*, and Nathaniel Hawthorne's Journal, the men's accounts were written up afterwards.

Hawthorne's 1997 editors, Thomas Woodson and Bill Ellis, show how that couple, at least, functioned as they travelled round England from his post as American consul in Liverpool between 1853 and 1857: 'It is hard to know how much husband and wife shared the separate accounts of the day as they sat down to write each evening.' As Sophia wrote to their daughter Una, 'Papa wrote in his journal and I to you till half past ten, when we went soberly to bed' (p725). It is not as easy to compare their separate published accounts as it is of those who have chapters of their own.

Anyone who has travelled knows that writing a diary while travelling is tough work, particularly at the end of a long day, particularly when you are not feeling well. Writing letters to a friend or a relative is spontaneous, and informal and influenced by similar restraints, including how tired one's arm gets.

If someone else is keeping a diary or writing regular letters, the temptation to let one's own slide, for both parties to rely on one account, is overwhelming. The most revealing comments on this aspect of literary endeavour come in relation to Fanny Stevenson. Charles Neider, the editor of Fanny's letters, writes in his introduction to *Our Samoan Adventure* (1956):

> Fanny was in the habit of keeping diaries partly for her own use and pleasure, partly so they could be used when needed to refresh Louis's memory of events and places for the benefit of his various literary projects, essays, novels, letters public and private. (pp12–13)

And Sidney Colvin, the recipient of Louis's *Vailima Letters* (1895), and their editor, writes:

> During the period of his odyssey in the South Seas, from August 1888 until the Spring of 1890, the remoteness and inaccessibility of the scenes he visited inevitably interrupted all correspondence for months together; and when at long intervals a packet reached us, the facts and circumstances of his wanderings were to be gathered from the admirable letters of Mrs Stevenson (who had this feminine accomplishment in perfection) rather than from his own. (p16)

Rose de Freycinet's editor, Marnie Bassett, writes in *Realms and Islands* (1962), 'She kept a journal that was probably used by de Freycinet for many details of his narrative account' (pxiv). Robin Hanbury-Tenison, who remarried following Marika's death, and has travelled extensively with Louella, often on horseback, is happy to admit on reading this section, 'I have ... relied greatly on Marika's and Louella's meticulous keeping of diaries'. (It is worth noting that, over nearly two centuries, the de Freycinets, the Hanbury-Tenisons and the Forbes all visited the island now known as East Timor or Timor Leste.)

It may well be more congenial and inspirational to sit down and write a polished travel account from the diaries and letters written by your companion which supplement your own terse notes and fading memory. Not only that, men did not always like writing the descriptive bits; it shows in Henry Forbes' account that Anna's observations formed the basis for at least some of his

11.5   Rose and Louis de Freycinet arrive at Dili, Portuguese Timor
(from Bassett, *Realms and Islands*)

descriptive passages. And both Xavier Hommaire de Hell and Percy Sykes quite openly left their companions to write the descriptive parts of joint books – so that they could get on with the clever bits.

Whatever moral stand one wishes to take over the less scrupulous borrowing, it is as well to note that it is in a literary tradition. According to Hilary Simpson (in Dale Spender's *Man Made Language*, 1980), D.H. Lawrence, for example, 'solicited notes and reminiscences from Jessie [Burrows], from his wife Frieda, from Mabel Dodge Luhan and others ... he also took over women's manuscripts and rewrote them, as in the cases of Helen Corke and Mollie Skinner.' In *Sons and Lovers*, 'It is clear that some of the most vivid scenes in the novel derive from Jessie's reminiscences. Lawrence often takes sentences directly from her manuscript ...' Dale Spender also instances Samuel Richardson, Thomas Hardy, Scott Fitzgerald and William Wordsworth as indulging in 'appropriation' (pp222–3).

There are other ways that women travellers' words have been misused. Marnie Bassett also suggests, concerning copies of Rose's original letters, which are all that survive, and in contrast to her journal, that 'In these copies, the lack of reference to important personal matters mentioned in her journal proves that they are incomplete and sometimes the style suggests that they were "improved"' (px).

Maggie Whitecross Paton's editor protests his scrupulousness, as does Fanny Stevenson's, but Fanny's family had previously deleted several passages, some about her relationship with Louis, not all of which he was able to resurrect.

And I have shown from Florence Baker's diaries how the most well-meaning editor can unintentionally distort.

I have suggested, too, how Anna Forbes rewrote her own text to conform to what was expected from a woman in her published account. We cannot know just what Lucy Atkinson meant, particularly in the context of her correspondence with her publisher, when she wrote in her introduction, '… I have bethought me to collect some of the letters written on the spot to friends; and these, with slight omissions and alterations, I now venture to present to the public' (pvi). Then there are the co-writers, the Blunts; Winstone notes,

> Wilfrid persuaded Anne to write up her diary of their recent travels, much more detailed and complete than his own, and to publish it … *Bedouin Tribes of the Euphrates* bore her name as author; underneath were the words 'edited with a Preface and some account of the Arabs and their Horses by W.S.B'. Subsequent scholarship would show that Wilfrid's contribution amounted in the main to interference of a kind that was not always helpful or disinterested.

Winstone also quotes an equestrian authority:

> Blunt's alterations to the Journals are far in excess of the wildest hopes of the most zealous editor. In the first place he allowed himself licence to rearrange the material in a general way and to transpose events in both time and place … Passages were then added or subtracted according to his own recollections. By and large, the descriptions of individuals were lengthily embroidered and those relating to horses omitted or emasculated.

Winstone adds further damning detail and concludes, 'Certainly Anne was the better scholar, fitted by temperament and an orderly mind to systematic study' (p145).

Blunt's meddling has emphasised the question of distortion. It is strange, in view of what has emerged in the ten chapters about particular couples, that men should have a reputation for objectivity and intellectual rectitude, in contrast to the reputation that women have. Annie Brassey notes of her husband's opinion of her, 'Tom declares I weave a complete legend for every bit of wood we meet floating around' (p398). That is nicely ironic. But then Thomas Brassey's account is very unlike that of his wife – and undoubtedly free from distortion. As well as being a Member of Parliament, he belonged to a rich Railway family to whose company he was expected to report back on what he saw, particularly about prospects in South America. His account, when he is not describing scenery which he likes, is full of the reports of experts, often British consuls, and often about exports. Would an MP be thought not quite serious if he strayed further than the scenery. Is it, in that instance, macho to be boring?

The travelling men are specialists in a wide range of interests and it seems to be acceptable, perhaps *de rigueur*, that the passages on their specialism should be slow-moving, sonorous even – for their findings are a serious matter. The good writers leaven this with a lively style in between times – though even this is, on occasion, consciously literary. From their books (and the findings therein) come their reputation, their identity.

That brings us back to Fussell's contentions on style and the opportunity he takes to put down Freya Stark's writing. It is all to do with who is writing and who they are writing for. Fussell, an American historian of the two world wars, is interested in male travel writers of the 1930s. They tended to be men caught between those wars; they had missed out, perhaps, on the first and they could begin to see the world crumbling around them as another approached. All the great exploration had been done. Adventure, under those circumstances, takes on a new meaning; it becomes internalised. Thus their books – and Peter Fleming and Graham Greene are hallowed exponents – become an exercise in a refined machismo more marked than in the journey itself. Freya Stark and her books do not fit into that masculine category, nor am I happy with Lindsay Simpson's description of some women travel writers as 'quasi-male', 'occupying that space between the masculine and feminine'. Unless she means what Virginia Woolf suggests in *A Room of One's Own* (1928; **1945**). That 'in each of us two powers preside, one male, one female' and that in the man's brain the man predominates, and in the woman's, the woman (p93). By the end of this Conclusion readers who are not already familiar with Freya and her writing may begin to place her to their own satisfaction.

Perhaps the most telling dichotomy in women's 'travel writing', at least in modern times, is revealed by the American anthropologist Laura Bohannan in the preface to her 'novel' *Return to Laughter* (1956) – another side of her fieldwork (with her husband) in Nigeria – which she published under the pseudonym Eleanor Smith Bowen:

> When I write as a social anthropologist and within the canons of the discipline, I write under another name. Here I have written simply as a human being, and the truth I have tried to tell concerns the sea change in one's self that comes from immersion in another and alien world. (pxix)

So Far as a Woman Could

The books of most of our women travellers stem from their diaries or letters. Those who refined a narrative were, on the whole, and at least on the surface, writing for women. That was part of the literary tradition. Men's writing was 'public', women's was 'private'. The poet Southey (1774–1843) wrote to Charlotte Brontë (quoted by Dale Spender):

> Literature cannot be the business of women's life and it ought not to be. The more she is engaged in her proper duties, the less leisure she will have for it, even as an accomplishment and a recreation. (p194)

And Anne Finch, Countess of Winchelsea (1660–1720), who refused to be put down, confirmed that 'a woman who attempts the pen' is 'an intruder on the rights of men'. Women were socialised to accept that writing letters was women's business. Annie Brassey notes, for example, that 'Tom and the gentlemen went for a walk, whilst we ladies rested and chatted and wrote letters' (p425). That is the reason why our women travellers – and there is evidence too from the world of literature – who exposed their writing to the public gaze felt the need to apologise, as well as the other sorts of modesty that I have highlighted.

When Henry Forbes writes in his preface about the work of the renowned traveller in the Eastern Archipelago, Alfred Russel Wallace,

> I should desire [my] volume ... which is a mere transcript of what I have thought the more interesting of the field notes made during my wanderings, to be considered in the light of an addendum to – unfortunately without any of the literary elegance and finish of that model book of travel ... (pv)

That is not the same sort of thing at all, for he goes on, 'No detailed account of the Timor-laut Islands has appeared before the present.' It is false modesty, good manners, correct form.

I have given examples of female humility in the Introduction and subsequent chapters; what we have not yet seen is how Mildred Cable and Freya Stark present their work. Do they do it on their knees? Part of Mildred's Prologue reads:

> After living for more than twenty years in the province of Shansi in North China, I took the old trade-route and, with my companions Eva and Francesca French, trekked northwest past the Barrier of the Great Wall and into the country which lies beyond. For many years we travelled over the Desert of Gobi and among its oases as itinerant missionaries, and we came to know the country and its people intimately ...
>
> Once the spirit of the desert had caught us it lured us on and we became learners in its severe school. The solitudes provoked reflection, the wide space gave us a right sense of proportion and the silences forbade triviality. The following record of what we saw and found in the Desert of Gobi may help others to appreciate its unique charm. These experiences were shared by three people, but for obvious reasons the record is written in the first person singular. (p11)

Is that last sentence a womanly modesty? Probably not. And is her book directed towards women? Probably not.

Freya Stark writes in her introduction to *The Valleys of the Assassins* (1934):

> I may confess at once that I had never thought of why I came, far less of why I came alone: and as to what I was going to do – I saw no cause to trouble about a thing so nebulous beforehand. My sense of responsibility was in

11.6   Mildred Cable
(from *Why Not for the World?*)

effect deficient, and purpose non-existent. When excessively badgered, the only explanation I could think of for being so unwontedly in Asia was an interest in Arabic grammar – a statement rarely accepted in that candid spirit in which I offered it to unconvinced enquirers.

I came to the conclusion that some more ascetic reason than mere enjoyment should be found if one wishes to travel in peace: to do things for fun smacks of levity, immorality almost, in our utilitarian world. I know in my heart of hearts that it is a most excellent reason to do things merely because one likes the doing of them. I would advise all those who wish to see unwrinkled brows in passport offices to start out ready labelled as entomologists, anthropologists, or whatever other -ology they think suitable and propitious.

But as this book is intended for the Public, and is therefore necessarily truthful, I must admit that for my own part I travelled single-mindedly for fun. I learned my scanty Arabic for fun, and a little Persian – and then went for the same reason to look for the Assassin castles and the Luristan bronzes in the manner here related. (ppxiii–xiv)

That is not false modesty but relish of self-knowledge from a woman supremely comfortable with her position and confident of her style. She is not writing for women, necessarily, and she is unafraid to rank herself with male travellers of the 1930s with their throwaway style.

Mildred Cable and Freya Stark were accepted on the same level as white men in the societies in which they travelled. Note how Owen Lattimore writes of a meeting with the governor of Chinese Turkestan:

> I had ... a semi-official audience of His Excellency the Governor, who talked with apparent freedom and with what seemed to me to be excellent observation and straight-forward intelligence; though he may not have believed everything he said. (p30)

And here is how Mildred Cable, not a mere fly-by-night, was received by the same man:

> When I met Governor Yang, I understood something of the power he wielded, for he was a most impressive man, tall and stately in his long grey silk gown, and bore himself with the dignity of a Chinese gentleman of the old school. His strong, intelligent, commanding face revealed one who could grasp a situation quickly and deal with it unhesitatingly. He spoke of the difficult problem created by widespread illiteracy, and declared himself convinced that the education of women was essential to the well-being of a nation, suggesting that after my companions and I had completed the journey on which we were launched, we should return to Urumchi, and help in organising women's educational work in his province. (p218)

Men were 'primary' people in the eyes of the world through which they travelled; the women who accompanied them were 'secondary'. Women who travelled alone were 'primary'. They had one added advantage over men – they could move at ease among both women and men. That is well illustrated by Freya Stark's description of arriving in Shibam and starting to revisit old friends. She is taken by Husain to his house:

> Here Husain and his three brothers settled for a few moments in avid silence to their hookah, after the day's fast; and presently took me to the harim above, where the wives and sisters dallied with samovar and tea things spread about them on the floor ...
> ... I felt happy in this friendly atmosphere. They invited me to stay, and showed me the room where Doreen [Ingrams] slept when she came, in a brass bedstead netted with pink tulle and decorated with ribbons. The brothers and I sat round a central dish of rice with eleven planets of excellent dishes round it. After I had climbed to another feast of cake and tea with the ladies upstairs, I walked back with Husain in the darkness. (pp30–1)

How about our travelling companions when they travelled without their partner (though perhaps with local companions)? Doreen Ingrams is the best example. Then she tended to be treated in some ways as if she were 'primary'; but she was still known as 'Ingram's Woman'.

What is also interesting is the contrast between travelling companions and lone women travellers when it comes to being mobbed. We have seen how Doreen Ingrams and Anna Forbes were pulled this way and that by a crowd of women and how Diana Shipton finally got irritated by one woman's importunities. Annie Brassey and Barbara Greene were stroked in approval by women. But Freya Stark has it her way:

> Wave after wave of beduin surged towards us and above, struggling for a glimpse of the stranger. They were friendly but terrifying by sheer numbers. Volunteers appeared to beat at them with sticks; like the air in the Ancient Mariner, the human mass 'opens from before and closes from behind'; a strange wild head with hair parted down the middle in long locks like Charles I appeared and reappeared persistent as a dream before me, tossed on the living waves. When we reached the doors of the little house, the wooden key, of course, would do nothing in a hurry. Three men held the crowd while a knife with a crooked blade was tried. Iuslim now emerged worried and dishevelled. When the key turned we made a rush; our three assistants held the onslaught for a second with their arms, and the door was closed behind us. I showed myself like royalty from the terrace, and was greeted with cheers or their Arabian equivalent by the mass of people which now stretched almost out of sight below. (p49)

What is more, Freya's account does not have the immediacy of the other women's – how can it when she has time to quote *The Ancient Mariner*!

The question of courage and endurance follows on from that. All our women, even Anna Forbes who down-played her courage for the benefit of her readership, were immensely brave. They do not appear to be different in that respect from lone women, or men. From the earliest of the women, and from the most trivial fear to the highest, there is a sort of stalwartness that is enviable.

Lady Fanshawe writes in her *Memoirs*, composed in 1676, published in 1829, of an incident during the journey to Spain:

> We saw coming towards us, with full sails, a Turkish galley well manned, and we believed we should be all carried away slaves, for this man had so laden his ship with goods for Spain, that his guns were useless, though the ship carried sixty guns: he called for brandy, and after he had well drunken, and all his men, which were near two hundred, he called for arms and cleared the deck as well as he could, resolving to fight rather than lose his ship, which was worth thirty thousand pounds; this was sad for us passengers, but my husband bid us be sure to keep in the cabin, and not appear, the women, which would make the Turks think that we were a man-of-war, but if they saw women they would take us for merchants and board us. He went upon the deck, and took a gun and bandoliers, and sword, and, with the rest of the ship's company, stood upon deck expecting the arrival of the Turkish man-of-war. This beast, the Captain,

had locked me up in the cabin; I knocked and called long to no purpose, until, at length, the cabin-boy came and opened the door; I, all in tears, desired him to be so good as to give me his blue thrum cap he wore, and his tarred coat, which he did, and I gave him half-a-crown, and putting them on and flinging away my night clothes, I crept up softly and stood upon the deck by my husband's side, as free from sickness and fear as, I confess, from discretion; but it was the effect of that passion, which I could never master. (pp91–3)

They were not morally weak and there is much evidence that they were not physically weak – they did not, through illness, hold the party up any more than the men. Only Anna Forbes was constantly very ill and she put it behind her better than anyone could have expected of her.

How about the encumbrance of children? Lone women travellers tended to be unmarried, childless. What is interesting is that women travelling companions tended, too, to be childless, relative to the female population of their time – an exception being Lady Fanshawe: she had four miscarriages, one of them triplets and, of the 14 children she carried to term, only five survived. Her endurance is in a class of its own.

Looking at the figures, it is worth noting that women like Lady Brassey already had children when they started travelling; several of the others, it may be remembered, were on their 'wedding journey'. So far as is apparent, Rose de Freycinet, who was at sea for over three years, Florence Baker, travelling in Africa twice for long periods, Anna Forbes, in the Eastern Archipelago for three years, Louise Bryant, Ella Sykes, and Ella Maillart had no children. Lady Londonderry had one and Lucy Atkinson had one, seven months after she began travelling, and then no more over the next four years of travel. Maggie Paton sent her children – most of them born on Aniwa – to Australia for their well-being. Fanny Stevenson had none by Robert Louis Stevenson. Eleanor Lattimore had one child later. Doreen Ingrams, having adopted a Hadhrami girl whose mother could not look after her, had one of her own a few years later. Diana Shipton left her baby in England; she later had another by Eric Shipton and one by her second marriage.

Did prolonged travel, or the exigencies of travel, affect fertility? Samuel Baker had seven children by his first wife. Whatever the reasons for childlessness, having and looking after children was not a brake on the travelling party. Even Lucy Atkinson, the only one (apart from Lady Fanshawe) to have a child while travelling, did not allow it to hold her back.

Reading about the endurance of my travelling sisters of even 50 years ago, I cannot help wondering how I would have managed. Barbara Greene added a useful postscript to the subject in the letter already quoted from, written after she had read the Introduction, the chapter about her and her cousin, and an earlier draft of this Conclusion:

I do believe that the average girl of today (of the educated class) has her feet on the ground more firmly than we had fifty years ago, though in a

11.7 Lady Fanshawe (from Fanshawe, *Memoirs*)

way (and in spite of our more privileged way of existence) we were brought up to be tougher about physical hardships and putting up with pain and discomfort. The stern words of our educators 'pull yourself together or leave the room' still ring in my ears! (2 January 1988)

And what of that other weakness of women – vanity? It looks as if another myth must go. Few of the women write about their appearance. Even Florence Baker is somehow practical and rather moving, rather than vain, about clothes. It is Sam for whom clothes are of great importance, and many of the other men are surprisingly interested in a way that harks back to Percy Sykes and Lord Curzon and the stricture that 'a dress suit is the most essential article of outfit, even for those who would attempt to reach Llasa'. The only time Lady Fanshawe writes about clothes is when she describes her husband on his way to kiss hands:

Then my husband, in a very rich suit of clothes of a dark fillemonte brocade laced with silver and gold laces, every one as broad as my hand, and a little silver and gold lace laid between them, both of very curious workmanship; his suit was trimmed with scarlet taffety ribbon; his stockings of white silk upon long scarlet ones; his shoes black, with scarlet shoestrings and garters; his linen very fine, laced with very rich Flanders lace; a black beaver, buttoned on the left side, with a jewel of twelve hundred pounds value. A rich curious wrought gold chain, made in the Indies, at which hung the King his Master's picture, richly set with diamonds, cost 300 [livres] which his Majesty, in great grace and favour, had been pleased to give him at his

11.8   Sir Richard Fanshawe by William Fairthorne

coming home from Portugal. On his fingers he wore two rich rings; his gloves trimmed with the same ribbon as his clothes. All his whole family were very richly clothed, according to their several qualities. (pp214–15)

And if you thought Peter Fleming was all burnt knees and who cares:

I opened my suitcase. Alas for foresight! A plague on vanity! The suitcase was full of water. And not of water only. Thus diluted, the fine dust of the desert, which habitually found its way through the chinks of all our luggage, had become a thin but ubiquitous paste of mud. One by one I lifted out the soggy garments ... the suit, the precious suit, came last of all. Wet it was bound to be, and soiled with mud; what I had not bargained for was that it should turn out to be bright green in colour. The dye from a sash bought in Khotan had run ...

... I had now to decide whether to enter Kashgar disguised as a lettuce, or looking like something that had escaped from Devil's Island. It seemed to me that, if there is one thing worse than wearing bright green clothes, it is wearing bright green clothes which are also soaking wet; I therefore sadly resumed the shorts and shirt of every day and prepared to let down the British Raj. (p318)

Don't say he had his tongue in his cheek; he had carried that suit all the way from Peking for that moment. Ella Maillart writes:

Every time he opened the case during these months past I had noticed the beautiful material and the impeccable crease of the trousers. I foresaw that in my pleated skirt (rolled up in a bundle ever since our departure) I could hardly expect to be taken for much more than Peter's cook when the time came for him, in his elegance, to take me out in Kashgar high society. Of course it was vexatious that his suit should have been ruined ... But I wonder whether I felt as sorry as I ought to have done. (pp248–9)

Some of the women are good at the tongue-in-cheek style, especially as it affects their men. Quotations from Lucy Atkinson, Maggie Paton, Ella Sykes and Ella Maillart have contained the term 'Lord and Master' used mockingly. Doreen Ingrams uses it in the more literal sense when she refers to Fatima and 'her lord'. Is there more to the mocking? There is enough evidence now deployed to ask, how feminist were our travelling companions and how feminist is their writing?

A couple of days after the last chapter was completed a letter arrived from Diana Shipton (Drummond) in response to an early version of the Introduction. It contained this paragraph:

I wonder if your very strongly held feminist views are not going to overload what you have to say on the travelling couples? Are you forcing the writings to fit a mould which interests you? I hope this query will not annoy you? Due, possibly, to the big difference in ages, but also just difference in attitudes, I am not in sympathy with excessive and aggressive feminism. (27 October 1987)

What a joy that after one meeting and with 7,000 miles and 27 years between us Diana felt able to be frank. It would also be rewarding to think that, if she had had the chance to read the whole book, she would not have been put off by any aggression. One cannot help being feminist – indeed, one can rejoice in it. Nor, I think, should one apologise for attempting to give one's work a spine. Ella Maillart, when I first wrote to her about the book, described another book about travellers as lacking 'a dominant look or philosophy'. Not that she was necessarily in sympathy with the line I have taken; she had her own questions about life.

A woman historian of women cannot help bearing in mind Virginia Woolf's lovely line in the essay 'Woman and Fiction' (1979): '... in those unlit corridors of history where the figures of generations of women are so dimly, so fitfully perceived' (p44). Disinterring their forgotten lives – forgotten mainly through the neglect of male historians and publishers – linking up with them through the generations, we not only forge a link that is our birthright but we learn from them how we may better enjoy and value our own. It is for others, those intent on a more theoretical approach, to fit the women into the history from which they were hitherto omitted, and analyse the whole – what is now called gender history (rather than women's history).

I quote Diana's letter happily; this book was conceived for her and women like her, as well as those with a more 'feminist' interest. Then there is the nice ambiguity of Sigrid Weigel in 'Double Focus' (*Feminist Aesthetics* 1985): 'All too many heroines whose biographies are more characterised by the wishful thinking of their creators than by the life of the women in question are put before us nowadays' (p66).

It is certainly true that of the 20 women travelling companions on the list at the front of this book only one declares herself to be a feminist. Louise Bryant writes, 'I am enough of a feminist to be pleased with the fact that the Cronstadt Soviet has been headed by a woman for more than half a year' (p162). And in her interviews Louise, where appropriate, takes a line firmly directed towards women's issues in the feminist sense. Of Marie Spirodonova – a respected and long-standing revolutionary – she writes:

> We talked about women and I wanted to know why more of them did not hold public office since Russia is the only place in the world where there is absolute sex equality.
> Spirodonova smiled at my question.
> 'I'm afraid I will sound a feminist,' she confessed, 'but I will tell you my theory. You will remember that before the revolution as many women as men went to Siberia; some years there were even more women ...
> Now that was all a very different matter from holding public office. It needs temperament and not training to be a martyr. Politicians are usually not very fine, they accept political positions when they are elected to them – not because they are especially fitted for them. I think women are more conscientious. Men are used to overlooking their consciences – women are not.' (p169)

No other travelling companion follows this direct feminist approach. Lady Fanshawe was not a feminist in anyone's sense:

> Both my eldest daughters had the small pox at the same time, and though I neglected them, and day and night attended my dear son, yet it pleased God they recovered, and he died, the grief of which made me miscarry, and caused a sickness of three weeks. (pp133–4)

But if most of our women were not feminists in today's terms, we have seen their indignation at the way women were treated in places they visited. Their evidence tends to suggest that women in the traditional societies they observed were often beasts of burden both in the metaphorical and physiological sense. But can we take it at face value?

Intellectuals from the developing world are quick to suggest that such outsider perceptions are false. Building on Edward Said's 'Orientalism' which criticises a concept of non-European cultures seen through the filter of European cultural and intellectual development (mainly from a male point of view), feminist anthropologists such as Denise O'Brien and Marilyn Strathern also warn against culturally loaded valuations of gender, sex and power.

Our women were not anthropologists; most of them were not even self-trained observers, and they were on the whole kept on the margins of cultural and intellectual development enjoyed by their men. They described what they saw, felt and experienced in a rather unencumbered way.

How ill-conceived it is possible for subjective observation to be can be illustrated (and turned on its Eurocentric head) by the comment of an eighteenth-century male, Islamic traveller to France quoted in Kumari Jayawardena's *Feminism and Nationalism in the Third World* (1986):

> In France, women are of higher station than men, so that they do what they wish and go where they please; and the greatest lord shows respect and courtesy beyond all limits to the humblest of women. In that country their commands prevail. (p11)

Thus when reading our travellers' descriptions I have tried to take into account both their subjectivity and the influences brought to bear on my own interpretation, such as the fact that I have lived in colonial climes both before and after I became conscious in the feminist sense, and have written about women in general and my relations with individuals.

Having said all that, Kumari Jayawardena also contends that feminism is not necessarily a 'product of "decadent" Western Capitalism'; it existed 'hidden from history' in several non-European countries in the nineteenth and early twentieth centuries. Some women were aware of their inferior position (often exacerbated by foreign intervention and, paradoxically, often brought to light by comparison with Western women) in countries such as China, Indonesia and Persia described by our travelling companions.

There are levels and levels of women's subjugation. Ella Sykes is completely liberated in the eyes of Persian men and yet the introduction to her book, written by a man, puts her down. None of our women complains about being badly treated by her society or her male companion (except perhaps Ella Maillart). Where there begins to be a consciousness of themselves as women is in their relations with other women – these are very often 'sisterly' in a feminist sense. In fact 'sisterhood' is one of the most attractive features of these accounts.

Louise Bryant illustrates this caring when she goes to interview members of the 'Women's Battalion', a rather over-publicised adjunct of the Provisional Government in Russia in 1917:

> Anna and Kira had virtually no clothes at all. They had thin summer clothing, pieced out with all sorts of rag-tags they had managed to gather together, and they didn't know where to get their next meal. I offered them money and clothes. At first they both wept and refused and then they were quite happy in accepting ...

... It was almost dawn when I bid the women soldiers farewell. One of them walked a little way with me in the night. It was painfully cold. 'Be sure to come back,' she urged sweetly as we shook hands.

'I give you my word of honour,' I said, feeling terribly solemn. I looked down and suddenly I realised her feet were bare ...

When I think back now she personifies Russia for me, Russia hungry and cold and barefoot – forgetting it all – planning new battles, new roads to freedom. (pp216; 219)

In Her Own Right

Why did our men travellers travel? Superficially the answer is obvious enough in individual cases – they were specialists and travelling was necessary to their work. But Percy Sykes makes a comment that gives the question another chance: he talks of the days – in classical times – when 'traveller and hero were interchangeable' (p160). And Mildred Cable came across a reference to the central government envoy in first-century Chinese Turkestan: 'A hero should not waste his days over pen and ink but ... he should seek fame in foreign lands' (p214).

In more modern times, in Europe during the Crusades, for example, it was arms and religion that gave men their self-image as the bravest of the brave; today it is sport; in between it was exploration and travel.

Exploration made heroes, and Samuel Baker was a good example. He was lionised on his return home, almost as a pop star or a sportsman might be today. And it tickled Sam's fancy to have his woman tough enough to accompany him. For Thomas Atkinson, on the other hand, it was preferable that there be no woman there, else how could there have been danger and travail? By the time Percy Sykes' sister joins him, chronologically and in his book, he no longer needs to prove anything to himself or his public; he can afford to write:

We had another unpleasant experience ... we were nearly blinded by the gale of sand, and I experienced the greatest difficulty in keeping on the track. That night we were all knocked up – men, horses, and mules, ... (p185)

For 'men' read, 'men and a woman'. (Only Annie Brassey ever writes 'his or her' (p350).)

Henry Forbes is the same as Percy Sykes: Anna joins him when his self-image is established. Of course, the British man tells it all, particularly the worst parts, low key, so that tennis shoes can become an image: at 10,000 feet Percy Sykes was 'at a disadvantage, as I was reduced to an old pair of tennis shoes as footgear' (p140). Peter Fleming uses the same image in the desert, a style aptly described by Nicholas Rankin, writing of his brother Ian, as a 'façade of nonchalance'.

The British man travelled differently because he was British and he told it as was expected of him. British pride, as we have seen, affected men and women. Sam Baker's imperialism was full blooded. Thomas Brassey's was a little more refined. Talking of development in South America he writes:

> In the task of accomplishing that desirable consummation English enterprise is certain to play a part. In years to come I see before me a glowing vision of the Anglo-Saxon race issuing forth from California on the East, and Australia on the West, spreading itself with vigorous energies to all the islands of the Pacific, and bringing the now secluded and benighted people of Polynesia into a close, prosperous, and a beneficent intercourse with the most advanced and civilised communities of the world. (p163)

And Annie, coming across some shoddy British goods in the Pacific, declaims, 'It will be a bad day when the confidence in England's honesty as a nation throughout the world, and consequently her well-earned supremacy in commerce, have passed away' (p453).

All that meant, of course, the keeping up of appearances of which there have been many examples. Even Barbara Greene, who had very few cares in the world, was determined 'not to let the men see that I was puzzled' (p12). And Maggie Paton kept her grief from the women of Aniwa – even though she often shared theirs.

Sometimes being white is almost as good as being British. Percy Sykes writes that 'It has been my good fortune to be the first European to follow in the footsteps of the mighty Iskander-i-Remi [Alexander the Great]' (p168). It is almost as good if their woman can be the first white woman, or Englishwoman, to go somewhere. Most of the men manage to claim that.

Thomas Brassey, when Annie climbs up the rigging, pronounces, 'She is, I am very confident, the first lady who has ever looked down on a coral reef from an equally elevated position' (p153). And yet Annie, trying to explain to some Polynesians that they were not traders or slavers, goes to the other extreme: 'We were only making a voyage of circumnavigation in a yacht' (p217). The American Lattimores decried the British imperial mode of travel: only its 'lawless eccentricity' lingered through the 1930s.

Women were alter egos; what else were they? Were they, in terms of the expedition, people in their own right? Most of them were able administrators, housewives and dogsbodies. Their talents should not be demeaned, if only their status were not. Lady Fanshawe tells of how her husband,

> received me in his arms, and gave me a hundred pieces of gold, saying, 'I know thou that keeps my heart so well, will keep my fortune, which from this time I will ever put into thy hands as God shall bless me with increase;' and now I thought myself a perfect queen. ... (pp44–5)

Only Barbara Greene – who was used at home to being waited on – steers clear of any of that side of the Liberian trip; but that was because Graham Greene ordered it that way. Their party had 26 porters and Barbara and

Graham each had their own servant. Barbara perks up the moment she is allowed to take any initiative.

That is a common feature even in the account of such an experienced traveller as Ella Maillart. And Annie Brassey, with the large yacht (the interior of which she designed, furnished and stocked) and the large dinner parties of important people when they were in port (which she organised) was easily roused. 'What a charming task it would be,' she wrote, 'thoroughly to survey these parts, and to correct the present charts where necessary, and how much I should like to be one of the officers appointed for service' (p200).

The question of initiative has another side. The bad times must have been worse for the woman who did not have the compensation of her 'work' to help her cope with them. As naturalist Henry Forbes wrote:

> But the worst road has always something to brighten it, for where it approached or rose above 2000 feet I was gratified by finding broad fields of brightly coloured purple, yellow and white balsams, and close to the edge of the path many low herbaceous Cyrtandreae, a family with chaste foliage and flowers; tall terrestrial orchids of numerous sorts, and many species of ferns. (p167)

But it could be worse than that. When Louis de Freycinet's ship was foundering just past Cape Horn on one of today's Falkland Islands, Rose recalled,

> Apart in my own quarters, given up to all the horror of our situation, my own position was all the more frightful because, having nothing to do for the common good, I was entirely at the mercy of my distressed speculation as to how this grievous affair was going to end. (p202)

It was after that that Rose came into her own. Crew member, the artist Arago, wrote (quoted by Marnie Bassett),

> She prayed without feebleness; no coward yet she wept. Some of our stock of biscuits had been brought up from the store and thrown into one of the rooms on the poop; the poor little thing arranged it all with the minutest care. (p202)

That was a male observer's perspective. When they were forced to abandon ship and take to a hostile shore, Rose herself wrote,

> I have been entrusted with the packing of the books, charts and so on, of the expedition, particularly anything of especial value to us; today I have numbered the 22nd case and I have perhaps still ten more. (p225)

And Rose's editor notes, 'Once more indisposed and in bed, unable to write with his own hand the dispatches to the Minister that Hale had promised to take, the Commandant dictated them to Rose' (p233). And the captain who eventually saved them wrote of Louis:

> But he enjoyed the sympathising consolation of his lady, who was young and very agreeable ... it was reported, that in the midst of the greatest danger and confusion, she retained a most surprising firmness and composure of mind. (p235)

Rose died of cholera, having nursed Louis through it. She was only 38.

Gleaning Only Women's Lore

Women travelling alone did not particularly concern themselves with women – every aspect of life was available to them in a way that was not always so in their home country, and they grasped it eagerly. Women companions were expected to mix with the women, while their men concerned themselves with higher things, especially in societies where women and men were segregated – and a fine body of ethnographic detail is the result.

If the men had travelled by themselves we should have been left, on the whole, with glimpses of picturesque women in fields. Tom Brassey finds it difficult even to mention the word woman; we have seen him with 'nymphs', now, watching the junks in Hong Kong waters he observes,

> the petticoated crew generally takes things easily, and seem able to endure the Siberian rigour of the winter in thin cotton robes without suffering the slightest inconvenience. (p182)

Does he mean women? It is difficult to tell, when writers indulge in euphemism. (And, in passing, in ten years of living in Hong Kong, I never experienced a winter that could be called Siberian – or is that a useful clue that the climate has changed?) Annie is easier to follow:

> I was awake and writing from half-past four this morning, but before I got up, a woman who comes here every day to work brought me some small ordinary shoes which I had purchased as curiosities, and took the opportunity of showing me her feet. It really made me shudder to look at them, so deformed and cramped up were they. She took off her own shoes and tottered about the room in those she had brought, and then asked me to show her one of mine. Having minutely examined it, she observed, with a melancholy shake of the head, 'Missy foot much more good, do much walky, walky; mine much bad, no good for walky. (p389)

Not all women were happy at the segregation imposed upon them. Lady Londonderry, for all that she enjoyed the company of Russian women and, anticipating Constantinople, wrote, 'I own I was very anxious ... to penetrate the Seraglio', regarded herself as a personage in her own right. At the Swedish court, where Napoleon's former comrade Bernadotte reigned, she had occasion sharply to record:

> We dined at court. About forty people were there. I was presented 1st to the Queen and afterwards to the King whom I was very anxious to see. This interesting man fully repaid my curiosity. I found him most agreeable and kind. However, he conversed principally with Lord L and left me to the Queen and the Prince Oscar. (p37)

11.9   Lady Londonderry and her son by Sir Thomas Lawrence
(courtesy of the Marquess of Londonderry)

A Lot More Fun

There is no doubt that most of the couples complemented each other personally in a way that was rewarding to both. Whatever the merits of travelling alone, sharing an experience has its compensations and, as far as the men were concerned, long-term travel without a little home-maker and 'devoted companion' could become wearing. Both Thomas Atkinson and Henry Forbes started off alone and then went off and got themselves a wife. John Paton, left a widower, returned to Scotland from the Pacific to remarry.

It is noticeable that the accounts of the nineteenth century do not discuss relationships between wife and husband. Widowed Lady Fanshawe in the seventeenth century was not so reticent:

> Now you will expect that I should say something that may remain of us jointly, which I will do though it makes my eyes gush out with tears, and cuts me to the soul to remember, and in part express the joys I was blessed with in him. Glory be to God, we never had but one mind throughout our lives. Our souls were wrapt up in each other; our aims and designs one, our loves one, and our resentments one. We so studied one the other, that we knew each other's mind by our looks. Whatever was real happiness, God gave it me in him. (p8)

In private, however, Sam Baker confessed to Lord Wharncliffe that his feelings for Florence were 'perhaps more intense than is often bestowed upon women by their husbands' (Hall p170). And Martha Bradford, whose husband was chaplain to the British Embassy in Vienna when Lord Londonderry was the Ambassador, observed, 'He is her most humble slave and casts on all besides such looks of condescending protection that one involuntarily bursts out laughing at the suppress'd pride of the creature' (p4). Rose de Freycinet, who dressed as a boy, and was smuggled aboard her husband's French man-of-war, wrote to her mother:

> I will follow my husband on his expedition round the world; I will share his fate and soften his anxieties if there should be any ... Ah! however great the trials of such a voyage may prove for your daughter, believe that a hundred times worse would be the absence of the one she so loves ... (p5)

It seems fairly clear, reading between the lines, that travelling together brought a bloom to the relationship of a Victorian couple which life at home did not always do. They were together much more than they would have been, and they shared the harrowing and the beautiful experiences. They had time and opportunity to laugh together, as well as toss on beds of fever.

By the 1920s, Victorian restraint about relationships had lifted: Eleanor Lattimore is quite open about her feelings for her husband, but she does not discuss their relationship the way Ella Maillart and Peter Fleming do theirs, nor the way Barbara Greene does in her travel account and her cousin does in his retrospective look at their journey together. Perhaps husbands and wives have to be more circumspect. Robin Hanbury-Tenison, in his email to me, provides a satisfying modern image:

> I have always relied heavily on the skills of both my wives, each of whom have been, in very different ways, superb travelling companions. There is ...

a vast difference between travelling alone and with a loved one. I have done much of both and each has its attractions, but there is something special about a clearly affectionate couple which breaks the ice more quickly when meeting people from different cultures.

One can certainly come unstuck by assuming that one can interpret relationships from what people write, even when it is not for publication. The letters of Effie (Euphemia) Ruskin (1828–1897) from Venice show a shallow hypochondriac whose husband was rather tolerant. To read the letters more sympathetically, one needs the information provided by her editor, Mary Lutyens, that Effie's six-year marriage to John Ruskin (1819–1900), learned author of *The Stones of Venice* (1851), was unconsummated.

However loving the relationship, and however strong the woman, she only had her way so far. Lady Londonderry, depicted in contemporary literature as a bit of a tyrant, records of their journey to Russia:

> We consulted much and long as to our future journey, Lord L. being desirous to see Denmark and Sweden, and I only anxious to arrive in Russia. The Riga road, which I wanted to take, was rejected as long and tedious. The passage of four days' sea from Lubeck to St Petersburg which we adopted for our heavy carriages and servants was declined and, against my consent, the journey through Denmark and Sweden was determined on. (p24)

And he writes airily in *Recollections of a Tour in the North of Europe 1836–1838* (1838) – note how, at a certain point, the passive is used in both quotations:

> The horror of a long passage presented itself on one side, and the inconvenience of a very bad land journey on the other. At length the latter was determined on, with the precaution of sending the heavy carriage and all the baggage by sea to Russia. (p27)

And Annie Brassey, organiser par excellence, observes,

> I have been trying to persuade Tom to steam out five or six hundred miles, so that we may make a quick passage and economise our time as much as possible but he is anxious to do *the whole voyage* under sail ... (p185)

Not for the first or second time we see disagreement about the mode of travel, with the woman coming off second best. Annie got very seasick, as did many of the crew.

When it comes to the accounts complementing each other, there is a paradox. It is obvious that the reader receives a more rounded picture from two separate accounts, sieved as they are through different perceptions and from different perspectives. But sometimes, as we have seen, the woman's account tears little holes in the man's – leaves it open to question; perhaps that is one of its merits. No wonder Graham Greene wrote, 'Only in one thing did she disappoint me – she wrote a book' (p38).

The Making of a Woman

'In Her Own Right' asked what travelling companions contributed to the expedition. Now the question is, what did they get out of it? What were they like at the beginning and how different were they at the end? And what sort of difference was there in attitude between different women over time?

Rose de Freycinet's voyage round the world took three years and 57 days and during that time she went through harrowing moments and long periods of unpleasantness. Towards the end, when they were safe again, she observed, 'It is true that what I have experienced in the last two years has darkened my disposition and made me philosophical, and that the gay, thoughtless madcap Rose has become grave' (p244).

Barbara Greene, on the other hand, after three months in Liberia during which she was often bored, tired and dirty but never affected by hostile nature or natives, felt that, consciously at least, nothing much had changed. Her son, Rupert Strachwitz, wanted to elaborate. After reading this conclusion long after his mother's death, he wrote back to me,

> I really do believe that this adventure changed my mother's life completely. Of course, she looked forward to a life of luxury on the trek but the truth is, when she came home, she couldn't live that way. She started writing and travelling and eventually plunged into an even greater adventure – and enjoyed it. (28 July 2011)

That adventure is sketched in Jeremy Lewis's *Shades of Greene*, and will no doubt be more intimately described in Rupert's planned biography of his parents.

The length of the journey, as well as what she experienced, must be relevant to how much a woman changed. But what did it all really mean in the long run? Lady Londonderry was probably much the same woman at the end of a ten months relatively undemanding journey through Europe to Russia and back; but later she travelled through Spain and Portugal and spent time in Vienna when her husband was ambassador there. Did travel broaden her mind? She was considered spoilt and immature when young, but Disraeli, whom she had helped, could write in 1861, when her husband had been dead for seven years:

> This is a remarkable place, and our hostess a remarkable woman. Twenty miles hence she has a vast palace in a vast park ... and all the splendid accessories of feudal life. But she prefers living in a hall on the shores of the German Ocean, surrounded by her collieries, and her blast furnaces, and her railroads, and unceasing telegraphs, with a port hewn of the solid rock,

screw steamers and four thousand pitmen under her control. In the town of Seaham Harbour, a mile off, she has a regular office, a fine stone building with her name and arms in front, and her flag flying above; and here she transacts, with innumerable agents, immense business – and I remember her five-and-twenty years ago, a mere fine lady; nay, the finest in London! But one must find excitement, if one has brains ... (p18)

Lucy Atkinson was far from 'civilisation' for five years. What is more, she had taken the initiative eight years earlier to leave England for Russia. She was betrayed by her 'husband', left in straightened circumstances, published her apparently anodyne but explosive letters, and then returned to Russia for an indeterminate time. From the letters written after her first return, however, she seems, not surprisingly, to have lost a confidence that is marked in her travel account. But then we have her put-down of George Meredith!

How much publication meant to the other letter and diary writers is impossible to know, but possible to guess. The psychological rewards of literature to women were in general substantial for it was one area where they could gain public recognition. Also, it was possible for women writers generally to make money and enjoy a measure of economic independence. (Until the Married Women's Property Acts of 1870 and 1882 – campaigned for by women – any money married women earned, including the copyright in their publications, belonged in law to their husbands.)

Of our travelling companions, only Ella Maillart had published a book before (and she continued to do so). After her first venture, Anna Forbes was to write again, both a joint book with Henry and a novel. Annie Brassey and Ella Sykes were to write several books; Eleanor Lattimore did the same, often with Owen. Doreen Ingrams had a career that followed her expertise in Arab affairs – writing, lecturing and broadcasting; Barbara Greene became an author. It is probably true to claim that, quite apart from the happy and unusual memories, travelling gave them the confidence and impetus to lead a fuller life thereafter than they might otherwise have done. Reading that suggestion, Doreen wrote to me,

> I agree with this 100%. My later career was entirely due to the confidence and impetus given me by working with Harold and the circumstances of life in Arabia. After experiencing the difficulties of the stage I was lacking in confidence and gained it 'behind the scenes' as it were. (10 December 1987)

As for whether or not women as a whole changed their attitudes over time, discussion, let alone judgement, can only be tentative when two twentieth century women travelling together can have such fundamentally conflicting views as Freya Stark and her companion:

> ... The Archeologist, under this first shock of genuine Arabia, is outraged to the very depth of her well-regulated heart. I have promised to keep her, as far as possible, separate from the inhabitants of this land; but alas! what will she make of a country whose chief if not only charm lies in its people ... (p27)

But there was more to those apparently conflicting views than Freya suggests, for the archaeologist was Gertrude Caton-Thompson, who also liked to be leader and was five years older. In her short biography, *Freya Stark: The Greatest Woman Explorer and Travel Writer of Her Age* (1985), Caroline Moorehead deliciously summarises Gertrude's opinion of Freya 40 years later:

> In 1983 she brought out her autobiography, *Mixed Memoirs*; the Freya who emerges from Chapter 23, clearly named and identified, is inefficient, quarrelsome, imperious, unscrupulous and, noted the ninety-year-old author with a kind of tart relish, had been called a 'bloody bitch' by the pilot who had come fruitlessly in search of her when she was ill. 'Which,' she concluded somberly, 'I thought moderate in the circumstances.' (p65)

For the full low-down from Gertrude's point of view you should refer to the original.

In the end, I am all too conscious of the dangers of generalising about women, even the small selection of women who travelled with men, who travelled in tandem. For all their similarities, they were different one from the other; they were themselves; and their writing, often by chance surviving, shows their individuality, however great the reputation of their men.

11.10   Fanny Stevenson in Samoa, 1893
(courtesy of Edinburgh Museums
and Galleries: The Writers' Museum)

Picture Fanny Stevenson (1840–1914) as she writes in their house, Vailima, in Samoa. She was 50 years old when she arrived there to live in 1890 and took to agriculture to help them survive. Her husband, aged 40, was a famous author, dying, and she:

> We have had a very heavy rainstorm, with thunder and lightning. At night the rain fell with such violence that we could not hear each other speak, and it seemed as though the house must be crushed by the weight of the water falling upon it. In the middle of the night Louis arose, made a light, and fell to writing verses. I was troubled about the taller corn which I feared might be broken down and spoiled. The verses turned out not badly, and the corn stood as straight as I might wish it to do. (p56)

Bibliography

Allen, Alexandra, *Travelling Ladies: Victorian Adventuresses* (London, Jupiter, 1980).

Arago, Jacques, *Narrative of a Voyage Round the World* (London, 1823).

Atkinson, Lucy, *Recollections of Tartar Steppes and Their Inhabitants* (London, Frank Cass, 1972; first published 1863).

Atkinson, Thomas, *Oriental and Western Siberia* (New York, Arno Press, 1970; first published 1858).

Atkinson, Thomas, *Travels in the Regions of the Upper and Lower Amoor* (London, Gregg International, 1971; first published 1860).

Baker, Anne, *Morning Star: Florence Baker's Diary ...* (London, William Kimber, 1972).

Baker, Samuel, *The Albert N'yanza* (London, Macmillan, 1866).

Baker, Samuel, *The Nile Tributaries of Abyssinia* (London, Macmillan 1868).

Baker, Samuel, *Ismailia* (London, Macmillan, 1874).

Banks, Russell, 'Too Late to Turn Back: Barbara Greene', in Michael Ondaatje, ed., *Lost Classics* (London, Bloomsbury, 2003).

Barlow, Henry, 'Anna Forbes: A Naturalist's Companion in the Far East', in John Gullick, ed., *Adventurous Women in South East Asia: Six Lives* (Kuala Lumpur, Oxford University Press, 1995).

Bassett, Marnie, *Realms and Islands: The World Voyage of Rose de Freycinet in the Corvette 'Uranie' 1817–1820* (London, Oxford University Press, 1962).

Bassnett, Susan, 'Travel Writing and Gender', in Peter Hulme and Tim Youngs, eds, *The Cambridge Companion to Travel Writing* (Cambridge, Cambridge University Press, 2002).

Bell, Gertrude, *The Letters of Gertrude Bell* (Harmondsworth, Penguin, 1987).

Belzoni, Sarah, 'Mrs Belzoni's Account of the Women of Egypt, Nubia and Syria', appended to Giovanni Belzoni, *Narrative of the Operations and Recent Discoveries ... in Egypt and Nubia* (London, 1820).

Bent, Mrs Theodore, *Southern Arabia* (London, Smith Elder, 1900).

Bent, Mabel, *The Travel Chronicles of Mrs J. Theodore Bent* (Oxford, Archaeopress, ca 2006).

Birkett, Dea, *Spinsters Abroad: Victorian Lady Explorers* (Oxford, Blackwell, 1989).

Blackman, Winifred, *The Fellahin of Upper Egypt* (London, Harrap, 1927).

Blake, Susan, 'What Difference Does Gender Make', in Nupur Chaudhuri, et al. (eds), *Western Women and Imperialism: Complicity and Resistance* (Bloomington, Indiana University Press, 1992).

Blodgett, Harriet, *Centuries of Female Days: Englishwomen's Private Diaries* (Gloucester, Alan Sutton, 1989).

Blunt, Lady (*see also* Winstone, H.V.F.)

Blunt, Lady Anne, *The Bedouin Tribes of the Euphrates* (London, John Murray, 1878).

Blunt, Lady Anne, *A Pilgrimage to Nejd* (London, Century, 1985; first published 1881).

Bohannan, Laura (*see* Bowen, Eleanore Smith).

Bowen, Eleanore Smith, *Return to Laughter* (London, Victor Gollancz, 1956).

Bradley, John, ed., *Ruskin's Letters from Venice 1851–1852* (Newhaven, Yale University Press, 1955).

Brassey, Lady, *A Voyage in the Sunbeam: Our Home on the Ocean for Eleven Months,* (London, Longman, 1899; Century, 1984; first published 1878).

Brassey, Lady, *The Last Voyage: To India and Australia in the Sunbeam* (London, Longman, 1889).

Brassey, Thomas (*see* Eardley-Wilmot, S.).

Brassey, The Earl, *The 'Sunbeam' RYS: Voyages and Experiences in Many Waters* (London, John Murray, 1917).

Bryant, Louise, *Six Red Months in Russia* (London, Journeyman, 1982; first published 1918).

Burton, Isabel, *The Inner Life of Syria, Palestine and the Holy Land* (London, H.S. King, 1875).

Burton, Jean, *Sir Richard Burton's Wife* (London, Harrap, 1942).

Butcher, Tim, *Chasing the Devil: On Foot Through Africa's Killing Fields* (London, Vintage, 2011).

Cable, Mildred, *The Gobi Desert* (London, Hodder & Stoughton, 1942).

Cable, Mildred, and French, Francesca, *Why Not For the World?* (London, British and Foreign Bible Society, 1952).

Caton-Thompson, Gertrude, *Mixed Memoirs* (Gateshead, Paradigm, ca 1983).

Chaudhuri, Nupur, and Strobel, Margaret, *Western Women and Imperialism: Complicity and Resistance* (Bloomington, Indiana University Press, 1992).

Coates, Jennifer, *Women, Men and Language* (London, Longman, 1986).

Cole, Mabel Cook, *Savage Gentlemen* (London, George Harrap, 1920).

Collins, David, 'Anglophone Travellers in the Russian Altai, 1848–1928, Part I: 1848–1904', *Sibirica: Journal of Siberian Studies*, vol. 2, issue 1, April 2002, 43–68.

Crawford, Anne, et al., eds, *The Europa Biographical Dictionary of British Women* (London, Europa Publications, 1983).

Crawford, Patricia, 'Women's Published Writings 1600–1800', in Mary Prior, ed., *Women in English Society 1500–1800* (London, Methuen, 1985).

Crocombe, Ron, and Ali, Ahmed, *Politics in Melanesia* (Fiji, Institute of Pacific Studies, University of South Pacific, 1982).

Cross, A.G., 'Early Miss Emmies', *New Zealand Slavonic Journal*, 1981, no. 1.

Cross, Anthony, 'The Testament of a Forgotten "Wife"', in *Anglo-Russica: Aspects of Cultural Relations between Great Britain and Russia in the Eighteenth and Early Nineteenth Century* (Oxford, Berry, 1993).

David, Caroline, *Funafuti: Or Three Months on a Coral Island* (London, John Murray, 1899).

Dawes, G., *A Dream of Islands* (Queensland, Jacaranda Press, 1980).

De Freycinet, Louis (*see also* Kelly, Marion).

De Freycinet, Rose (*see* Bassett, Marnie; Duplomb, C.; Rivière, Marc Serge).

Dictionary of National Biography and *Oxford Dictionary of National Biography* (online).

Dolan, Brian, *Ladies of the Grand Tour* (London, HarperCollins, 2001).

Duplomb, C., ed., *Campagne de l'Uranie ... Rose de Freycinet* (Paris, 1927).

Dutton, T., *Police Motu* (Waigani, University of Papua New Guinea Press, 1985).

Eardley-Wilmot, S., ed., *Voyages and Travels of Lord Brassey from 1862–1894*, 2 vols (London, Longman, 1895).

Ecker, Gisela, ed., *Feminist Aesthetics* (London, The Women's Press, 1985).

Ellis, S.M., ed., *A Mid-Victorian Pepys: The Letters and Memoirs of Sir William Hardman* (London, C. Palmer, 1923).

Faderman, Lillian, *Surpassing the Love of Men* (London, The Women's Press, 1985).

Fanshawe, Lady, *Memoirs* (London, Henry Colburn, 1829).

Fanshawe, Sir Richard, *Extracts from Correspondence* (London, Henry Colburn, 1829).

Fleming, Peter, *Brazilian Adventure* (London, Jonathan Cape, 1933).

Fleming, Peter, *One's Company* (London, Jonathan Cape, 1934).

Fleming, Peter, *News From Tartary*, London, Jonathan Cape, 1936).

Forbes, Annabella (Mrs Henry O.), *Insulinde* (Edinburgh, William Blackwood, 1887); published as *Unbeaten Tracks in Islands of the Far East* (Singapore, Oxford University Press, 1987).

Forbes, Annabella, *Helena* (Edinburgh, William Blackwood, 1905).

Forbes, Henry O., *A Naturalist's Wanderings in the Eastern Archipelago* (New York, Harper & Bros, 1885; reprinted 1989).

Foster, Shirley, and Mills, Sara, eds, *An Anthology of Women's Travel Writing* (Manchester, Manchester University Press, 2002).

Fraser, Antonia, *The Weaker Vessel* (London, Methuen, 1984).

Fraser, Mrs Hugh, *Seven Years on the Pacific Slope* (New York, Dodd, Mead, 1914).

Fussell, Paul, *Abroad: British Literary Travelling Between the Wars* (Oxford, Oxford University Press, 1980).

Galton, Francis, *Memories of My Life* (London, Methuen, 1908).

Gardner, Virginia, *Friend and Lover: The Life of Louise Bryant* (New York, Horizon Press, 1982).

Geikie, Archibald, *Life of Sir Roderick Murchison* (London, John Murray, 1875).

Gelb, Barbara, *So Short a Time: A Biography of John Reed and Louise Bryant* (Berkley, Berkley Books, 1981).

Gill, Isobel, *Six Months in Ascension: An Unscientific Account of a Scientific Expedition* (London, John Murray, 1878).

Gladstone, Penelope, *Travels of Alexine* (London, John Murray, 1970).

Greene, Barbara, *Too Late to Turn Back* (London, Settle Bendall, 1981; first published as *Land Benighted*, 1938).

Greene, Graham, *A Sort of a Life* (London, The Bodley Head, 1971).

Greene, Graham, *Journey Without Maps* (Harmondsworth, Penguin, 1971; first published 1936).

Greene, Graham, *Ways of Escape* (London, The Bodley Head, 1980).

Haggis, Jane, 'White Women and Colonialism: Towards a Non-recuperative History', in Clare Midgley, ed., *Gender and Imperialism* (New York, Manchester University Press, 1995).

Hall, Richard, *Lovers on the Nile* (London, Quartet, 1980).

Halsband, Robert, *The Life of Lady Wortley Montagu* (Oxford, Clarendon Press, 1956).

Halsband, Robert, 'Women and Literature in the 18th Century England', in Paul Fritz, ed., *Women in the 18th Century* (Toronto, Samuel Stevens, 1976).

Hanbury-Tenison, Marika, *A Slice of Spice* (London, Hutchinson, 1975).

Hanbury-Tenison, Robin, *A Pattern of Peoples* (London, Angus & Robertson, 1975).

Harding, Susan, 'Women and Words in a Spanish Village', in Rayna R. Reiter, ed., *Toward an Anthropology of Women* (New York, Monthly Review Press, 1975).

Hart-Davis, Duff, *Peter Fleming* (London, Jonathan Cape, 1974).

Hawaiian Star, The, Obituary of Alatau T. Atkinson, 24 April 1906.

Hawthorne, Nathaniel (see also Woodson, Thomas).

Hawthorne, Nathaniel, *Passages from the English Notebooks* (Boston, 1870).

Hawthorne, Sophia, *Notes in Italy and England* (London, Putnam, 1869).

Hickman, Katie, *Daughters of Britannia: The Lives & Times of Diplomatic Wives* (London, HarperCollins, 1999).

Hill, Bridget, *Eighteenth Century Women* (London, George Allen & Unwin, 1984).

Hoagland, Edward, *African Calliope* (New York, Random House, 1979).

Hodgson, Barbara, *No Place for a Lady: Tales of Adventurous Women Travellers* (Vancouver, Greystone Books, 2003).

Hoe, Susanna, 'White Women in the Colonies: Were They Responsible for Setting Up Racial Barriers', *Bikmaus: A Journal of Papua New Guinea Affairs, Ideas and the Arts* (Port Moresby), vol. v, no. 2 (June 1984).

Hoe, Susanna, *Chinese Footprints: Exploring Women's History in China, Hong Kong and Macau* (Hong Kong, Roundhouse (Asia), 1996).

Hoe, Susanna, *At Home in Paradise: A House and Garden in Papua New Guinea* (Oxford, HOLO Books: The Women's History Press, 2003).

Hoe, Susanna, *Watching the Flag Come Down: An Englishwoman in Hong Kong 1987–97* (Oxford, HOLO Books: The Women's History Press, 2007).

Hoe, Susanna, and Roebuck, Derek, *The Taking of Hong Kong: Charles and Clara Elliot in China Waters* (London, Curzon Press, 1999; Hong Kong University Press, 2009).

Holmes, Richard, *Footsteps* (Harmondsworth, Penguin, 1986).

Hopkirk, Peter, *Setting the East Ablaze* (Oxford, University Press, 1986).

Hommaire de Hell, Adèle, and Hommaire de Hell, Xavier, *Travels in the Steppes of the Caspian Sea ...* (London, Chapman and Hall, 1847).

Huie, Shirley Fenton, *Tiger Lilies: Women Adventurers in the South Pacific* (North Ryde, NSW, Angus and Robertson, 1990).

Hulme, Peter, and Youngs, Tim, eds, *The Cambridge Companion to Travel Writing* (Cambridge, Cambridge University Press, 2002).

Ingrams, Doreen, *A Time in Arabia* (London, John Murray, 1970).

Ingrams, Harold, *Arabia and the Isles* (London, John Murray, 1966).

Jayawardena, Kumari, *Feminism and Nationalism in the Third World* (London, Zed Books, 1986).

Justice, Elizabeth, *A Voyage to Russia* (York, T. Gent, 1739).

Kelly, Marion, ed., *Hawaii in 1819* (Louis de Freycinet) (Honolulu, Bernice P. Bishop Museum, 1978).

Kennedy, Valerie, 'Graham and Barbara Greene in Liberia: Two Accounts of a Journey Without Maps', in Conference Proceedings (Cyprus, Department of Foreign Language Education, Middle East Technical University, 2005).

Kenyon, Olga, *800 Years of Women's Letters* (Alan Sutton, 1992).

Lady Margaret Hall, Register, Oxford. Lady Margaret Hall (1939) (Brown Book, Oxford, 1879–1881).

Lattimore, Eleanor Holgate, *Turkistan Reunion* (London, Hurst & Blackett, 1934; reprinted 1975 and 1994).

Lattimore, Eleanor Holgate, and Lattimore, Owen, *The Making of Modern China*, (London, Allen & Unwin, 1945).

Lattimore, Eleanor Holgate, and Lattimore, Owen, *Silks, Spices and Empire* (London, Tandem, 1972).

Lattimore, Owen, *The Desert Road to Turkestan* (London, Methuen 1928).

Lattimore, Owen, *High Tartary* (Boston, Little, Brown, 1930; reprinted 1975 and 1994).

Lawrence, Karen R., *Penelope Voyages: Women and Travel in the British Literary Tradition* (Ithaca, Cornell University Press, 1994).

Leacock, Eleanor Burke, *Myths of Male Dominance* (New York, Monthly Review Press, 1981).

Levine, Philippa, *Victorian Feminism 1850–1900* (London, Hutchinson, 1987).

Lewis, Jeremy, *Shades of Greene: One Generation of an English Family* (London, Jonathan Cape, 2010).

Londonderry, Marchioness of, *Journal of a Three Months Tour in Portugal* ... (London, J. Mitchell, 1843).

Londonderry, Lady (*see* Seaman, W.A.L., and Sewell, J.R.).

Londonderry, The Marquis of, *Recollections of a Tour in the North of Europe 1836–1838*, 2 vols (London, Richard Bentley, 1838).

Londonderry, The Marquis of, *Journal of a Tour in the Southern Part of Spain* (London, printed privately, 1840).

Lutyens, Mary, *Young Mrs Ruskin in Venice* (New York, Vanguard Press, 1965).

Macartney, Lady, *An English Lady in Chinese Turkestan* (Hong Kong, Oxford University Press, 1985; first published 1931).

MacClancy, Jeremy, *To Kill a Bird With Two Stones* (Vanuatu, Cultural Centre Publications No. 1, 1980).

MacKay, Margaret, *The Violent Friend: The Story of Mrs Robert Louis Stevenson 1840–1914* (London, J.M. Dent, 1970).

Maillart, Ella K., *Turkestan Solo* (New York, G.P. Putnam, 1934).

Maillart, Ella K., *Forbidden Journey* (London, William Heinemann, 1937).

Maillart, Ella K., *The Cruel Way* (London, William Heinemann, 1947).

Maillart, Ella K., 'My Philosophy of Travel', in M. Michael, ed., *Traveller's Quest* (London, William Hodge, 1950).

Maillart, Ella K., 'Tibetan Jaunt', in Odette Tchernine, ed., *Explorers' and Travellers' Tales* (London, Jarrolds, 1958).

Maillart, Ella K., *Voyages Vers le Réel* (mélange dédiés à) (Geneva, Editions Olizane, Collection Artou, 1983).

Manley, Seon, and Belcher, Susan, *O, Those Extraordinary Women* (Philadelphia, Chilton Book Co., 1972).

Melman, Billie, *Women's Orients: English Women and the Middle East, 1718–1918* (Ann Arbor, University of Michigan Press, 1995).

Mendelson, Sara H., 'Stuart Women's Diaries and Occasional Memoirs', in Mary Prior, ed., *Women in English Society 1500–1800* (1985).

Middleton, Dorothy, *Baker of the Nile* (London, Falcon Press, 1949).

Midgley, Clare, *Gender and Imperialism* (New York, Manchester University Press, 1995).

Miller, Jean Baker, *Toward a New Psychology of Women* (Harmondsworth, Penguin (Pelican), 1978).

Mills, Lady Dorothy, *Through Liberia* (London, Duckworth, 1926).

Mills, Sara, *Discourses of Differences: An Analysis of Women's Travel Writing and Colonialism* (London, Routledge, 1991).

Moers, Ellen, *Literary Women* (London, The Women's Press, 1978).

Montgomery-Hyde, H., *The Londonderrys* (London, Hamish Hamilton, 1979).

Moore, Katharine, *Victorian Wives* (London, Allison & Busby, 1985).

Moorehead, Caroline, *Freya Stark* (London, Penguin, 1985).

Morgan, Susan, *Place Matters: Gendered Geography in Victorian Women's Travel Books about Southeast Asia* (New Brunswick, Rutgers University Press, 1996).

Morris, Mary, ed., *The Virago Book of Women Travellers* (London, Virago, 1993).

O'Brien, Denise, and Tiffany, Sharon W., *Rethinking Women's Roles: Perspectives from the Pacific* (California, University of California Press, 1984).

Okely, Judith, and Callaway, Helen, *Anthropology and Autobiography* (London, Routledge, 1992).

Okin, Susan M., *Women in Western Political Thought* (London, Virago, 1980).

Ondaatje, Michael, et al., *Lost Classics* (London, Bloomsbury, 2003).

Paton, John, *Missionary to the New Hebrides* (London, Hodder & Stoughton, 1889; reprinted 1994).

Paton, Margaret W., *Letters and Sketches from the New Hebrides* (London, Hodder & Stoughton, 1896; reprinted 1994).

Pearson, E.A., 'Memories of the Hall', in Brown Book (Oxford, Lady Margaret Hall, 1928).

Pickering, Anna Maria, *Memoirs* (London, Hodder & Stoughton, 1903).

Philips, Susan U., Steele, Susan, and Tanz, Christine, eds, *Language, Gender, and Sex in Comparative Perspective* (Cambridge, University Press 1987).

Plowden, Alison, *Women All on Fire: The Women of the English Civil War* (Stroud, Gloucestershire, Sutton, 1998).

Prior, Mary, ed., *Women in English Society 1500–1800* (London, Methuen, 1985).

Reed, John, *Ten Days that Shook the World* (Harmondsworth, Penguin, 1977; first published 1919).

Reiter, Rayna R., *Toward an Anthropology of Women* (New York, Monthly Review Press, 1975).

Rivière, Marc Serge, trans., *A Woman of Courage: The Journal of Rose de Freycinet on her Voyage Round the World, 1817–1820* (Canberra, National Library of Australia, 1996).

Robinson, Jane, *Wayward Women: A Guide to Women Travellers* (Oxford, Oxford University Press, 1990).

Robinson, Jane, *Unsuitable for Ladies: An Anthology of Women Travellers* (Oxford, Oxford University Press, 1994).

Robinson, Jane, *Parrot Pie for Breakfast: An Anthology of Women Pioneers* (Oxford, Oxford University Press, 1999).

Routledge, Katherine, *The Mystery of Easter Island* (London, Sifton Praed, 1920).

Routledge, Katherine, and Routledge, William Scoresby, *With Prehistoric People* (London, Edward Arnold, 1910).

Rowbotham, Sheila, *Women, Resistance and Revolution* (Harmondsworth, Penguin (Pelican), 1974).

Ruskin, John (*see* Bradley, John).

Russell, Mary, *The Blessings of a Good Thick Skirt* (London, Collins, 1986).

Said, Edward, *Orientalism* (New York, Vintage Books, 1979).

Seaman, W.A.L., and Sewell, J.R., *Russian Journal of Lady Londonderry 1836–37* (London, John Murray, 1973).

Searight, Sarah, and Taylor, Jane, *Yemen: Land and People* (London, Pallas Athene, 2002).

Shipman, Pat, *The Stolen Woman: Florence Baker's Extraordinary Life from Harem to the Heart of Africa* (London, Bantam Press, 2004).

Shipton, Diana, *The Antique Land* (London, Hodder & Stoughton, 1950; reprinted 1987).

Shipton, Eric, *The Mountains of Tartary* (London, Hodder & Stoughton, 1951).

Shipton, Eric, *That Untravelled World* (London, Hodder & Stoughton, 1969).

Showalter, Elaine, ed., *The New Feminist Criticism* (London, Virago, 1986).

Simpson, Lindsay, 'Lying Truths: Diaries as Historical Documents and the Craft of Fiction'. Association of Writing Practitioners Conference Proceedings, 2007, internet article.

Skrine, C.P., and Nightingale, Pamela, *Macartney at Kashgar: New Light on British, Chinese and Russian Activities in Singkiang, 1890–1918* (Hong Kong, Oxford University Press, 1987; first published 1973).

Smeeton, Beryl, *Winter Shoes in Springtime* (London, Rupert Hart-Davis, 1961).

Spencer-Stanhope, Lady Elizabeth (*see* Stirling, A.M.W.).

Spender, Dale, *Man Made Language* (London, Routledge, Kegan, Paul, 2nd edition 1985).

Stark, Freya, *The Valleys of the Assassins* (London, John Murray, 1934).

Stark, Freya, *A Winter in Arabia* (London, John Murray, 1940).

Steele, Peter, *Eric Shipton: Everest and Beyond* (Seattle, The Mountaineers, 1998).

Stevenson, Fanny, and Stevenson, R.L., *Our Samoan Adventure* (London, Weidenfeld & Nicolson, 1956).

Stevenson, Mrs Margaret, *From Saranac to the Marquesas and Beyond* (London, Methuen, 1903).

Stevenson, Mrs Margaret, *Letters from Samoa 1891–1985* (London, Methuen, 1906).

Stevenson, R.L., *In the South Seas* (London, Chatto & Windus, 1888).

Stevenson, R.L., *A Footnote to History: Eight Years of Trouble in Samoa* (London, Cassell, 1892).

Stevenson, R.L., *Vailima Letters: Being Correspondence Addressed by RLS to Sydney Colvin*, 2 vols (Michigan, Scholarly Press, 1972).

Stirling, A.M.W., *The Letter-bag of Lady Elizabeth Spencer-Stanhope*, 2 vols (London, 1913).

Strachwitz, Rupert, 'Barbara Greene'. Unpublished talk, Berkhamstead, 28 September, 2007.

Strathern, Marilyn, ed., *Dealing with Inequality: Analysing Gender Relations in Melanesia and Beyond* (Cambridge, University Press, 1987).

Summers, Anne, 'An Object Lesson in Women's History', in Jan Mercer, ed., *The Other Half* (Ringwood, Penguin, 1975).

Sykes, Ella, *Through Persia on a Side Saddle* (London, John Macqueen, 1901).

Sykes, Ella, *Persia and Its People* (London, Methuen, 1910).

Sykes, Ella, *A Home Help in Canada* (London, Smith, Elder, 1912).

Sykes, Ella, and Sykes, Percy, *Through Deserts and Oases of Central Asia* (London, Macmillan, 1920).

Sykes, Percy M., *Ten Thousand Miles in Persia* (London, John Murray, 1902).

Sykes, Percy M., *History of Persia* (London, Macmillan, 1915).

Tchernine, Odette, ed., *Explorers' & Travellers' Tales* (London, Jarrolds, 1958).

Teichman, Eric, *Journey to Turkistan* (Hong Kong, Oxford University Press, 1988; first published 1937).

Tiltman, Marjorie H., *Women in Modern Adventure* (London, Harrap, 1935).

Todd, Janet, *A Dictionary of British and American Women Writers 1660–1800* (London, Methuen, 1987).

Trollope, Joanna, *Britannia's Daughters* (London, Hutchinson, 1983).

Tuchman, Barbara, *Practising History* (London, Papermac, 1983).

Uglow, Jennifer, *The Macmillan Dictionary of Women's Biography* (London, Macmillan, 1982).

Vicinus, Martha, *Independent Women: Work and Community for Single Women, 1850–1920* (London, Virago, 1985).

Wandor, Michelene, ed., *On Gender and Writing* (London Pandora, 1983).

Ward, Mrs Humphry (Mary), *Robert Elsmere* (London, 1888).

Weigel, Sigrid, 'Double Focus: On the History of Women's Writing', in G. Ecker, ed., *Feminist Aesthetics* (London, The Women's Press, 1985).

Wilkinson, J., *Worthies of Barnsley* (Barnsley, privately printed, n.d.).

Wilson, Katharina M., ed., *Medieval Women Writers* (Manchester, University Press, 1984).

Winstone, H.V.F., *Gertrude Bell* (London, Quartet, 1980).

Winstone, H.V.F., *Lady Anne Blunt: A Biography* (Manchester, Barzan, 2005).

Woodson, Thomas, and Ellis, Bill, *The English Notebooks 1853–1856/Nathaniel Hawthorne* (Columbus, Ohio State University Press, 1997).

Woolf, Virginia, *A Room of One's Own* (Harmondsworth, Penguin, 1945; first published 1928).

Woolf, Virginia, 'Women and Fiction', in *Women and Writing* (London, The Women's Press, 1979).

Wynn, Antony, *Persia in the Great Game: Sir Percy Sykes, Explorer, Consul, Soldier, Spy* (London, John Murray, 2003).

Youngs, Tim, 'Buttons and Souls: Some Thoughts on Commodities and Identity in Women's Travel Writing', *Studies in Travel Writing*, no. 1, Spring 1997.

Index

Also from HOLO Books: The Women's History Press

Of Islands and Women 1
Susanna Hoe   MADEIRA: WOMEN, HISTORY, BOOKS AND PLACES
paperback 180pp published 2004 1 map and 25 illustrations ISBN 9780953773084
Madeira – Travel – History (update www.holobooks.co.uk 2005)

In the 19th century, many people visited Madeira in the hopes that the dry, warm winter might help them recover from illness – usually consumption (tuberculosis). Today, travellers still go for the winter sun and for the magnificent walking, tropical and temperate gardens 100 or more years old, glorious wild flowers and trees and unparalleled mountain views. The history of Madeira's women and the writing of women travellers about the island are less well known than they should be. This livret combines a flavour of all these elements for the visitor or the armchair traveller.

Of Islands and Women 2
Susanna Hoe   CRETE: WOMEN, HISTORY, BOOKS AND PLACES
paperback 408pp published 2005 2 maps and 31 illustrations
Crete – Travel – Archaeology – Legend – History ISBN 9780953773077
(updates www.holobooks.co.uk 2007)

Once upon a time, Europa emerged from the waves at Matala on the back of a bull – the god Zeus in disguise. There, too, the author broke her ankle as she followed Europa to nearby Gortyn – whose famous law code has much to say about women. Europa was the mother of Minos, of the Minoans, (and of the concept of 'Europe'). Millennia later, Harriet Boyd was the first woman archaeologist to discover and direct her own dig, at Gournia – a perfect Minoan town. This livret links legend and archaeology by writing and place, but does not neglect the island's other women. Over the centuries they were subject to numerous violent changes of overlord – Mycenean, Roman, Byzantine (twice), Saracen, Venetian, Ottoman – but somehow have emerged as Cretans.

Of Islands and Women 3
Susanna Hoe   TASMANIA
Paperback 436pp published 2010 ISBN 9780954405663

In 1792 Louise Girardin – disguised as a French sailor – was the first white woman to visit Van Diemen's Land (Tasmania). She was followed by Martha Hayes who stepped ashore in 1803 among the first British settlers and convicts; she was the pregnant 16-year-old mistress of their leader. But Aboriginal women had already lived on the island for perhaps 40,000 years. The first to be named in exploration literature is Ouray-Ouray; the best known is Trukanini, erroneously called the last Tasmanian when she died in 1876. In the 1970s, Aboriginal rights became a live issue, often with women in the forefront, as they were, too, in environmentalism. This book gathers together these strands, and that of a vibrant women's literature, linking them to place – an island of still unspoilt beauty and unique flora and fauna.

Susanna Hoe   AT HOME IN PARADISE: A HOUSE AND GARDEN IN PAPUA NEW GUINEA
paperback 208pp published 2003 1 map 215 × 240mm ISBN 9780953773091 – Papua
New Guinea – Travel – Autobiography/Biography

*How would Margaret have written her story if she had been able to? I tried to help her
to learn to read and write but I could never see into her mind – there was too much that
divided us, in spite of all that drew us together. But sometimes, and once in particular, I
felt that she knew I was recording everything she told me.*

This is how the author introduces us to the family's cleaner in her diary of a stay in
Papua New Guinea – home of the bird of paradise. Through the gradual accumulation
of detail, the reader gets to know Margaret, her extended family, her unreliable husbands
and her independent spirit. Then there is Kaman, the outrageous gardener, who has to be
prised away from his creation so that his employers can enjoy planting and tending, as
well as admiring and eating its produce. There is endless scope for misunderstanding and
enlightenment as the tropical seasons come and go and relationships develop.

CHINA

**Susanna Hoe   WATCHING THE FLAG COME DOWN: An Englishwoman in Hong Kong
1987–1997**
Paperback 224pp published 2007 1 map ISBN 9780954405670
Hong Kong – China – Autobiography – Biography – Travel – Politics – History –
Women's Studies (updates www.holobooks.co.uk 2007)

At midnight on 30 June 1997 Hong Kong reverted to Chinese sovereignty after 150 years
of British rule. The moment when the British flag came down was dramatic enough but
the 10 years leading up to it were full of surprising incident and change. These 'Letters
from Hong Kong', written by an Englishwoman who was involved in those events from
1987, are both an unusual historical record and a heartwarming account of women's
domestic, intellectual and political activity. An epilogue brings Hong Kong up to date ten
years after the Handover.

Susanna Hoe   WOMEN AT THE SIEGE, PEKING 1900
Paperback 430pp published 2000 4 maps 44 illustrations ISBN 9780953773060
China – History – Women's Studies

The Boxer uprising; the siege of the legations; 55 days in Peking; foreign troops looting
China's capital; these are images from books and films over the past 100 years. Now the
story is told from the women's point of view, using their previously neglected writings and
giving a new dimension.

HOLO Books is agent in the United Kingdom for:

Susanna Hoe   CHINESE FOOTPRINTS: EXPLORING WOMEN'S HISTORY IN CHINA, HONG KONG AND MACAU
Roundhouse Publications (Asia) 1996 paperback 351pp 41 illustrations
ISBN 9789627992035
China – Hong Kong – Macau – History – Historiography – Women's Studies – Travel

This book is as much about the author's task of historical re-creation as it is about the lives, loves and struggles of women such as the 1930s civil rights campaigners Shi Liang, Agnes Smedley and Stella Benson; autobiographical writer Xiao Hong; Olympic sportswoman, traveller and writer Ella Maillart; icon of revolutionary China Soong Ching Ling; philanthropist Clara Ho Tung; and Clara Elliot, who lived in Macau at the time of Hong Kong's cession to Britain.

Nan Hodges & Arthur W. Hummel (eds)   LIGHTS AND SHADOWS OF A MACAO LIFE: THE JOURNAL OF HARRIETT LOW, TRAVELLING SPINSTER
Bear Creek Books (USA) published 2002 2 vols paperback 833pp 10 illustrations (set) ISBN 9780938106296
China – History – Historiography – Women's studies

Lights and Shadows of a Macao Life, the title chosen by Harriett Low for her journal, aptly describes the conflicting emotions of the first American woman to live in China. Making a rude transition from the tranquillity of Salem, Massachusetts into a world of sampans and sedan chairs, women with bound feet and men with queues, the lively young American records a detailed portrait of her life in Macao from 1829–1834. In these diaries, published for the first time as a complete edition, Harriett Low displays wit and courage as she metamorphoses from a socially naive girl into a mature, independent woman. This is an important addition to the historiography of the China Coast.